CRADLE OF AUSTRALIAN POLITICAL STUDIES:
Sydney's Department of Government

Cradle of Australian Political Studies

Sydney's Department of Government

Michael Hogan

connorcourt
PUBLISHING

Connor Court Publishing Pty Ltd

Copyright © Michael Hogan 2015

ALL RIGHTS RESERVED. This book contains material protected under International and Federal Copyright Laws and Treaties. Any unauthorised reprint or use of this material is prohibited. No part of this book may be reproduced or transmitted in any form or by any means, electronic or mechanical, including photocopying, recording, or by any information storage and retrieval system without express written permission from the publisher.

PO Box 224W
Ballarat VIC 3350
sales@connorcourt.com
www.connorcourt.com

ISBN: 9781925138511 (pbk.)

Cover design by Ian James

Printed in Australia

CONTENTS

Preface   vii

Foreword   xi

1 **Origins of the Department of Government**   1
Public Administration and Politics in the Faculty of Economics. The first in Australia?

2 **Establishing the Department of Government (1947-62)**   31
The Partridge interlude. Availability to students in the Faculty of Arts. After Partridge.

3 **The Dick and Henry show**   54
Technology change. Publishing and entrepreneurial work. Management style.

4 **The expanding department**   82
Government I challenges. Internationalisation of staff. Decision-making style. Budgeting. After Dick and Henry. The Merewether Building. A community of scholars?

5 **Real politics in the 1970s**   109
The Political Economy dispute. Women's movement. Gay and lesbian politics. The Philosophy Department dispute. Democratisation in the Department. An elected head? Aftermath.

6 **Redesigning the curriculum**   153
Redesigning Government I. Short units for second and third year. An Honours program. A postgraduate program. Political science methodology. Curriculum reform?

7 The corporate university 179
Some coping mechanisms. Postgraduate coursework degrees. Kolej Antarabangsa. Hung out to dry in a business school (1999-2008).

8 Into the Faculty of Arts and Social Sciences 217

9 In Australian political science 224
A defining character? Ranking the Department of Government. Contribution to the discipline.

10 Challenges and opportunities 242
The competitive university. The continuing electronic revolution.

Appendix 256

Bibliography 259

Index 265

Preface

Why a history of the Department of Government?

As the Discipline of Government and International Relations was coming to terms with the decision of the University to move it from its traditional academic location in the Economics Faculty, Professor Graeme Gill sent round an undated memo [c. 2007] on the subject of a "History Project":

The shift from the Faculty of Economics and Business to the Faculty of Arts provides an opportunity to take stock of the Department's history, to identify and consolidate the resources we have and to think about producing some kind of enduring 'product' (book, website, etc.) to record and showcase our history.

The memo set out the framework of questions to ask, resources to collect, and people to be interviewed. As is the frequent reaction to memos that suggest that something should be done, very little was done. This is not surprising, since writing up the history of the department is a major project, and the transition from one faculty to another has provided more than enough for overworked staff in the department to manage. Perhaps a retired member of staff would be interested?

Sometime in 2013 I was waylaid by two of my ex-colleagues, both themselves retired – Sue Wills and Bob Howard – and told that I should do the job. Although I had just completed one large project, and was contemplating genuine retirement from writing, I expressed an interest. After consulting with Graeme Gill and Michael Jackson, both of whom were enthusiastic, I accepted the task. This may not be the history that Graeme was contemplating in his memo, but I could see other reasons beside the transition from one faculty to another. Many of the leading figures from the department of Dick Spann and Henry Mayer have already died, and there is some urgency if the insights of the remaining septuagenarians and octogenarians are to be collected. Moreover, the origins of the department lie in appointments of two lecturers in Public Administration in 1917, so the centenary of the institution is rapidly approaching.

This account represents a personal viewpoint – that of someone who has been an undergraduate and postgraduate student, then a temporary and contract tutor and lecturer, then a member of tenured teaching staff. I began the study of Government, with lectures from Ken Turner and tutorials with Lex Watson, in 1967. The advantage is that I am part of a small group that constitutes the institutional memory of the department. The disadvantage is that I can be regarded as rather intellectually inbred (if it were not for a previous formation in philosophy and theology in quite a different academic tradition, but even that was in Sydney). If this book had been written by any of the majority of staff members who came to Sydney after studies and careers in other universities and countries it would be quite different in style and approach. (I have occasionally speculated about Ernie Chaples reading over my shoulder as I write: "That's crap, Hogan. Don't be such an asshole"! He is sadly missed.) Living readers are invited to contemplate how they would have corrected for my biases.

I have taken the opportunity of this book to provide brief sketches of some of the department's illustrious graduates. The ones highlighted are merely a small sample, and by no means constitute the "top 20" or anything like that. They are meant to span careers in politics, public service, business, journalism, and the arts. I could have provided a completely different set of names that would have been just as notable, although I have found it hard to find candidates for that final category of novelists, poets, painters or musicians. Our alumni are the measure of our success or failure.

The main difficulty in writing has been that the department has not kept its records; lack of space means that successive heads of department have trashed old files to make room for new ones. Faculties are little better, while university databases are accessible only with great trouble. Fortunately some enlightened head sent most of the minutes of the department's Board Meetings of the 1970s to the Archives, which also contains Dick Spann's papers. Some individuals have kept files for some years, so I have been able to collect considerable random information and ephemera. Can I encourage future heads of department to send material to the University Archives?

Acknowledgements

There are many acknowledgements due to people and organisations who helped in this study. At the suggestion of Graeme Gill some money was set aside by the Faculty of Arts and Social Sciences, as also by the School of Social and Political Sciences, for research and publication expenses. This helped pay for valuable research assistance by Rosa Evaquarta, and transcription of oral history interviews by Lisa Campano, Bonnie Kelly and Jack Kelly – as well as for assistance in publication costs. For cooperation in the oral history part of the project I am very grateful to the University Historian, Julia Horne. A number of colleagues read individual chapters and offered valuable suggestions: thanks to Graeme Gill, Sue Wills, Michael Jackson, Dennis Altman, Frank Stilwell and Ken Turner. I am grateful to the past and present members of staff who consented to be interviewed for the record; the interviews and transcripts are deposited in the University Archives. In the University Archives, Nyree Morrison has always been a delight and eager to help. Ian Jack introduced me to the resources of St Andrew's College concerning Dick Spann. Sue Wills kept sending me interesting tidbits of information from her voracious reading that have enriched the work, while I have been privileged to be able to bounce ideas off colleagues such as Ken Turner, David Clune and Lex Watson (now sadly departed). Professor Marie Carroll helped gain me access to some of the university's statistical records. I have used illustrations by courtesy of the National Portrait Gallery, the NSW Parliamentary Archives, the University of Sydney Archives, St Andrew's College, the Department of Government and International Relations, and from individuals such as Mary Pollard, Terry and Sue Irving.

Foreword

*Michael Lambert, Chair, External Advisory Committee,
Department of Government and International Relations*

Michael Hogan has written an engaging and informative book about what would normally be considered a dry and specialist topic, the history of what is now the Department of Government and International Relations at Sydney University. The book engages, partly because of the wide range of national issues that have impacted on the department and in which staff and students have been actively involved, partly because it reflects the research and publications that have informed and influenced public debate, and partly because of the big and influential personalities that have led the department – such as Francis Bland, Dick Spann and Henry Mayer.

The origins of the department extend back to 1917 when various public administration courses were taught within the Economics Faculty, leading to a chair in Public Administration in 1934 with Bland becoming the first Professor in 1935. This was followed in 1947 by the establishment of the Department of Government and Public Administration. It is arguably Australia's oldest political science department and certainly one of its most successful.

With the post war baby boom and the rising expectations regarding education, the department experienced a dramatic growth in students and staff. It was also heavily involved in the issues of the day, including the Vietnam War and conscription, the Iraq Wars, women's liberation, gay rights, aboriginal rights, the interaction of media and politics, political corruption and ethics, and the nature of democracy and individual rights. Academics such as Henry Mayer, Peter King, Denis Altman and Lex Watson, among others, were prominent in leading public discussion on major issues.

The Department also has a substantial number of prominent graduates who have both contributed on public issues and have gone on to major careers, including writer and journalist Geraldine Brooks, Anne Summers, one of the founders of the women's liberation movement in Australia, Jeff Angel, a leading player in environmental politics, Martin Indyk, who achieved high office in the US State Department, Jim Spigelman, who took a leading role in highlighting aboriginal disadvantage in the freedom rides of the 1970s and was a Chief Justice of NSW, and Mark Scott, head of the ABC.

For students a department is the prime contact with the university as they progress through courses, interacting with the lecturers and tutors as well as forming a more abstract but nevertheless real relation with the department. Occasionally the association becomes a lifetime one.

There have been major changes over time in the way the department has functioned. In the immediate post-World War I period it was focussed on teaching undergraduates. Since that time it has broadened and deepened its academic offerings, with research and coursework Masters, Masters degrees designed for mid-career professionals and a PhD program for research students. The students' backgrounds have also changed, with students in 1946 being nearly all local whereas today it draws on students and staff from around the world.

In terms of its area of study and teaching, the department has moved from a focus on public administration in Australia and public policy to a broader range of interests including political theory, comparative politics and international relations.

Organisationally the department has changed significantly, starting out as a part of the Economics Department and then gaining autonomy as the Department of Government and Public Administration. At the beginning of the present century its location was the Faculty of Economics and Business, and then it found its current home as the Department of Government and International Relations in the Faculty of Arts and Social Sciences. Along the way it faced a form of internal competition with the creation of the Graduate School of Government and the Centre for International Security Studies. Thankfully cooperation is appearing to replace competition in this area.

As Michael Hogan sets out quite clearly, the forces of technology and corporatisation of the university have and will continue to impact on the university and the department. There will be tension and conflict between the model of providing training for business and the broader role of research and scholarship which is concerned with the wider society and world.

The department has always maintained a broad perspective on society and this is reflected in the work of the External Advisory Committee, consisting of past alumni with the enthusiastic support of Michael Jackson, its secretary and tireless organiser, and of Graeme Gill, chair of the department. The role of the committee is to establish and nurture relations with relevant external organisations on behalf of the department and in furtherance of its role.

I congratulate Michael Hogan for conceiving, researching and writing *Cradle of Australian Political Studies*. The work will be of great interest to alumni who participated in the courses of the department by reminding them of their experience and putting this into a larger context. I trust it also inspires others to do like histories of their departments, each being a foundation block of the whole, of the University of Sydney.

1

Origins of the Department of Government

At the beginning of the 20th century the separate discipline of political science had barely emerged onto the world academic stage. There was little interest in having it arrive in Australia. During the 19th century one of the parents of modern political science was called "political economy", and Peter Groenewegen chronicles the spasmodic and largely unsuccessful attempts to have it taken seriously at the University of Sydney.[1] There was some academic debate about the need for the new discipline of sociology in the years before the Great War, but not much for political science.[2] This does not mean that the academic study of politics (disregarding the name "political **science**") was either new or neglected. Political philosophy and theory can be traced back to the Greek pre-Socratic philosophers, while both Plato and Aristotle are (or should be) fundamental sources for any appreciation of the study of politics. There is debate about the beginnings of an academic discipline separate from philosophy, history or law – one claim has been made that a Dutch professor of history, Justus Lipsius, suggested the creation of a separate chair for the study of politics at Leiden University in 1587. Subsequently, according to this claim: "The world's first chair in Political Science was established at Leiden University when Daniel Heinius (1602-1655) was appointed 'Professor Politices' in 1602."[3] Nevertheless, it is also the case that, mainly for reasons of feared political partisanship, such appointments and courses tended to be short-lived.

> **Ignoring the study of politics**
>
> Since the founding of the University the conviction we then had has been growing upon us, that no department of study is more imperatively required to be provided for than the whole science of Political Economy. The public is well aware that this branch of knowledge has been entirely overlooked in the arrangement of that institution ... By Political Economy we mean something more extensive than what is commonly applied to commercial and financial science exclusively. In our opinion it should include the whole range of public and general social relations, duties, and interests as objects of practical concern ... The science exists, and imperatively calls, side by side with the philosophy of which it is to be the application, for the endowment of a professorship.
>
> The Empire (Sydney), 2 January 1854. Quoted in Gavin Butler, Evan Jones & Frank Stillwell, Political Economy Now!, p. iii.

Nor does such academic reluctance to study politics mean that there was little popular interest in politics in Australia. A community interest in political debate was given a major fillip with the conclusion of the Great War, followed by international debate about constructing a new international order based on the League of Nations. Australians responded to the inspirational leadership of America's President Wilson, wondered at the collapse of empires and the redrawing of national boundaries in Europe, generally believed in a world of disarmament, and worried about the ever more frequent challenges to the new world order. By the 1930s and the Great Depression the institutions of democracy in Australia were themselves facing challenge from home grown versions of authoritarian and populist leadership. Local Australian fascist organisations even presented Mussolini and Hitler as models for a new political system to take the place of democratic institutions seemingly incapable of confronting the Depression in this country.

Other than the major newspapers one early important organisation concerned with politics was the Round Table, arriving in Australia from Britain at the beginning of the century. It was a small, largely secret, body whose members came to be a who's who of Australian academic, business, and political networks. The main concern was commentary on political, economic and social conditions throughout the British Empire, of which Australia was an important part. The British group published a quarterly review, called the *Round Table*, which was very influential in political debate, even in Australia. The Sydney branch, founded in the 1920s, included important members of the NSW government and the University of Sydney who will feature later in the story.[4]

One of the important Australian organs of debate was the journal *Australian Quarterly*, established in 1929 to discuss economic and political issues of the day. Its treatment of these matters gave it a claim to be the first political science journal in Australia. In 1932, a new association, the Australian Institute of Political Science (AIPS) was founded in Sydney and took over management of *Australian Quarterly*. In 1933 an interest in the place of Australia in the world led to the blending of a number of earlier bodies to form the Australian Institute of International Affairs (AIIA). One can say that political science had arrived, even if not yet in a significant institutional way in the universities.[5]

Another British implant in the Australian scene relevant to the study of politics was the Workers' Educational Association (WEA), an adult education organisation which had a special interest in political and economic issues. Judith Brett has stated:

> For the history of the social sciences in Australia the most important institutional expression of both social liberalism and the aspiration to incorporate sociology into the Australian academy was the workers' education association …[6]

The WEA was certainly of fundamental importance to the foundation of politics and administration as a discipline seeking a toehold in the University of Sydney. Arriving in Sydney in 1913, under its Sydney leader Meredith Atkinson, it immediately established an intimate relationship with the University of Sydney. Organisation, funding and choice of courses were the responsibility of the WEA. The university provided most of the lecturers through its tutorial outreach (called "extension courses"), while giving academic legitimacy to courses where students wanted a diploma qualification as a result of their studies.

An increase in popular interest in politics was given a boost by technological change that began to permeate Australian society in the 1920s – radio. It changed the nature of electoral campaigning, so that large public meetings were partly replaced by the more intimate chat by politicians on the "wireless". Political parties became keenly aware of the new technology, to such an extent that the NSW Labor Party purchased control of one of the early Sydney radio stations, 2KY, to be used as an instrument of political propaganda.

Studying politics at the University of Sydney

The University of Sydney was typical of the Australian universities of the time in that politics appeared as a component in a number of disciplines, but with very little crossover of influences. Most obvious in Sydney was the Department of History in the Arts Faculty which concentrated heavily on political history, especially British and imperial history. Many of the central themes of political science schools – political institutions, international relations, effective policy and administration, political leadership, to mention a few – were highlighted, although with little attempt to generalise. A good example of a book that could just as easily have issued from a political science school came from a professor of history in the 1930s – Stephen Roberts' *The House that Hitler Built*.[7]

In the Department of Philosophy in the same faculty it must have been hard to avoid the political ramifications of "traditional" philosophers like the ancient Greeks, or more "modern" thinkers such as David Hume or JS Mill, but the teachers for most of the first half of the century managed very well in downplaying the importance of political philosophy. With the arrival of the controversial Professor John Anderson there were obvious political implications in his teachings on libertarianism and the public role of powerful social institutions like the churches, but explicit academic treatment of political philosophy seemed to be discouraged. In 1934 a young Perce Partridge was appointed a Lecturer in the Philosophy Department with almost no scope for his interest in teaching political theory until he completed further study in Britain and returned as a lecturer in political theory (1943-47). In 1939 Alan Stout was appointed Professor of Moral and Political Philosophy, partly, according to his biographer, to be a counterbalance to the influence of Anderson and his "corrupting influence on impressionable young students".[8]

In the Law Faculty subjects with a strong political content, such as constitutional law or international law, were generally taught in such a way as to push politics into the background. Perhaps to balance this tendency, a reform of the curriculum in 1902 introduced a minor second year subject with the title of Political Science.[9] The term did not yet have the connotation of a behavioural, much less behaviourist, study of quantifiable facts that it acquired by the 1950s. In the first half of the 20th century such courses tended to be more prescriptive and normative than descriptive. Professor Pitt Corbett lent his name to a prize for political science to the best students in the course; in 1910 the recipient was Francis Bland, later to be the foundation Professor of Public Administration.[10] After the Great War the prize was renamed to honour the memory of Morven K Nolan, who had been killed in the war. By 1935 the prize seemed to have disappeared, but Political Science was still being taught by Charles Currey, by inclination more historian than lawyer:

> This subject will comprise an account of (a) the elements of Political Science, and (b) legislation in New South Wales and the Commonwealth with respect to social and economic matters.[11]

To this course in the Law School was added another in 1940 on Political Theory, taught by Professor Stout from the Philosophy Department, but that disappeared during the war years. When Julius Stone arrived in 1942 he brought a much wider social science perspective to the study of International Law. In a number of societies, notably in continental Europe, law faculties have provided an institutional base for the development of political science schools, but that was never likely in Sydney. The Sydney Law School's insistence on a "black letter" interpretation of law pushed matters like the political and social environment of legislation firmly into the background.

There was some interest in social issues and public administration in the Department of Social Studies (the school for professional education of social workers), where Francis Bland and Tom Kewley gave courses throughout the 1930s. Kewley was a lecturer in that department throughout the 1930s, while Bland and other teachers like Duncan MacCallum, were members of related departments.

Michael Jackson, searching through university records for more specific information on prizes for politics, also noted the arrival of a university interest:

> Now that I have been reading Calendars looking for prize winners, what I see from 1910 onward is politics here, there and everywhere: political philosophy in Philosophy, politics in History, federalism and constitutions in Law, public administration in Economics, prizes for political theory, etc. Bland's efforts may explain why it ended up in Economics, but the development was general and over a generation or more.[12]

Public administration and politics in the Faculty of Economics

The institutional origins of the eventual Department of Government lie in courses offered by the Faculty of Economics and the WEA from the years of the Great War. A young public servant and law graduate, Francis Armand Bland, was appointed as a Lecturer in the Department of Economics in 1917. According to the 1918 Report of the Senate referring to new appointments: "Department of Economics. — Mr. P.R. Watts, B.A. LL.B., and Mr. F.A. Bland, B.A., LL.B., were appointed Lecturers in Public Administration."[13] They were not mainstream lecturers in Economics, but specifically for the new discipline of Public Administration. They were also apparently half-time and temporary appointments that needed regular reappointment by the Senate. In 1918 Bland was also appointed assistant director of tutorial extension classes at the University of Sydney, with the two positions making up one full-time job. Incidentally, the Report of the Senate seemed unaware that Bland had recently graduated with an MA to add to his undergraduate Arts and Law degrees.

Francis Bland came from a modest background, attending a number of schools until he found work as a clerk. He studied at night and eventually passed the public service entrance exam. In 1901 he began work in Treasury, then in 1903 moved to the Public Service Board – a powerful body controlling administrative procedures and recruitment for the whole public service – where he was an assistant to Robert F Irvine. He continued his studies at night to achieve matriculation, and then graduated in Arts (1909), Law (1912), before gaining an MA (1914). Through all his studies he remained attached to the Public Service Board. He began his involvement in extension teaching for the WEA and the university after Irvine became head of the Department of Economics in 1914. Many years later he told *Honi Soit* that he had succeeded maverick politician and later judge, George Beeby, in teaching public administration for the WEA. Beeby had apparently taken up this task after he abandoned the NSW Labor Government in

1912 to try with limited success to start a new "progressive" country party. When Beeby went back into Parliament Bland took his place. He took time off in 1916-7 to travel to Britain, where he studied public administration at the London School of Economics under Professor Graham Wallas.[14]

The same 1918 Report of the Senate noted the structural change in the Bachelor of Economics, which became a four-year rather than three-year degree. Like most university strands at that time the heart of the degree was a "major", a sequence of full-year courses. In the new BEc the core was a four-year sequence of Economics I, II, III and IV. To that could be added other majors, or a minor sequence, or a mixture of a full sequence and some half courses. (Only much later did the Economics and Arts Faculties change to a structure of "units" with a mathematical value.) At its beginning Public Administration was not a full minor sequence, but rather a mixture of optional half-courses. A full unit of study normally involved 90 lectures per year, with three lectures a week, while a short or half-course involved 45 lectures per year. Bland and Watts taught an optional fourth-year course in Public Administration, while Bland offered a short course on Municipal Administration, and Watts presented a similar option on Elements of Political Science.[15] Public Administration was also approved as an optional course for the Master of Economics degree.

Some idea of Bland's expansive interpretation of administrative studies can be gathered from his summary of his Municipal Administration course in the 1922 University Calendar:

> The course will deal with Municipal Administration from the socio-political point of view. In addition to outlining the forms and functions of Local Government, an attempt will be made to estimate the social and economic effects of Municipal Administration.
>
> A review will be made of the chief features of the municipal systems of England, Germany and the United States, and, in

greater detail, of Australia. The subjects of City Government, Housing and Town Planning, Municipal Finance, and Municipal Trading will also be considered.[16]

Bland renewed a professional relationship with Professor Irvine, by 1920 now Dean of the newly established Faculty of Economics. Irvine had previously been his patron when they were both working for the Public Service Board. The appointment of Bland to the Department and then Faculty was clearly designed, presumably by Irvine, to bring into the curriculum some kind of study of the public sector and political institutions. Bland had already been giving WEA classes in Helensburgh and Wollongong at the urging of Atkinson. He was now helping administer the university tutorial system under GV Portus, a lecturer in the Economics Department, having already developed within the WEA a course in "Public Administration". During the early 1920s he mainly left the teaching of WEA courses to others while he concentrated on his work in the faculty, although he remained the university's assistant director of its tutorial program until 1933. He resumed the WEA courses in a more formal way when the Diploma of Public Administration was set up by university by-laws in 1928, to commence the following year. He eventually published a number of books based on his classes – *Shadows and Realities of Government* (1923), *Budget Control* (1931), *Planning the Modern State* (1934), and *Government in Australia* (1939). Their content makes a convincing case that Bland's vision of public administration was set within a very wide context of modern political institutions.

In 1929 the course on Public Administration, along with mainstream Economics courses, had become the centrepiece of a new three-year Diploma administered within the faculty as part of the university's tutorial program.

Diploma in Public Administration.

40. On the recommendation of the Faculty of Economics, the Senate has instituted a new Diploma Course styled "Diploma

in Public Administration". Matriculation is not required of candidates for this course, which extends over at least three years. Candidates are required to specialise in such subjects as Economics, Public Administration, and Modern Political Institutions. The course will be of great value to members of the State Public Service.[17]

Bland had been able to get the support of the NSW Public Service Board to have the new Diploma given preferred status in promotion of public servants. While courses in the Diploma in Public Administration were available for members of the public service, (the Intermediate Certificate was normally required for both purposes) the Faculty took the opportunity to expand the offerings for undergraduates in the BEc so that Bland managed an abbreviated three-year sequence. The original half-course became a full-year course, and a second offering, Public Administration II, joined it as a half-course, while Bland's colleague PR Watts, appointed Lecturer in Public Administration at the same time as Bland, continued teaching a half-course entitled Modern Political Institutions for the diploma and the degree.

The diploma course also had the support of public servants themselves and their trade union. In 1931 the Public Service Association (PSA) welcomed the new diploma with a gift of £430 to fund a prize named after John S D'Arcy, a former senior public servant and chairman of the PSA, that would be awarded to the best pass and honours students in Public Administration I and II. The PSA John S D'Arcy prize is still awarded to students excelling in Government I and II.[18]

In 1934 the New South Wales State government made provision for increased funding for the Faculty of Economics.

> Financial Assistance from the N.S.W. Government.
> 62. The Premier informed the Senate in October that he had made provision in the Parliamentary Estimates for an

increase in the Parliamentary Grants of £2,000–£500 for Veterinary Science and £1,500 for the Faculty of Economics. The Premier expressed regret that the position of the public finances precluded the Government from doing more. The additional income has greatly strengthened the Department of Economics by making possible—

(a) Establishment of a Chair of Public Administration.

(b) Provision for full-time Lecturer in Economics.

(c) Provision for full-time Lecturer in Economic History.

(d) Appointment of an additional full-time Assistant Lecturer in Economics.[19]

This seemed an extraordinary measure at a time when the iron grip of the Depression was forcing cuts in government funding for universities. At an early meeting of the University Senate in 1935 the decision was made to use the money to fund a chair in Public Administration. The Senate immediately awarded the Chair to Bland:

Chair of Public Administration.

20. In February the Senate was informed by the Finance Committee that, on account of the increased Parliamentary Vote for the Department of Economics, funds were available for the establishment of a Chair of Public Administration. The Senate resolved at the meeting that such a Chair be established in the University and decided to offer the Chair to Mr. F.A. Bland, M.A., LL.B., as from the 1st March, 1935. It was felt that no good purpose would be served by advertising the position throughout Australia or Great Britain since the Senate was convinced that the best candidate available was Mr. Bland, who had held the Lectureship in the subject since 1916.[20]

The 1916 date is slightly confusing. The 1918 Report of the Senate had noted Bland's appointment in 1917, but he had been teaching the subject for some time before that as a casual lecturer for the WEA, whose courses were supervised by the university. Bland now became a full-time member of the Faculty staff and its second professor.

The University of Sydney was still a small academy in 1935 (especially compared with 21st century Australian universities). To be awarded a Chair carried considerable status throughout the city and State community, as there were only about 40 professors in total on the Professorial Board, in a university with just over 3,000 students.[21] It was still the only university in New South Wales. Other than the professional Faculties of Medicine and Law, most teachers and students pursued their activities in or around the Main Quadrangle of the original building.

The origins of the modern academic study of public administration can be traced to the reforms of the British civil service (soon followed in the Australian colonies) in the late 19th century, following some ideas developed by John Stuart Mill, and given some American salience in a ground breaking article by future US President Woodrow Wilson in 1887. However, as two Dutch scholars have argued:

> Any claim that the 'real' start of PA [Public Administration] as a scholarly discipline did not take place until the end of the 19th century would be met with well-founded objections from Europe. There the PA discourse goes back to the Middle Ages and, ... for instance, experienced a first golden age in the 17th and 18th centuries with discipline known as Cameralism.

In the 20th century the strongest influence was the German sociologist, Max Weber, whose seminal study of the links between bureaucracy, public policy and politics, *Economy and Society*, was published posthumously in 1922. Both Bland and his later successor, Dick Spann, were strongly influenced by Weberian ideas.[22]

Upon Bland's appointment to the Chair of Public Administration the university also approved the creation of a new "Department of

Public Administration" in the Faculty of Economics.[23] Modern readers should be cautious of giving too much weight to this name. In some ways it was merely the confirmation of the fact that any professor of that time had considerable autonomy in the teaching of matters embraced by the title of the Chair. Bland had a small team of teachers who taught at his direction – his colleague Percy Watts along with Tom Kewley from Social Studies and some occasional part-timers. Bland would have had a secretary and some research funds available for him. In most other matters the small Faculty of Economics functioned as a single administrative unit, with various strands of academic disciplines. Not having a compete "major" sequence, Bland's new

Professor Francis Bland. (Drawing by Cyril Dubois, courtesy of the Department of Government)

department had neither Advanced courses nor Honours graduates, while any Masters student completing a dissertation on public administration issues (such as later ANU professor, Robert Parker) would graduate simply with the Master of Economics degree, with no mention of the separate discipline. Nevertheless, in the history of the later Department of Government, the creation of the Department of Public Administration was a significant step.

The decisions of 1934 and 1935 were clearly connected, and they cry out for some explanation. According to Peter Groenewegen, the driving force was the Premier of New South Wales, Bertram Stevens, who was very impressed with Bland's work in the professional development of public servants, which he supported strongly.[24] Stevens, who had himself been a career public servant, would also have been impressed with the political views of Bland, who had made a number of public interventions attacking the previous Premier, JT Lang, a few years before, while Bland became a frequent advisor to the Premier, as he had been previously when Stevens was head of Treasury. Yet there was probably another network of influences. Bland was an active member of the Sydney chapter of the Round Table. Fellow members around that time were his university colleagues Tom Kewley, Hermann Black, Sidney Butlin, Charles Currey and GV Portus; another was the former Nationalist Premier, Thomas Bavin, who was still on the backbench of the United Australia Party (UAP) government of Stevens. Nor should one forget Bland's Dean, RC Mills, nor the Chancellor of the University of Sydney, Sir Mungo MacCallum, who were also members of the Sydney chapter of the organisation.[25] No wonder that the promotion of a part-time lecturer to a Chair received Senate approval without dissent. There is no doubt that Bland was very well connected. It should be pointed out that there is no firm evidence that this network was involved; perhaps these matters were all entirely coincidental.

Judith Brett has given a nice description of the academics who were closely associated with the WEA:

> Bland and Portus, and many others who began university teaching in the 1920s, came into the academy through an organisation that was built to link not just town and gown but labour and learning, and which they imbued with missionary zeal. As well as civics, the syllabus they taught covered economics, sociology, and economic and industrial history, including the history of trade unionism. These men began their teaching with a broad palette and an elevated sense of social purpose.[26]

There certainly seems to have been a missionary zeal in Bland's makeup. This was welcomed by some (mostly students) and criticised by others (notably other academics). As well as being an enthusiastic lecturer Bland also set the precedent that was continued through most of the second half of the century in that his team was the most productive in the Faculty in terms of published research. Some of Bland's successors in the emerging Australian discipline of political science were not impressed with his writings. Brett points out:

> From the vantage point of the emerging professionalism of the 1950s, Rufus Davis and Colin Hughes (1958) were condescendingly dismissive of Bland's work, describing it 'almost entirely as a missionary literature, full of earnest diagnosis, alarums and calls to action'.[27]

That judgement was probably not unfair, although "alarums and calls to action" were very typical of Australian political writings of the 1920s and especially the Depression of the 1930s. It was easy to be condescending in the postwar optimism of the 1950s, and when the new discipline was well on the way to setting its own standards. On the other hand, there were more positive responses from equally eminent political scientists, writing in the 1980s. One of Bland's students from the 1930s, Robert Parker (later professor at the ANU), appreciated both Bland's enthusiasm and his wide interpretation of the scope of public administration:

> From the time I sat under Bland it was inevitable that I would always see and treat public administration (so far as it concerned my own work) as part of the study of government, and hence of political science. Bland himself did not write books about 'public administration', but about Shadows and Realities of Government, about Planning the Modern State, about Government in Australia.[28]

One of Bland's successors at Sydney, Professor RN Spann, also wrote with admiration for a kind of 'engaged' and 'interventionist' tradition represented by Bland that was shared with many teachers of politics in Britain and America, (even if public political controversy was not Spann's own style).[29]

Bland's teaching style

His lecture began with the characteristic 'Well, peoples' and was delivered – more than one student has coined the phrase – in machine gun staccato, an outpouring of ideas, critical comment, anecdotes, and factual record. After the first lecture or two, the student realised that Bland meant it when he said that the 'synopsis' was meant to obviate note-taking, but that, unlike similar systems used in some other University departments, this did not mean that everything in the lectures was already in the typescript. In a sense, nothing in one way was in the other; the lecture was comment on, extension of, digression from the condensed material of the typescript, to which one could listen with close attention and interest.

Bland was a great success with students, inspired them in their work and sometimes influenced them in their outlook. He had always held strong political and social views, and was not afraid to disclose them to his students ... The students felt always that here was a man who knew the material of his subject, and was widely read in its theory, and who held his views with a passionate, even religious conviction.

Mills and Butlin, p.132-3; also quoted in Groenewegen, p.31.

The new Professor of Public Administration was now one of two professors in the Faculty, along with the Dean, RC Mills. Yet the whole Faculty in 1935 was still one small teaching unit, with only 12 teaching staff, including part-timers. The formal division of the Faculty of Economics into separate Departments, irrespective of the holders of chairs, was still many years in the future. Patrick Weller described the situation under Bland at that time as "a department for practitioners and without a staff".[30] That is not quite the case; Bland's colleague, Percy Watts, had been appointed as Lecturer in Public Administration along with Bland in 1917, and taught his course on Modern Political Institutions alongside the Public Administration courses in both the BEc and Diploma. A majority of students were probably "practitioners", that is, public servants, but the Faculty under Professor Mills was very insistent that future economists should be exposed to the historical, social and political context of economic choices.

Francis Bland's politics were firmly on the right of the spectrum, featuring a life-long distrust of the Labor Party. His basic belief was that the state was the most direct threat to individual freedom, so any manifestation of a social welfare state was anathema. During the 1940s he was active in campaigns against the Federal Labor Government's policies on wartime censorship, the referendums of 1944 and 1946 to extend Commonwealth powers over postwar reconstruction and social services, and the attempt of the Chifley Government to nationalise the banks. His attitude to referendums was resolutely in defence of States' rights:

> Any proposals that aim either at shifting the balance of the Federal system, or at widening the field of uniformity in legislation and administration should be opposed irrespective of the specific character of the proposals.[31]

He was a member of the ideologically anti-Labor Institute of Public Affairs, and chairman of the similarly right-wing NSW Constitutional

League. It should have been a surprise to no one when, after he retired from the university, he was preselected for the safe Liberal seat of Warringah for the 1951 Federal election.

> **Bland letting himself go**
>
> *In lectures the synopsis headings provided the stimulus for Bland to let himself go, in an outpouring of frankly biased comment on current affairs. His political theory was old-fashioned liberatica of 1900 vintage stiffened with emphasis on 'correct' finance and he spoke at a rate which excluded all note-taking. A count of what a licensed court reporter could get down showed that his normal lecturing speed exceeded 250 words a minute, but all delivered with clarity, fire and passion and conviction. Hearing Bland during the Lang regime with a full head of steam was a fascinating and enjoyable experience even for the majority who profoundly disagreed with him.*
>
> Butlin, p.11, Also quoted in Turney, Bygott & Chippendale, Vol.1, p.578.

There is some doubt about how coherent Bland's teaching team was. Watts was appointed as a lecturer in Public Administration in 1917, and the 1921 Economics Handbook has him teaching a course called Public Administration A, which was a comparative analysis of "executive institutions in various countries", while Bland taught Public Administration B. However, in the 1924 Handbook Watts was listed as a lecturer in Modern Political Institutions, while his appointment came to an end on 31 December 1939 when his personnel record notes that the position was "terminated".[32] One suspects that Watts and Bland did not get along very well. During the 1930s Bland cooperated much better with Tom Kewley (who was still in the Social Studies Department). It helped that Kewley had been one of his star pupils as a graduate student in the Diploma in Public Administration a few years previously. Watts was eventually replaced in 1944 by Kewley, who was appointed as Lecturer in Public Administration. During the war years Professor Stout from Philosophy also briefly taught a course on Political Theory for Economics students. Bland's biographer in the *Australian Dictionary of Biography*, Ross Curnow, recalls that Bland was not averse to expecting junior colleagues, such as Kewley, to act as his personal assistants, even before Kewley came onto his staff in 1941.[33] Perhaps Watts did not take kindly to such professorial exploitation, or perhaps he wanted to distance himself from Bland's style of politics.

Professor Bland tended to annoy editors of university handbooks because he constantly changed the descriptions of his courses. Yet, even with such changes there were constants in his approach. The description of his Public Administration I course for 1935 is a good example. The university year still followed the British tradition of teaching in three terms – Lent, Trinity and Michaelmas – rather than semesters, which were introduced only much later in the century. The course consisted of 90 lectures, which, spread over three academic terms of 10 weeks, meant three lectures per week, on Mondays, Wednesdays and Fridays at 7 pm.

> This course is intended to introduce the student to the more important changes which have taken place in the nature and content of Government, consequent upon the emergence of the Social Service State. It will examine the problems which confront Federal, State and Municipal Governments in regard to such matters as delimiting and coordinating the functions of each; the determination of suitable administrative areas and agencies (including New States); the recruitment, training, and organisation of officials; the relations between officials and popular representatives, and the desirability of revising our political institutions to enable Parliament to exercise an effective control on behalf of the people over the executive and administrative activities of Government.[34]

The content of Public Administration II was more narrowly professional, as it offered a half-course (45 lectures) with "special subjects of which the following are illustrations": Budgetary Methods and Practices, the Administration of Transport, the Administration of Social Services, and the Administration of State Industrial Undertakings.

As part of the sequence available to undergraduates, Percy Watts offered his half-course of Modern Political Institutions, which, in that same year of 1935, had this description:

> A course of forty-five lectures divided into two parts.
>
> The first part will be devoted to an examination of the principal conceptions underlying the various forms of modern political organisation. The State. Sovereignty. Organs and functions of Government. The Legislature. The Executive. The Judiciary. Theories as to the separation and division of powers.
>
> The second part will be devoted to a comparative survey of modern political institutions in the United Kingdom, the United States, France, and Switzerland.[35]

Clearly students completing the abbreviated three-year sequence of one full-course and two half-courses offered by the Public Administration team in 1935 were not exposed to the full range of a modern political science major. Political theory and international relations were notably absent until the former was added a few years later. Yet, just as clearly, this was not a narrow how-to-administer course designed for practitioners. It was a good introduction to a comparative analysis of modern political institutions and the modern state. It was the study of politics appropriate for students of economics at that time.

Not that most Sydney students of economics were all that interested. The course on Modern Political Institutions was compulsory as a half-course in second year, while Public Administration I and II were available as options in the third and fourth year of the degree, competing against other offerings in Economic History, Accountancy, Statistics and a short course in Commercial and Industrial Law. Throughout the 1930s Bland's courses attracted the fewest undergraduate students among those choices. As an illustration, at the 1934 examinations, 57 students completed the compulsory Modern Political Institutions course, while 21 completed Public Administration I, and only four completed Public Administration II.[36] It was only the presence of students in the diploma that lifted the numbers in class to a more impressive level. This pattern continued until after the Second World War. Numbers would pick up only when the sequence was made available to students from the Faculty of Arts.

At the end of 1939 the unit on Modern Political Institutions, previously taught by Percy Watts, was replaced by a half-course on Political Theory, taught in the second year of the degree initially by Professor Stout from the Philosophy Department. This now became the first offering in the three-year sequence, followed by full-courses in Public Administration I and II in years three and four of the degree. When Percy Partridge joined the team part-time in 1943 political theory became the established introductory course to the sequence. Partridge taught his half-course in the Public Administration strand, and another half-course in Social Philosophy for the Department of Social Studies, and a course in Political Philosophy in the Philosophy Department which was his primary location. Until the 1950s the small Faculty of Economics was physically located in the Western Quadrangle of the university. Other related academic units such as the Departments of Philosophy, History, and Social Studies were nearby, making the exchange of staff for particular courses very easy.

The Diploma in Public Administration ran into strong opposition within the Faculty of Economics during the Second World War. Courses for non-matriculated students were seen as affecting academic teaching standards and as inappropriate for a professional faculty. In 1943 the Faculty resolved to eliminate its Diplomas in Commerce and Public Administration: "to work for their abolition or conversion into post-graduate diplomas".[37] The following year

> **Bland against wartime censorship**
>
> *The detailing of Commonwealth Peace Officers to investigate the actions of University students is almost as extraordinary as were the outrageous events that led to their action. I may lack Dr. Evatt's experience of political practice, but he and I share a common University tradition which demands that we measure University conduct by a different standard of values than he is applying. Surely he has lost his sense of perspective as well as his appreciation of his duties as a Minister. What justification was there for this wanton waste of public funds? If he did not authorise this investigation, is this just another illustration of the intimidatory practices of unrestrained officialdom, and if it is, then what happens to the doctrine of Ministerial responsibility? Apparently these things are less important than that University men and women should be traduced for having shown a clear appreciation of issues that are fundamental to their work.*
>
> SMH, 15 May 1944, p. 4.

the by-laws were changed to demand the Leaving Certificate as a minimum qualification. That was terminal for most public servants, who traditionally completed only the Intermediate Certificate at that time. By-laws were eventually altered so that no new students could be admitted into the Diploma in Public Administration after 31 December 1945. Students already committed under the old by-laws could attend classes and be examined for a few years, but effectively the diploma was dead. For the teaching of politics the main result was that class sizes, especially in Public Administration I, were reduced. During the 1930s there had always been more students from the diploma than from undergraduates at that level. On the other hand, student numbers in the diploma had always dropped off drastically in the second and third years of their sequence. During the war even entry levels had collapsed since recruitment was restricted because of the men and women going into the services, and few applicants had completed the Leaving Certificate. One reason that the Diploma could be eliminated so easily was that completion rates had always been very low. Graduate courses for public servants found a new home within the Faculty half a century later when the Graduate School of Government was introduced in 2003 with precisely that as one of its principal objects.

It was not only the diploma that the Faculty of Economics was uneasy about. Nor was it only that faculty. Roger Scott, briefly a teacher in the Department of Government, has written about the difficult relationship between political science and public administration, especially when the second title was dominant:

> It is fair to say, however, that the study of public administration experienced significant resistance within universities. On the one hand, it was regarded as too soft by accountants and economists and, on the other hand, it was suspected by pure scholars in Arts of dirtying its hands through close involvement with the community of public servants. Part-time study was seen as not quite proper and the Faculty of Arts in Sydney was typical in not recognising public administration as an Arts subject.[38]

One can add that at the University of Sydney part-time study was associated with evening classes, so that both the Arts and Economics Faculties largely abandoned part-time and evening students from the 1960s until later in the century, although there were still occasional evening lectures. That task could be left to lesser universities like UNSW or Macquarie! Moreover, in Sydney the reputation of Professor Bland was already under attack. His discursive evangelical lecturing style, along with his endeavour to widen the interpretation of classes in public administration to a general discussion of modern politics, made him suspect in the Faculty of Economics.

At the final meeting of the Senate in 1946 approval was given to Bland's request for a further lectureship in Public Administration.[39] The result of that decision was the appointment of a science graduate, Neville R Wills, who joined Bland and Kewley, while Partridge left to head the Melbourne political science department during 1947.

However, it is clear that plans were afoot to reorganise the team in the light of the decision already taken to divide the Faculty of Economics into separate Departments.

In August 1947 Bland would reach the standard public sector retirement age of 65. Folklore among veterans of the Department of Government is that Bland was forced out by the university. The record does not support that. The university had resolved in 1935 that the normal retirement age for professors in the future should be 65, with discretion to extend it but not beyond the age of 70.[40] At the end of 1946 the Registrar informed the Senate that three professors – of Public Administration, Architecture and Oriental Studies – would reach retirement age during 1947. Senate resolved to initiate the process of replacing them by advertising for the three Chairs. Bland, who was a member of the Senate, agreed that the Chairs should be advertised, and offered to stay on until the replacement could take over. His offer was accepted, and he remained for nearly a further year beyond his 65th birthday, retiring at the end of June 1948. The controversy came not from Bland but from another member of the Senate, Sir Henry Barraclough, who insisted that it was profligate of the university to be getting rid of senior staff at a time when enrolments by students were expanding rapidly in the immediate postwar years.[41]

Bland agreed with Barraclough at least in his appreciation of the consequences of a flood of students. He took advantage of the process of his replacement to get extra staff for his Department. When he reported that Percy Partridge was moving to the University of Melbourne and was thus unavailable to teach his political theory course in the Department he got approval for two temporary lecturers to teach in 1947 – CH Currey from the Law School and WGK Duncan who was director of the university's tutorial classes. That was only a start:

> Professor Bland said that in view of the increased numbers of students taking Public Administration in 1947 it was

necessary to provide additional assistance during the year. He moved that Mr AW Coady, BA, BEc, Mr JT Monaghan, LLB, and Miss Ruth Atkins BA, BEc, be appointed as part-time Lecturers for the year, with remuneration in each case of £100.

That also was approved. So, during 1947, the Departmental team had increased to three full-time members, Bland, Kewley and Wills, plus two temporary lecturers and three part-timers. Bland hoped he would be handing over a good working team to his successor.

In April 1947, as part of the process of advertising the Chair, the Senate resolved that: "the present Chair of Public Administration be designated 'Chair of Government and Public Administration' ".[42] The Faculty of Economics had already determined that the Department would have that name. The title was a compromise, recognising the origins of the unit in the teaching of public administration, yet insisting that its concerns were much wider, encompassing the whole sphere of modern politics. Both terms – government and public administration – took their origins in the University of Sydney decision from the terminology used by Bland.

If Bland was not pushed aside, he must have realised that a new era needed new leadership. He had suffered a number of setbacks in the mid-1940s. The decision of the Faculty to cripple, then terminate, the diploma course must have been a deep disappointment, especially as Bland remained the chairman of the university's Joint Committee for Tutorial Classes. Bland was also firmly committed to the Public Administration title of his team and courses, even though he recognised that it did not adequately describe what his courses were about. In the handbook entry for Public Administration I in 1947 the first sentence read: "This course might otherwise be described as an introduction to the study of government, although its emphasis is upon administrative aspects".[43] One indication of continuing disappointment was a brief discussion in the Professorial Board in September 1947 when the appointment of Professor Partridge came up for confirmation. Bland was not present at the meeting, but two other professors moved that the appointment be sent back to the committee to see if there were not other candidates "with Mr Partridge's academic qualifications, together with greater experience in Public Administration".[44] The motion was lost on the voices, but it is easy to speculate that Bland was not happy that a political theorist, rather than a public administration specialist, was replacing him.

The new environment was also evident in student interest in politics (rather than professional public administration courses). In June 1946 the inaugural meeting of a "Political Science Association" was held at the university, where JA McCallum addressed the question of "What has science to do with politics?".[45] By 1947 the University of Sydney, along with other Australian universities, must have been considering what form it wanted for a sequence in political science available to students in Faculties other than merely Economics. A sequence with the title of Public Administration, or a dominant concentration on it, would hardly have been appealing to professors in the Faculty of Arts as something that their students might like to pursue.

The first in Australia?

In a recent survey of political science in Australian universities, Patrick Weller states that: "Sydney was the first. In 1934 it created the Department of Public Administration and in 1939 Bland was created professor of public administration".[46] Bland's Chair and the creation of his Department both date from 1935. Weller dismisses the Department of History and Political Science founded in 1934 at the University of Adelaide as a candidate since during the 1930s it was in effect a normal history department with little interest in political science. Nevertheless, the statements and dates about Sydney are misleading. A good case can be made that Sydney did lead the field in the teaching of politics, but the argument is rather more complicated than Weller asserts. In 1929 the University of Sydney beefed up the Faculty of Economics offerings in Public Administration and Modern Political Institutions as part of the decision to inaugurate the diploma course for public servants. According to Weller, the University of Melbourne gave departmental status to politics in 1939, but again (as with Sydney's Department of Public Administration) that was probably not what modern readers would recognise as a separate "department". In a paper on the development of political science in Australia, Dick Spann commented that "it was still true in 1945 that no Australian university had given full status to political science".[47] Perhaps a better term to use (to avoid the scourge of nominalism) would be "teams"; the Sydney and Melbourne teams were vestigial until after the Second World War. In Sydney Bland was not on his own because others regularly taught in the Sydney program under his authority as Professor; Tom Kewley shared the Public Administration courses with Bland long before joining the Economics Faculty in 1944, while Percy Watts taught his course on Modern Political Institutions alongside Bland until the start of the Second World War. In Melbourne McMahon Ball was alone until he acquired a part-time tutor in 1939.

By 1944 the Melbourne team had three full-time members and one part-timer. In the same year the Sydney team had increased to two teachers plus the part-time use of Percy Partridge to teach political theory as the first offering of the three-year sequence. The Melbourne team certainly grew more strongly in the later 1940s, partly because of its location in the Faculty of Arts, where there was more student interest in the subject than in Sydney's Faculty of Economics, and also because the Sydney course was not available for first year students until well into the next decade. When Spann published his survey of political science in Australia in 1955 he noted that the Melbourne Department had twice as many students and staff as the next largest Department (Sydney).[48]

Sydney can claim some priority in that Bland became Professor of Public Administration in 1935, while McMahon Ball managed his team as a Senior Lecturer. Again there is some semantic confusion in that Weller states that Percy Partridge became the first "political science professor in the country" when he took a chair in the newly named Department of Government and Public Administration in 1947. The inclusion of the new term "government" was meant to make the point that the scope of teaching and research would be much wider than just "public administration", but the reality was that under Bland and his small team that had always been the case. Bland should be given his due as the first political science professor.

Sydney's strongest claim to be the first is based on the origins of the eventual Department. There was an almost seamless transition from the appointment of Bland and Watts as lecturers in Public Administration, teaching undergraduate and WEA courses since 1917, to the beginning of the Diploma of Public Administration under university by-laws in 1929, to the Chair and Department of Public Administration in 1935, to the Department of Government and Public Administration in 1947, to the Department (briefly the Discipline) of Government and International Relations from 2000.

---

1 Peter Groenewegen, *Educating for Business, Public Service and the Social Sciences: A History of the Faculty of Economics at the University of Sydney 1920-1999*, Sydney, SUP, 2009, pp. xiii-xv.

2 Judith Brett, "The Inter-war Foundations of Australian Political Science" in RAW Rhodes (ed.), *The Australian Study of Politics*, Melbourne, Palgrave Macmillan, 2009, p. 34.

3 Rudy B Andeweg, "Lipsius to Lijphart and beyond", in Joop van Holsteyn, Reineke Mon, Ineke Smit, Henk Tromp, Gezinus Wolters (eds.), *Perspectives on the Past: 50 years of FSW*, Leiden, Faculty of Social and Behavioural Sciences, University of Leiden, 2013, pp. 6-7.

4 Leonie Foster, *High Hopes: the Men and Motives of the Australian Round Table*, Melbourne, MUP, 1986.

5 Judith Brett, *op.cit.*, p. 38.

6 Judith Brett, *op.cit.*, p. 34.

7 Stephen Roberts, *The House That Hitler Built*, London, Methuen, 1937.
8 Philip Gissing, "Stout, Alan Ker (1900-1983)", *Australian Dictionary of Biography*.
9 John and Judy Mackinolty (eds.), *A Century Down Town: Sydney University Law School's First Hundred Years*, Sydney, Sydney University Law School, 1991, p. 45.
10 Ross Curnow, "Bland, Francis Armand (1882-1967)", *Australian Dictionary of Biography*.
11 *University of Sydney Calendar*, 1935, p. 251.
12 Michael Jackson to Michael Hogan, 3 May 2013.
13 *University of Sydney Calendar*, 1918, p. 614.
14 Ross Curnow, *op.cit.;* RWM, "Goodbye to all that", *Honi Soit*, 30 October 1947.
15 *University of Sydney Calendar*, 1918, p. 88.
16 *University of Sydney Calendar*, 1922, p. 217.
17 "Report of the Senate for the year ended 31 December 1928", *University of Sydney Calendar, 1929*, p. 883.
18 *University of Sydney Calendar*, 1952, pp. 365-7.
19 "Report of the Senate for the year ended 31 December 1934", *University of Sydney Calendar, 1935*, p. 895.
20 "Report of the Senate for the year ended 31 December 1935", *University of Sydney Calendar, 1936*, p. 934.
21 *University of Sydney Calendar*, 1935, pp. 604, 858.
22 John Stuart Mill, *Considerations on Representative Government*, London, Parker, 1861. Woodrow Wilson, "The study of public administration", *Political Science Quarterly*, 1887. Fritz van der Meer & Gerrit Dijkestra, "Public Administration: from Rotterdam and Leiden to The Hague", in Joop van Holsteyn, Reineke Mon, Ineke Smit, Henk Tromp, Gezinus Wolters (eds.), *Perspectives on the Past: 50 years of FSW*, Leiden, Faculty of Social and Behavioural Sciences, University of Leiden, 2013, p.61. Max Weber, *Wirtschaft und Gesellschaft*, published in English as *Economy and Society: an outline of interpretive sociology*, New York, Bedminster, 1968.
23 I have not been able to verify this decision from any official document. Michael Jackson has seen an administrative memorandum dated 8 December 1937, apparently in the University Archives. Unfortunately the Bland personnel file in the Archives is still closed and was not available to me. In the Spann Papers in the Archives there is a Spann handwritten memo of the history of the Department of Government that refers to the creation of the Department of Public Administration in 1935 (Box 45, Folder "1980-81").
24 Peter Groenewegen, *op.cit.*, p. 30.
25 A list of members in the quite small Sydney chapter can be found in Appendix B of Leonie Foster, *op.cit.*, pp. 245-6.
26 Judith Brett, ibid., p. 35.
27 Judith Brett, ibid., p. 35-6.
28 RS Parker, "Understanding Public Administration: a Comment", *Australian Journal of Public Administration*, Vol. XI, No.3, September 1981, p. 229.

29 RN Spann, "Understanding Public Administration: Reflections on an Academic Obituary – 'Alas, Poor Yorick' ", *Australian Journal of Public Administration*, Vol. XI, No.3, September 1981, p. 239.

30 Patrick Weller, "Universities and the study of politics" in RAW Rhodes (ed.), *The Australian Study of Politics*, Melbourne, Palgrave Macmillan, 2009, p. 20.

31 RS Parker, "F.A. Bland's contribution to public administration in Australia", *Public Administration (AJPA)*, September 1948, p. 176.

32 University of Sydney, *Handbook of the Faculty of Economics*, 1921, pp.15-6; 1924, p.2; Employment record for Percy Richard Watts, University Archives.

33 Conversation with Ross Curnow, 18 March 2011.

34 *University of Sydney Calendar*, 1935, pp. 351-2.

35 *University of Sydney Calendar*, 1935, pp. 356.

36 *University of Sydney Calendar*, 1935, pp. 588 & 593.

37 Peter Groenewegen, *op.cit.*, p.49.

38 Roger Scott, "Political Science and Public Administration: The Saga of a Difficult Relationship", *Australian Journal of Public Administration*. Vol. 62, No 2, 2003, pp 113-120.

39 Peter Groenewegen, *op.cit.*, p. 60.

40 "Report of the Senate for the year ended 31 December 1935", *University of Sydney Calendar, 1936*, p. 935.

41 Minutes of the Senate, University of Sydney, 11 November 1946; 3 March 1947; 11 August 1947.

42 Minutes of the Senate, University of Sydney, 23 December 1946; 14 April 1947.

43 *University of Sydney Calendar*, 1947, p. 428.

44 Minutes of the Professorial Board, University of Sydney, 22 September 1947.

45 *Honi Soit*, 20 June 1946.

46 Patrick Weller, *op.cit.*, p. 20.

47 RN Spann, "Political Science in Australia", *Australian Journal of Politics and History*, Vol 1 No 1. 1955, p. 88.

48 RN Spann, *op.cit.*, pp. 89-90.

2

Establishing the Department of Government (1947-62)

During 1947 the Faculty of Economics established a separate Department of Government and Public Administration, which would offer courses in a sequence entitled simply "Government". The first Government courses were offered in 1948. They initially comprised a sequence of Government I, II and III, available to students in that Faculty in the second, third and fourth year of their degree (although the *Economics Handbook* of that year still called the courses by their old names, as did the *Sydney Morning Herald* when it reported the results). It was not yet available to Arts students, and not available to first year students. However, it now could accept Honours and postgraduate students, along with planning the appropriate courses for those levels.

The title "Government" needs some explanation. There was no consensus in the Australian academic community about either the desired content or name for the emerging discipline studying politics. There still is not. The term "political science" had a presence in the University of Sydney since the beginning of the century, but by the period after the Second World War it was already being associated with the dominant behavioural and "scientific" study favoured in the United States. There were a number of Departments of Government in Britain and America that could be taken as a precedent for Sydney

– for example at universities in Harvard, Georgetown, Manchester, Birmingham and the London School of Economics. The term had the connotation that the proper study of politics was the institutions of the state. That notion came under heavy attack by the 1960s – giving way especially to the study of power in all its social manifestations – but there is little doubt that most students of politics in Australia in the 1940s would have accepted it without cavil. In the Faculty of Economics, where there was a professional concern with questions of governance and public policy, it was accepted as a good title for what had long been taught in Professor Bland's courses. For the Faculty of Arts it was much more acceptable as a more inclusive term than those courses under the title of "Public Administration". It is impossible at this stage to say who was responsible for the title of the department and the chair.

In the Spann Papers in the University Archives a one-page set of jottings by Dick Spann on the history of the department offers two reasons for choosing the title of "Government":

> (1) That the Philosophy Department on paper taught Moral and Political Philosophy (they taught in practice very little Political Philosophy) and objected to a separate Department using the term "Political Science" or "Political Studies".
>
> (2) There was an Oxford Chair with the same title, occupied by an Australian, KC Wheare, whose advice was commonly sought at that time by Australian Universities.
>
> It was not warmly welcomed at first, and for many years the Faculty of Arts would not admit Government as a First Year subject."[1]

The best explanation is that it was a compromise acceptable to all interested parties at the University of Sydney at that time. It was managed while Bland was still the professor and a member of the University Senate. The tacking on of "Public Administration" was the minimum that he would have accepted without a public fight after 30 years of teaching under that banner.

A reorganisation of Economics Faculty by-laws undertaken about the same time meant that there was more scope for Economics students to choose Government in their degree, although a clear separation of the Faculty into two sections – business students and others – was already becoming obvious. Students wanting a professional qualification as accountants filled up their degree with Economics, Statistics, Accountancy and Commercial Law, and had little inducement to study subjects like Government, Economic History, Industrial Relations or more advanced Economics. In the title of his history of the Faculty – *Educating for Business, Public Service and the Social Sciences* – Peter Groenewegen suggests a threefold division, but it is clear that educating for the social sciences was not a high priority in the Faculty in the postwar period.[2] On the other hand, neither was it a school of commerce; the University of Sydney at that time preferred an academic education in Economics, leaving subjects like commerce, marketing or "business principles" to technical colleges or lesser (!) universities. That attitude would change in later years.

The context for decisions about a new department was the great influx of students into the University of Sydney immediately after the end of the war. Many of the newcomers were ex-service men and women who had postponed their studies during the war, or who took advantage of the Commonwealth funded retraining scheme, while others were a new generation of school leavers who were beginning to appreciate that a higher level of education would be both possible and necessary in the postwar world. (The baby-boomers did not arrive at university until the 1960s, which was when an even more spectacular explosion of enrolments occurred.) Between 1940 and 1950 the student intake to the university as a whole more than doubled (from 4,094 to 9,626). However, this was not reflected uniformly among Faculties. In Economics the numbers barely changed in those years, while the biggest increase was in the Arts Faculty where student numbers jumped by nearly 150%.[3]

The Partridge interlude

When Government I was offered for the first time in 1948 Professor Bland was still in charge, while Percy Partridge had been offered and had accepted the Chair of Government and Public Administration. Partridge had evidently done some hard bargaining. The Senate minutes record:

> A difficult position has arisen with respect to the Chair of Government and Public Administration. The Advisory Committee of the Professorial Board unanimously recommended the appointment of a man from Melbourne University, but it is felt that Sydney will lose him if the ordinary routine is adhered to.[4]

Partridge was the "man from Melbourne University". Negotiations were obviously successful. He arrived in Sydney to take up his post at the beginning of the second (Trinity) term in May, while Bland eventually retired on 30 June 1948. The Chair had attracted a strong field of 14 applicants, from whom the eventual choice was made to prefer Partridge over Gordon Greenwood (History, Sydney). One of the applicants not shortlisted was Robert Parker, then teaching at the ANU and later to be a distinguished professor and colleague of Dick Spann. Although Partridge was appointed to the Chair of Government and Public Administration, he preferred to be known as Professor of Political Theory (which must have enraged Bland in his retirement).[5] Moreover, the first new member of his staff appointed by Partridge was a political theory graduate of the Melbourne department of which he had briefly been the head – a young Henry Mayer, who took up his position as a teaching fellow in 1950.

Professor Percy Partridge (Photo courtesy of Archives, Australian National University)

The Partridge personnel file in the University Archives gives some insight into the straitened circumstances of postwar Sydney. A week or two before he was to arrive from Melbourne to take up his appointment he wrote to the Registrar explaining that he was having great difficulty finding somewhere to live. This was not surprising since in 1948 rental accommodation was virtually unobtainable in Sydney except at the very high end of the market. Apparently that problem was sorted out, because Partridge then asked the Registrar to provide a letter of support from the university so that he could have a telephone installed at his home. Otherwise he would just be put on an indefinite waiting list. He also wanted a similar letter so that the new car he had ordered could be delivered earlier than the 18-month period offered to him. The file does not record how successful such measures were.[6]

Percy Partridge (usually called Perce) came from a modest background, was educated at public schools in Yass in rural New South Wales and Sydney, graduated from the University of Sydney with First Class Honours in Philosophy (1930), then spent a few years teaching in secondary schools to serve out the bond on his Teachers' College Scholarship. He returned to study under Professor John Anderson to graduate MA with the University Medal (1937) while lecturing in Philosophy (1934-39). After a year studying in Britain at the London School of Economics and at Oxford, he returned to the Philosophy Department as lecturer in political theory (1943-6). He spent 1947 as the senior lecturer head of the department of political science in Melbourne, before accepting the Chair of Government and Public Administration. His biographer in the *Australian Dictionary of Biography*, Grant Harman, refers to him as "an inspiring teacher with formidable knowledge", but he was more comfortable with advanced students rather than undergraduates. In this he was quite different from Bland, who enjoyed the performance of teaching, and preferred minds that he could more easily mould. Harman quotes the comments of an ANU colleague, WD Borrie, about Partridge:

> There was not a trace of flamboyance in this man, who despised cant and denigration, and who always spoke and wrote as logical thinking and conclusions directed him to.[7]

During the war years, while lecturing on political philosophy, Partridge had gained a reputation as a political conservative. This was sparked by a resolute opposition to Stalinism in the Soviet Union, which he argued was being exported to the rest of the world. This was not an unusual attitude among Australian intellectuals at that time, although it did amount to an attack on one of the Australia's allies against Nazi Germany. When he used a lecture in a WEA course in 1943 to attack Communism, the NSW Trades and Labor Council disaffiliated from the WEA, while the State Labor journal, *Progress*, (run by the pro-Soviet Hughes-Evans group expelled from the ALP in 1940) condemned Partridge with the headline "WEA tutor emits pro-Nazi filth". This led Bland to come to the defence of Partridge and the WEA.[8] Not that Partridge was consistently on the right. A few years later he was criticised by Peter Coleman for exhibiting naiveté by praising Chinese communism after a short trip to China:

> It would be foolish to criticise those who went to China in 1956. One simply does not know what private contacts they made. But to return from a routine guided tour, as Partridge did – the same teacher (and friend) who had so effectively dismissed Soviet propaganda in the 1940s – and proclaim a great renaissance in Mao's China, a land of new freedom, stability and excitement, was for me a disheartening spectacle.[9]

Partridge's main support in the Department was Tom Kewley, who had also been a valuable back-up for Bland as a part-time lecturer during the 1930s and 1940s, even before he transferred from the Department of Social Studies to Government in 1944. From his experience in the Commonwealth Public Service, Kewley's interest was public administration, rather than a wider perspective on politics, and his particular policy concern was social welfare, which experienced strong growth in Australia during the 1940s. His textbooks on the subject, especially *Social Security in Australia, 1900-72*, remained the essential starting point for students of the subject for decades. He was a quiet, small, unfailingly polite person who preferred to remain in the background. His biographer in the *ADB* noted that: "His unfailing helpfulness, courtesy and encouragement to his students were widely admired." Despite his preferred low profile he was extremely well connected throughout the university as well as in the Commonwealth and NSW governments.[10]

Now that Government had become a fully separate department, with a three-year sequence of year-long courses, it was able to offer an Honours major and postgraduate degrees. There was no provision at that stage for a separate year of Government IV for Honours students. An Honours degree in the Faculty of Economics involved students doing extra work at Distinction level in the later years of any major sequence of courses. That meant performing at the higher level in Government I, II and III, then graduating with the customary First, Second or Third Class Honours. The department insisted also that students should complete a minor thesis or extended essay in Government III; this continued as a tradition in the department long after the transition to a special fourth year for an Honours degree. Honours students completed a small thesis in third year, then the major thesis in fourth year well into the 1970s before the third year thesis was dropped.

For postgraduate students the normal degree was the Master of Economics. The university had approved a PhD degree only in 1946, over the objections of the Faculties of Arts and Economics, who did not want to see their Masters qualifications downgraded, so it is not surprising that take-up by staff and potential students was slow. At the end of 1948 the Professorial Board recommended the admission of WF Browne, a graduate of New York University, as a candidate for the Master of Economics in Government.[11] Browne was probably the first postgraduate student in the department; there is no record of his finishing the degree. When the Government sequence was made available to students in the Arts Faculty the Master of Arts became available, but, again, take-up was very limited.

It is difficult to discover who taught what in the first year of courses, since Professor Partridge did not arrive till the second term, and Professor Bland retired in mid-year. At the beginning of the following year the first four Honours graduates of the new department got their results for the "School of Government (Political Theory and Public Administration)". There were no Firsts, and no Medal. John Wright was awarded Second Class Honours, while Brian Hurley, Arthur Fitzgerald and James Moran had to be satisfied with Third Class Honours.[12] In a department with no experience of advanced courses or students, and with a patched-together teaching staff, one could not expect brilliance in such a transition year.

In the Economics Faculty, Government may not have attracted many students, but those coming through from the beginning of Government tended to be high quality and motivated. In 1950, of the 21 students in the Faculty graduating with Honours eight were from the Government Department, including Laurence Corkery, the first student to achieve First Class Honours in Government.[13] This proportion was well beyond what could be expected purely from the numbers in the various disciplines of the Faculty, establishing a precedent for succeeding years.

Professor Partridge put his stamp on the department immediately. The curriculum for the sequence in the first year that he supervised completely (1949) was typical of political science offerings emerging in many Australian universities about that time. Most importantly, he transferred the course in political theory from the beginning of the sequence to the end. Government I became a general introduction to "the theory and practice of modern parliamentary democracy"; according to the Calendar it was taught by Partridge and Kewley. It was a classic institutional introduction, with different notions of democracy helping to explain the differences among democratic regimes. It was also a full-year course, where the introductory course had previously been a half-course.

> Attention is given mainly to the political institutions and problems of Britain and Australia, but some reference is made to the working of parliamentary government in the U.S.A. and other countries.[14]

A Distinction strand was available (since this was a second year course in the Faculty), with students concentrating on democratic theory.

Government II was closer to the pattern of the old Public Administration I, devoted to: "a study of the main social and economic functions of the modern state, and of the machinery which is being developed to carry out those functions". It was taught mainly by Tom Kewley, newly promoted to Senior Lecturer. There were subsections on: "Historical and theoretical introduction"; "Principles and problems of administration"; "The state and economic life"; "The social services"; and "Centralisation and decentralisation". Distinction students were asked to study a segment on "Labour and the state" which concentrated on working class ideology and organisation.

The topic for Government III in 1949 was entitled "Modern political theory". Its content, stressing the class theory of politics, Marxist and fascist theories, the state and nationalism, political parties, pressure groups, and public opinion, is instantly recognisable as a checklist of Henry Mayer's academic preoccupations at that time. Yet Mayer had still not arrived in Sydney. Presumably Partridge had consulted Mayer on the content, with a view to his appointment in the following year. Distinction students were given the task of studying Australian federalism and constitutional issues, which was more something for Professor Partridge.[15]

Conspicuously absent was any attention to international relations. Granted that this was typical enough of Australian political science schools in the late 1940s, it is still somewhat surprising. The United Nations Organisation (later simply the United Nations) was still new and full of promise, and Australia had taken a very positive role in its early years. Moreover, for a curriculum built on Bland's interest in the modern state, one would have thought that the interdependence of states, and the shortcomings of political activity by any one state on its own, were crying out for attention. Partridge was aware of the absence. A few years later, when he had moved on to a Chair at the ANU, he stressed the importance of international relations as an essential component of any set of courses aiming to educate students in politics:

> Usually international relations is not treated as being an essential part of the course but as an optional or extra. But I take the view that what is taught should be related throughout to the outstanding issues in the political life of the time, the problems and dilemmas which loom largest in the political thinking of the period. In our time, problems concerning the relations between states, the implications of national sovereignty, the issues concerned with international political authority and international law, and so on, are amongst the most pressing and pervasive political problems of the age. I maintain that a student cannot be said to have a good knowledge of modern politics unless he understands the fundamental general issues of international politics, and the forces which are affecting the relation of contemporary states to one another.[16]

The question to ask, of course, is why he neglected to do anything about it while he was in charge at the University of Sydney. The most likely answer is that he did not have the staff to teach such a course, and there was little likelihood that he would be allocated new teachers given the low level of student demand for Government while he was there.

Given his earlier career path as a lecturer in philosophy, developing a speciality in political philosophy, it was not surprising that Partridge wanted a strong strand of political theory. In a symposium in the *Australian Journal of Politics and History* on the question of what should be the content of courses in political science, Partridge made a strong appeal for the centrality of theory. What provoked some comment was his conviction that political theory was a very different field from the study of the history of political thought and of the great political philosophers:

> To begin with, political theory and the history of political thought are not the same thing: the development of theory in politics has long been retarded by the not uncommon assumption that the study of theory is merely the study of the texts of Aristotle, Hobbes, Locke, Burke or Rousseau. I don't want to deprecate the study of the history of political thought; no one will deny that a knowledge of it is necessary for an "educated understanding of contemporary politics" ... But it still seems obvious to me that political theory needs to be taught independently, and not merely by means of historical study.[17]

Partridge went on to argue that political theory refers to the need to provide explanations and generalisations about the institutions and ideologies that were the central topic of most politics courses. A course in history could be descriptive, concentrating on causes and consequences; a course in political science should look for wider generalisations.

Almost as soon as he took up his chair in Sydney Professor Partridge was persuaded to become the Dean of the Economics Faculty for a year. This had the advantage that he was in a better position to defend his small department from critics within the Faculty, and it extended his network of influence within the university generally. Yet it was a demanding job that took up time and energy needed to reorganise the curriculum, provide incentives for postgraduate students and manage his own research. There were problems in his department that were crying out for attention.

Most of the problems were inherited. Among those was the makeup of his established staff. Tom Kewley was a very experienced Senior Lecturer who was entirely dependable. The other established position was held by Neville Wills, who had been appointed as one of the final

> **Criticism of Partridge on theory**
>
> The main problem raised in Professor Partridge's paper, at least in its third and following sections, is how the disparate elements that enter into political courses can be so related to one another as to make political science a coherent academic subject. His contention is that integration can be achieved only if more, and more rigorous, political theory is introduced at all (or very nearly all) stages of the political science course. By this he does not primarily mean that the institutional or factual courses should be more theoretical; he rather means that strictly theoretical courses should be conducted along with, but separately from, the distinctively institutional courses. Professor Partridge, of course, does not base this separation of institutional and theoretical courses on any final logical distinction between theory and practice or theory and fact. On the contrary, he insists that the main thing is to relate the content of the theory courses to the content of the others.
>
> BD Beddie, "A Comment on Professor Partridge's Paper", AJPH, Vol 4 No 1. 1958, p. 31.

initiatives of Professor Bland at the end of 1946. The appointment had many of the characteristics of a patron-client relationship. Wills was a science graduate (Sydney, 1941) and economics graduand (Sydney, 1947). The appointment was pushed through the Senate personally by Bland. There seems to have been no process of advertising and selection (which by itself was not unusual at that time). The most likely explanation was that Wills' knowledge of politics stemmed more from his active involvement in some of the many anti-socialist campaigns that took up a great deal of Bland's free time in the 1940s than from his attendance at courses in Public Administration under Bland. The professor liked to be surrounded by like-minded people. He was no stranger to patronage himself, as he had spent many years in his youth under the close attention of Robert Irvine, both in the Public Service Board and in the Faculty of Economics. When Partridge took over from Bland, Wills began looking for more suitable employment. He took unpaid leave to accept a Nuffield Foundation Travelling Fellowship in Social Science in July 1948, then in July 1951 took four months leave to do research for the BHP company. He had published a number of articles on the steel industry. Both leaves were extended.[18] While Partridge was head of the department Wills was on duty for only about 18 months. Towards the end of 1951 he applied for a further extension of his second leave, which Partridge refused to support. Partridge had also refused to support an application by Wills for promotion to Senior Lecturer. One can only assume that Wills had been told by Bland that promotion would follow as a matter of course. Wills reluctantly handed in his resignation. Professor Bland, still a member of the Senate, moved that Wills' resignation should not be accepted and his leave should be extended – there was no support in the Senate for that. No doubt there are faults on both sides when a professional relationship breaks down so completely, but the consequence for Partridge was that he had to depend very heavily on part-time teachers and junior staff like Ruth Atkins and Henry Mayer. This was intensified by Kewley's absence on sabbatical leave for the whole of 1950. In fact, Partridge was able to use Wills' unused salary to extend Atkins' temporary appointment for 1949, and his later absence to have Mayer promoted to Temporary Lecturer in 1951.[19]

Enrolments in Government were still modest. The first years after the war had seen strong interest, but, somewhat surprisingly, general enrolments in the Economics Faculty were not experiencing the boom evident in the university as a whole. Perhaps its concentration on evening lectures was not attractive for full-time students straight out of school. It is very difficult to get accurate numbers of enrolments in individual courses from that era, so the most useful comparison uses completion numbers published in the *Sydney Morning Herald* along with an estimate of failures and "posts" (a second chance in January to pass examinations). According to this estimate, in 1946 about 161 students enrolled in the Public Administration sequence, with 79 in the first course (Political Theory). In the following year, 1947, numbers increased strongly to 212 in total, with 97 in the first year.

Figure 2.1

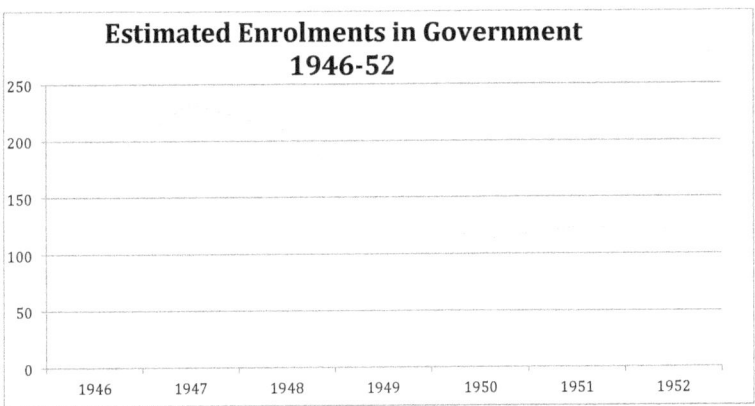

Source: *SMH* published results of end-of-year examinations, plus 10%

In 1948 they dropped back slightly to 190, with 80 in the first year. Then numbers collapsed, especially in the first year of the sequence. In 1949 Government I enrolled only 42 students, while 57 passed Government II, and 43 completed Government III. There had been a striking drop in student support for Government I in only the second year of the new regime – from 97 in 1947 to just 42 in 1949. Low enrolments in Government I would flow through inexorably to later year enrolments in 1950 and 1951. They continued low for the remainder of Professor Partridge's tenure, and picked up only well after Professor Spann arrived, and after Arts students started enrolling in numbers.[20]

Why was there such a relatively small number enrolled in Government I in 1949 and succeeding years? One could enrol in Government only in the second year of the degree, so it is unlikely that the reason for the low number was the university's custom at that time of failing a large proportion of first year students. (This was before any system of ranking Matriculation performance and setting quotas for university admission had been designed).[21] One possible reason was the retirement of Professor Bland; neither Percy Partridge nor Tom Kewley were renowned as stimulating lecturers, while Bland certainly was. The *Economics Handbook* for 1949 noted the presence of Ruth Atkins as an acting lecturer for that year, along with AW Coady and JT Monaghan as part-time lecturers. Another factor was that the introductory course (Political Theory) had been only a half-course till the department was established; many Economics students would not have had room in their degree for an optional full-year course. Perhaps students were being drawn to other optional courses, especially to Economic History; there was certainly a timetable clash for evening students. One can only guess about word-of-mouth reputation, and conflicts with the timetables of other courses and commitments, but the drop in enrolments must have been a concern for Professor Partridge. If quantity was a problem, quality was more positive; in 1952 the list of Economics Faculty students passing Government I included two future staff members of the department, Ken Turner and Peter Westerway. One advantage of this enrolment pattern was that class sizes were small and enabled face to face teaching rather than mass lectures. The disadvantage was that the small first year enrolments would have lowered any expectation by Partridge of increasing his teaching staff, and would certainly have endangered the continuation of the acting and part-time teachers.

Another possible explanation for the decline in numbers was a change in the timetable. In 1947, before the Department of Government was established, there was one lecture a week for Political Theory at 6 pm on Tuesdays; by 1950 the new program had Government I lectures at 5.15 pm on Mondays and 6.15 pm on Wednesdays, which certainly would have presented problems for some students.[22] When Government was accepted as an abbreviated sequence in the Arts Faculty after 1950 a separate set of day lectures was provided: Government I at 3 pm on Monday, Tuesday and Wednesday; Government II at 11 am on the same days; and Government III also at 11 am on the same days. The evening timetable remained, so that the department was committed to repeat lectures when enrolments were in decline, further stretching the meagre teaching resources. Yet timetabling problems cannot alone be blamed for the decline in numbers.

Availability to students in the Faculty of Arts

One solution to the problem of enrolments was already in process. In 1950 the Faculty of Arts rewrote its by-laws to provide for a social science set of choices. As part of this process Government was accepted as a sequence, first for the vestigial social science school in the Faculty and then for the general Bachelor of Arts.[23] Clearly, this was meant to provide further choice of subjects for the rapidly rising number of students in the Faculty. Yet the change was not without its difficulties. Firstly, the Arts Faculty refused to accept the version of Government II taught in the Economics Faculty – the one most closely modelled on the old Public Administration I course of Professor Bland – as it was regarded as too narrowly professional. The *Handbook* entry for Government II read:

> GOVERNMENT II (PUBLIC ADMINISTRATION).
> This is a course in the Faculty of Economics only; it does not form part of the sequence of Government courses in the Faculty of Arts (Social Sciences).[24]

Secondly, and presumably as a consequence of that refusal, Government I was not available to first year students (as was already, for a different reason, the situation in the Economics Faculty). The first year of a sequence of Government courses in Arts had to be either History or Philosophy (Scientific Method), followed by Government I and III. That would make up an equivalent three-year sequence of Government. Consequently, even though the Arts by-laws allowed for a sequence of three Government courses, only two were available until the Government Department re-arranged its curriculum to provide a Government II acceptable to the Arts Faculty.

For some reason Partridge did not move to provide a more acceptable Government II. Probably he was constrained by the limits of his staff; Tom Kewley, his Senior Lecturer teaching the existing course, had taught versions of that same course throughout the 1930s in both the Department of Social Studies and for Professor Bland. That was what he knew how to do. Moreover, he was still committed to teaching it for students in the Department of Social Studies. Until the department could get new staff much would depend upon enrolments picking up significantly, while any change in what Kewley taught would be mainly cosmetic. Yet enrolments were not likely to pick up strongly as long as Government courses were not available to first year students in the Arts Faculty, and as long as there was only an abbreviated sequence available. Moreover, the Economics Faculty would have resisted the dropping of the one course that was seen as professionally valuable for future economists. This stalemate continued till Partridge resigned at the end of 1951, to be sorted eventually under his successor, Professor RN Spann.

Another problem with the acceptance of Arts students was that an Honours degree in Arts required a fourth year in each discipline, whereas in Economics a three-year sequence was sufficient. A compromise had been negotiated so that Arts students could do a unique Government IV, which comprised two seminar courses – one on The Modern State and another on Political Parties and Pressure Groups. Presumably a minor thesis was required. Very few Arts students took advantage of this compromise. It was clearly to the advantage of a department with so few staff to work towards synchronising the requirements of the two Faculties.

Not surprisingly, the take-up of Government courses by Arts students was restrained. In 1951 only three students who had already completed the pre-requisite first year completed Government I. In

1952, which was the first year that most Arts students could expect to be able to enrol, 22 students from that Faculty completed Government I. A significant landmark was achieved in 1953 when for the first time Arts students outnumbered Economics students in Government I. That pattern would continue into the indefinite future. Nevertheless, the problem of enrolments remained. Even with the Arts students, the total number in Government I, and in the full sequence of three courses, was still considerably less in 1953 than it had been in 1948 and the few years before that.[25]

It took a dozen years for the degree requirements for Arts and Economics students enrolled in Government to become more or less compatible. In 1955 the department's curriculum tried to adjust to the unacceptability of the Government II course in the Arts Faculty. The theory course previously taught in the third year became Government II and the content of Government III was left open:

> Students of Government III work as far as possible under individual supervision. The lecture courses to be attended will be arranged with the Professor of Government.[26]

By the following year it was obvious that Professor Spann had been bluffing, since the Arts Faculty now wanted to know what was really in the new Government III. In 1956 it was revealed that it was little more than a re-working of the old Government II.

> A study of the activities of the modern state (in particular Australia, the United Kingdom and the United States), with special reference to administrative problems.[27]

That still was not acceptable for Arts and there were no changes in its by-laws to accommodate Government. There were still differences in the requirements for an Honours degree, and neither Arts nor Economics students could enrol in a Government course in their first year. It was not till well into the 1960s that the department was able to require a separate fourth year for all its Honours students.

After Partridge

At the end of 1951 the University Senate reported the resignations of two of the four staff members of the Department of Government. Neville Wills had resigned in circumstances discussed above. Then Partridge notified the university that he had accepted an offer to become the foundation Professor of Social Philosophy in the Institute of Advanced Studies, Australian National University (ANU). The Senate immediately began the process of advertising for the Chair of Government and Public Administration.[28] One can see the attraction for Partridge of moving to a well-funded research position at the ANU with no undergraduates, after his few years of frustration taken up largely with administration and teaching.

These two resignations left the department with Tom Kewley, a Senior Lecturer, and Henry Mayer to continue as an Acting Lecturer. Partridge stayed till mid-year, and Kewley became acting head of the department in August 1952 until a new professor could be appointed and arrive. Asking two teachers to manage three full-time pass and honours courses, with repeat classes for day and evening students, along with any postgraduate students, was asking a very great deal even though student numbers were still small. The interregnum would last 18 months till Professor Spann arrived for the 1954 teaching year. As an acting head, and with severe constraints on staffing, there was little that Kewley could do to sort out the problems with the curriculum and the Arts Faculty.

Even if there was no professor in charge, Kewley was not left without the administrative support that was normally a professorial privilege at that time. In 1949 the Senate Minutes noted the appointment of Barbara Delarue to the department, but when Professor Partridge resigned she was quickly appropriated by the Economics Department. In her place Marcia Daniel was appointed as graduate assistant in the department, one of only two in the Economics Faculty. Barbara Delarue and Marcia Daniel, followed by Shirley Harris, Jackie Walter and Mary Pollard, were the beginning of a long line of non-academic staff appointments that made the effective management of the department possible. From 1954 the formidable Joyce Fisher arrived, first in the Department of Economics and then as the manager of the Faculty. Nothing happened in the administrative area without the oversight of Joyce Fisher. Also employed in the department as research assistant during Kewley's regime was Joan Rydon, later professor of politics at La Trobe University, who was active producing publications on public administration. She left to spend a short period at the ANU, then returned in 1958 to be a research assistant for Professor Spann. She set a very high standard of research support that was matched by many of her successors.

In fact, Kewley coped fairly well in the interregnum. Mayer was reappointed as a Temporary Lecturer in February 1952, and at the end of the year the department gained approval to advertise for a new lecturer. In February 1953 Mayer won that position from six other candidates, but that meant, of course, that the department faced losing his teaching fellowship. That was eventually corrected in June 1954, after Spann's arrival, when permission was given to advertise for a new lectureship to fill the void. Meanwhile, Kewley got Ruth Atkins re-appointed as a part-time lecturer for 1953, along with three other part-timers. With two full-time staff and four part-time teachers it was a patched up team, but holding on.

In 1951 the Economics Faculty had moved from the Western Quadrangle into the new RC Mills Building. Unfortunately there was little space for the Government Department, some of whose junior members took up residence in temporary accommodation in what was known as the "lecturers' hut".[29] It was a small pre-fabricated and military-style building on the southern side of the Maclaurin Hall, still the Fisher Library at that time. The site is now a car park. Ken Turner, who spent some time in the hut, recalls the conditions:

> The hut was small scale, a block with about five single rooms and a long joint corridor. As I remember, its timbers were

unlined, offering little protection when the weather was very hot or very cold. It was also noisy and provided little privacy. A single telephone at the end of the corridor served us all.[30]

It was also close to the library, to the staff club and to one's colleagues in the Mills Building, so Ken remembers it with some affection. That had to be endured for about 15 years until the completion of the Merewether Building on the other side of City Road in 1966, although by that time most Government full-time staff had found space in the Mills Building.

There is no doubt that Percy Partridge was a first rate scholar and able administrator, and thus a very suitable appointment to the chair that FA Bland had held for so long. Yet the fact that he stayed in Sydney for only four years was a disappointment when there were major challenges to be faced. That was compounded by the delay in finding a successor. In effect, for the first five years of its formal existence the new Department of Government was simply marking time. Within the Faculty of Economics the profile had been lifted somewhat from the previous years of a sequence of Public Administration courses, but within the wider university little had changed.

---

1 Spann Papers, University of Sydney Archives, Box 45, Folder "1980-81".

2 Peter Groenewegen, *Educating for Business, Public Service and the Social Sciences: A History of the Faculty of Economics at the University of Sydney 1920-1989*, Sydney, SUP, 2009, pp. 57-63.

3 Bruce Williams, *Liberal Education and Useful Knowledge: a brief history of the University of Sydney 1850-2000*, Sydney, Chancellor's Committee, University of Sydney, 2002, p. 32.

4 Minutes of the University of Sydney Senate, 1 September 1947.

5 Minutes of the Professorial Board, University of Sydney, 22 September 1947; Groenewegen, p. 60.

6 Percy Partridge personnel file, University of Sydney Archives.

7 Grant Harman, "Partridge, Percy Herbert (1910-1988)", *Australian Dictionary of Biography*.

8 *Honi Soit*, 6 May 1943, 13 May 1943.

9 Peter Coleman, *Memoirs of a Slow Learner: An intimate and personal memoir*, Sydney, Angus & Robertson, 1994, p. 80.

10 TH Kewley, *Social Security in Australia*, Sydney, SUP, 1965; *Social Security in Australia from 1900 to 1972*, Sydney, SUP, 1973. Michael Horsburgh, "Kewley, Thomas Henry (1911-1989)", *Australian Dictionary of Biography*, Volume 17, Melbourne, MUP, 2007. For his connections, see Leonie Foster, *High Hopes: the Men and Motives of the Australian Round Table*, Melbourne, MUP, 1986, Index.

11 Minutes of the University of Sydney Senate, 1 November 1948.

12 *SMH*, 12 January 1949, p. 7.

13 Minutes of the University of Sydney Senate, 14 June 1950.

14 *University of Sydney Calendar, 1949*, p. 452.

15 Details of the three years of curriculum can be found in *University of Sydney Calendar, 1949*, pp. 452-5.

16 PH Partridge, "Politics as a University Subject", *AJPH*, Vol 4 No 1. 1958, p. 21.

17 PH Partridge, "Politics as a University Subject", *AJPH*, Vol 4 No 1. 1958, p. 24.

18 Minutes of the University of Sydney Senate, 5 July 1948, 2 July 1951.

19 Personnel file of Neville R Wills, University of Sydney Archives. Minutes of the University of Sydney Senate, 5 July 1948; 6 February 1950; 3 December 1951. Transcript of oral history interview with Ruth Atkins, University of NSW Archives.

20 The numbers cited are taken from the *Sydney Morning Herald* reports on examination results for each year, usually published in December or the following January. An additional 10% is a guess at the number of failures and deferred exams (posts) that were done at the beginning of the next academic year.

21 See comments by Groenewegen on this matter, *op. cit.*, p. 62.

22 *University of Sydney Calendar, 1947* and *1950*.

23 Minutes of the University of Sydney Senate, 5 June 1950; 6 November 1950.

24 *University of Sydney Calendar, 1951*, p. 479.

25 *SMH*, 9 January 1952, p. 11; 18 January 1952, p. 8; 10 December 1952, p. 6; 17 January 1953, p. 8; 26 December 1953, p. 4; 8 January 1954, p. 9.

26 *University of Sydney Calendar, 1955*, p. 1003.

27 *University of Sydney Calendar, 1956*, p. 1035.

28 Minutes of the University of Sydney Senate, 3 December 1951.

29 Groenewegen, *op. cit.*, p. 72.

30 Ken Turner to Michael Hogan, 26 April 2013.

3

The Dick and Henry show

Richard Neville Spann (he was always Dick Spann) took up his appointment to the Department of Government on 31 December 1953, so that he was in place for the beginning of the 1954 teaching year. An appointment had been delayed because the initial advertisement of December 1951 had received a mediocre set of applicants. The only two names with any resonance to modern ears were Tom Kewley and Neville Wills. The appointment committee received permission from the Senate to appoint by invitation, giving the names of two Oxford academics – Wilfred Harrison and HG Nicholas – who might be invited. Apparently neither wanted to come to Sydney, so in October 1952 the Chair was readvertised, attracting six further applicants including Spann. A search committee of Oxford dons had recommended that he should apply, and apparently his former colleague Heinz Arndt added his voice to that.[1] Professor KC Wheare interviewed him in Britain, providing a glowing reference. At the second round the committee was unanimous in recommending Spann, who was offered the Chair in June 1953. At the age of 37 he was relatively young and inexperienced for such a daunting task.

His friend, student and colleague, Ross Curnow, has provided a good summary of Spann's intellectual formation, with his choice of a career in political science and public administration evolving largely by chance.[2] Like his two professorial predecessors in Sydney,

Professor Dick Spann (Photo courtesy of St Andrew's College)

Spann did not come from a privileged background. Born in suburban Manchester in 1916, he graduated in 1937 with an Oxford degree in Modern Greats (Philosophy, Politics and Economics) and immediately took up a position in Oxford, first on his own research grant and then as a research assistant studying "public utility problems". That led him into the field of public administration, and to an assistant lectureship in the discipline in Oxford in 1939. During the war he served in the Royal Navy as a staff officer to the Home Fleet. There are suggestions that this involved an analysis of intelligence issues. The notion of Dick Spann as a spymaster may seem incongruous to those who knew him in Sydney, but he fitted the profile of many in that profession – Oxbridge education from a middle class background, and a seemingly confirmed bachelor. In 1946 he gained a lectureship at Manchester University in the Department of Government of the Faculty of Economic and Social Studies. During his period there he also spent a year in the United States as a Rockefeller Foundation Fellow studying the Federal Civil Service.

Never seen out of a grey suit, Dick Spann was a man of culture and scholarship. He was a charming conversationalist, happy to discuss literature, theatre or history as well as his professional concerns, with wit and irony. At heart he was a conservative, believing strongly that good manners and correct grammar were the foundations upon which to build any relationship. He was unfailingly courteous, and expected courtesy from others, although in conversation or in correspondence he could be quite waspish in his comments about colleagues. He would argue forcefully when his opinion was sought, but usually gave respect to opinions that he did not share. This characteristic became central to his leadership of the department, especially in the heated political controversies of the 1970s, when he was able to help resolve fierce ideological disputes where his own views were diametrically opposed to those of other staff members. He was also politically conservative, one of the earliest members of the Association for Cultural Freedom, and a regular contributor to the *Quadrant* journal that defended similar anti-communist views. Yet, while genuinely concerned about the threat to freedom posed by communism, he welcomed into his department a number of ideological Marxists and at least two former members of the Communist Party. One of his students, Martin Krygier, probably got close to the heart of the matter in an obituary for *Quadrant*:

> His attitude to political enthusiasms and enthusiasts was frequently one of detached, at times amused, scepticism. Partly this stemmed from "a certain perversity [which] has always affected my political outlook, a disposition to buck when presented with apparent inevitabilities or alleged fundamental contradictions". Partly, too, it stemmed from

Spann's healthy, probably instinctive, distaste for fashions and the fashionable. Though often sceptical, however, Spann was never a cynic, for he cared greatly about matters of politics, morals and education.[3]

This distaste for fashions extended to his attitude towards colleagues who became committed to feminist and gay political activity; initially he regarded these as a passing fad – not so much to be opposed, but not to be taken seriously. When Henry Mayer did take them seriously Spann revised his opinion of the academic relevance of such issues.

Spann on civility in political action

There is a high degree of courtesy and mutual respect and restraint in speech and action and obedience to established procedures; and I would also like myself to add a certain joy and delight in all such things as expressions of our essential humanity. Indeed I would argue to those people who are constantly talking about liberation, that one can have the most satisfying of all senses of human freedom by working within a framework of civility. There are radicals who regard it as the subtlest form of repression and false consciousness to have a situation like this. I regard that as wholly, morally wholly, perverse.

RN Spann, quoted in Martin Krygier's obituary for Spann, *Quadrant*, September 1981, p. 43.

More than for most academics the university was Dick Spann's life. He lived on campus at St Andrew's College, where he became Vice-Principal. In many ways he was the ideal professorial head of department for that era. He gained the highest reputation for work in his chosen field of public administration and policy; he was a generous, although hardly exciting teacher, who was willing to fit into any part of the curriculum where he could help; he was a first-rate administrator, becoming skilled at working the university networks for the benefit of his department and staff. He was happy to talk to any of his colleagues about their research and was very valuable in reading drafts of papers or chapters. His views on style and expression were always helpful, while he could often surprise a colleague by having detailed knowledge of the substantial content and argument.

Peter Coleman reports that Spann, "at once liberal and conservative" wrote a letter to the *Observer*, referred to by Coleman as Spann's version of Sydney Hook's "Ethics of Controversy". Its principles became part of the informal editorial policy of the magazine:

> Many more-or-less honest people (as well as a good many more-or-less dishonest ones) are deeply divided on some major issues of policy. That is all the more reason why they should recognise one another as tolerably honest opponents, open to conviction by the truth as they can be made to see it.
>
> We should not renounce this belief in one another's credentials until we are inescapably driven to do so.
>
> There are stupid, cowardly, opportunistic 'intellectuals'. There are also plenty of unpleasant fanatics, power-worshippers, power-seekers around. No doubt we are all, to some point affected by one or other of these characteristics.
>
> But it is a completely feeble and pompous thing to ask those of us who are proud of being 'committed' in this way or that, if some, at least, of our enemies are not friends in disguise, who could teach us something if we cared to learn it? And to whom we might also teach something if we could resist the temptation to hurt and rebuff them?[4]

Coleman conceded that the magazine was not always able to follow the Spann set of principles. The experience of Spann in the Government Department, where there was often a great deal of passionate conviction, was that he personally could and did implement them. So did most of his staff.

When Spann arrived in the department he found only two tenured staff members and a few part-timers. Tom Kewley, the Senior Lecturer,

> **Spann and the importance of history**
>
> *Political science has established its independence though there may be reasons for its remaining an appendage of history in a small university, or one where the subject has only recently entered the curriculum. History should clearly form some part of the political scientist's education. In particular, it is the best kind of introduction to the subject. From one point of view a political scientist is only a very modern historian. But he is an inveterate generaliser and system builder, who needs a certain emancipation from (at least) the spiritual heirs of Ranke.*
>
> Spann in 1956, quoted in Weller, p.23.

was a quietly spoken, modest and retiring personality, whose slight frame sometimes seemed to make him almost invisible. Henry Mayer, promoted to Senior Lecturer later that year, was none of those things. He was loud, assertive and dominated in any company. He was also unquestionably brilliant. So unlike Dick Spann in many ways, Henry became his closest ally, helping to make a formidable leadership team for the next quarter of a century.

Mayer had come to Australia on the *Dunera* in 1940, along with many other Jewish refugees from Nazism who would later contribute so much to Australian academic, business, political and artistic life. He served in the Australian Army until the end of the war, then studied at Melbourne University where he graduated with an MA after writing a thesis on Marxism. Recruited by Professor Partridge, who had known him in the Melbourne department, he ascended the promotion ladder with a sense of inevitability to become Professor in 1969, with a chair in Political Theory. He was larger than life, extremely productive, confronting, very generous of his time with colleagues and students as long as he thought them capable of benefiting from his contributions, and a giant in Australian political science. As Don Rawson noted in an obituary, he was "one of the true founding fathers of Australian political science and an important figure in Australian intellectual life more generally".[5]

A young Henry Mayer. photo by his friend and colleague, Hugo Wolfsohn (Courtesy of the National Portrait Gallery)

The term "confronting" applies to him in a singular way: he was generous and enthusiastic about the research of others, but had no hesitation in forcing colleagues and students to defend assumptions that were unspoken and taken-for-granted. Especially for Honours and postgraduate students who were cautiously feeling their way into a thesis this often came as an unwelcome shock. At one period he was asked not to come to seminars presented by postgraduate students on their research because too many students found the experience almost shattering. For students who were more self confident, more intellectually mature, or more eager to debate the fundamentals, he was the ideal advisor or supervisor. For many years he set an end-of-year exam for Final Honours students that was not based on any individual course or seminar that they had completed. This "General

Paper" sought to identify students with a spark of individuality and lateral thinking, and gave a choice of provocative statements that students were expected to "discuss". Typical examples were: "Reality is 32 frames per second", or "Nothing is predictable except death and taxes". Most students hated it, even though the weighting in the final assessment was almost negligible. Eventually, in the early 1970s, student rejection of the test forced him to abandon it.

> **One question from Government IV General Paper, 1973**
>
> (There were 12 questions, of which students needed to answer two or three.)
>
> 1 (a) 'The young are not fit students of political science. They are inexperienced in the actions that occur in life, which the subject starts from and is about. They also tend to follow their passions, so their study will be vain and unprofitable, aimed not at knowledge but action'. (Aristotle). Discuss.
>
> OR
>
> (b) 'I learned more about politics from the struggle over the Philosophy dispute than from any course given by the Department of Government'. Discuss.

Mayer also wanted students to confront their own prejudices. In one Honours course for second year students in the late 1960s he took delight in challenging two students – one a Catholic priest in uniform and the other a scruffy and bearded "Jack the Anarchist". The priest was told to read Bakunin, while the anarchist was expected to read some Aquinas. The anarchist was also challenged to explain why he had not blown anything up! Mayer enjoyed dissent and regarded conflict as the source of most advances in human society. Good intentions in political actors were not worthy of remark; only consequences, especially unintended, provided a basis for evaluation. Again, in the words of Don Rawson:

> Behind it all there was – to use a term which is not now as popular as in Mayer's earlier days – a deeply rooted sceptical pluralism. He suspected bigness, domination, complacency and even unity when he suspected that it was being used as a cover for these other qualities. This is perhaps as close

as we can get to identifying a common theme in his life and work. It applied to his research from electoral studies through 'group theory' to media studies. It led to his wish to see political science as an autonomous but not independent study. And, at a personal level, it led him, like an even more notable figure, to seek to put down the mighty from their seats and to exalt the humble and meek – as long as the latter could be persuaded to take a share in exalting themselves.[6]

Mayer was the driving force in the early Australian Political Science Association, as in its *APSA Newsletter*, which he helped transform into the journal *Politics* (later the *Australian Journal of Political Science*). Later in his career he became the virtual inventor of the Australian academic study of the mass media. The journal he helped establish produced a festschrift edition in 1985, where colleagues and students such as Joan Rydon, Herb Feith, Elaine Thompson, Anne Summers, Ross Curnow, Ken Turner, Dennis Altman, Jean Holmes, Don Aitkin, Dean Jaensch and many others reflected on aspects of Henry's academic career.[7]

Mayer's political leanings are very hard to classify. It is much easier to understand what he was against, rather than what kind of political program he favoured. He found many of the ideas of the philosopher John Anderson attractive, and for some time was a fringe member of the Sydney "push" where Andersonians tried to put into effect some of those ideas and values. In the 1950s his activities helped to provide a public image for the Government Department that was fairly controversial. Jill Ker Conway, in her autobiographical account of the period, contrasted this with the stodgy image of the History Department at that time:

> The most interesting circle at the University revolved around the philosophy and political science departments, and a small coterie of gifted faculty and students who were iconoclasts, cultural rebels, and radical critics of Australian society. I liked their ideas, and enjoyed the fact that their circle also contained

journalists and serious writers about Australian politics. The trouble was that their intellectual originality went along with a stultifying conformity to what were considered "advanced" sexual mores. Everyone regarded marriage and monogamy as bourgeois conventions, and it was more or less de rigueur to join in the sexual couplings of the group to share in its intellectual life.[8]

One can be confident that Conway was not referring to Dick Spann or Tom Kewley. But that, also, is significant. For most of the time until his retirement the image of the department for many outsiders was provided by Henry Mayer. Conway was not the only commentator to refer to Mayer's attitude to women. In the festschrift to Henry Mayer in the journal *Politics*, Elaine Thompson wrote of him, with affection but not completely with admiration:

> He conveyed a sense of caring passionately about his subject (whatever it was) and caring about his students. He liked and nurtured women students. These were the days before women's liberation and it must be said that Henry was sexist. He treated women students differently and had a roving eye for brains and beauty.[9]

This attitude to women was part of the paradox of the man (and Henry welcomed paradoxes) in that during the 1970s he was one of the strongest champions of research and political agitation by women in pursuit of the aims of women's liberation – as detailed in Chapter 5.

Mayer detested Nazism because of his personal experience of the persecution of Jews and other minorities. As the Soviet Union exhibited many similar totalitarian tendencies he was opposed to Communism as a contemporary political movement, and he was happy to follow Dick Spann in joining the Association for Cultural Freedom. Nevertheless, he had an enduring interest in Marxism as an ideology, and, although he would not have regarded himself as a

> **Mayer's objectivity**
>
> *Committed with great passion to passionless objectivity, he believed that joining any political movement meant losing all intellectual integrity. One of the rare times I saw him silenced, however briefly, was at a meeting in the old tumbledown rooms of <u>Quadrant</u> in Albert Street when he put that view to Hal Wootten, then something of a Savonarola of anti-communism. Wootten retorted that, on the contrary, it was only by serious and sustained involvement, and sometimes disenchantment, that one learned anything at all, including the capacity to observe objectively. After a long pause, Mayer replied brightly: 'Cheer up!'*
>
> Peter Coleman, *Memoirs of a Slow Learner*, p.125.

Marxist, he would have been on the left of the otherwise conservative ACF group. When Tony Crosland, of the British Labour Party, visited Sydney in 1963, partly to promote the values of a left critique of Communism, he met Mayer and was bemused. Mayer was described in his papers as: "v.v. bright, but mad".[10]

Dick Spann found himself the head of a small department seemingly stagnating in a university exploding with students. He had the assistance of Marcia Daniel as graduate assistant for himself and the department. Over the three-year sequence of Government classes about 130 students were enrolled, with just over 50 in Government I (divided into evening and day students). There was little interest from postgraduate students. Spann attracted considerable personal goodwill in the Economics Faculty, but it was anomalous that in the 1950s Government was the only separate discipline besides Economics with its own professor, while the schools of Accounting and Economic History (as well as Economics itself) attracted more students. He had inherited a curriculum that reflected the interests of the two previous professors, and that looked like a patchwork rather than a coherent program.

Initially, Spann moved slowly and made no significant changes. He found his feet in the Faculty and the university, setting up the networks that he came to exploit masterfully. During 1954 Henry Mayer gained

Caricature of Dick Spann (Drawing by Allan Gamble in The '54 Club, the University of Sydney: a fortieth year review, Sydney, privately published, 1994, copy in Fisher Library, Rare Books)

promotion to senior lecturer, and the department was allocated another lecturing position. Doug McCallum, yet another philosopher and theorist, was appointed at the end of the year, to begin teaching in 1955. In the first few years the department depended heavily on part-time teachers, who included the historian Ernest Bramsted, David Benjafield, an expert on administrative law from the Law School, Ruth Atkins moonlighting from the NSW University of Technology (later UNSW), Robert Parker visiting from the ANU for a term, EM

Higgins and Beatrice Myers. After Peter Westerway graduated in 1957 with First Class Honours in Government he came on to the full-time staff, initially as a Teaching Fellow or tutor.

It is fair to assume that Spann moved slowly on some of the issues because he did not see them as urgent problems – or rather that the likely solutions would bring worse problems. He was never an empire builder as head of department, and as a new professor he was content to manage a small department with the resources at his disposal. He did have firm ideas on the ideal content for the education of students in political science (as he expounded a few years later[11]), but for his first few years in Sydney his two senior staff members were teaching courses that suited their talents, and neither would appreciate much interference. Meanwhile, Spann was bringing himself up to speed with the details of public administration in Australia that would become his own preferred research, publication and teaching area. In the mid-1950s he would also have been keenly aware of the problems being experienced in some of the large departments in the Arts Faculty (especially English and History) that were confronting very rapid increases in enrolments. Meanwhile, one advantage of Government not being available for students in their first year at university was that almost all students enrolled in the subject had at least some interest in applying themselves.

In November 1955 Spann was elected Dean of the Faculty of Economics for a three-year term, which provided further distraction from issues in his department. He was also busy on his research, as were his colleagues. Groenewegen records that "after his arrival, in 1954 Spann published four articles" on public administration. To that could be added two articles by Doug McCallum, six by Henry Mayer, and three by Joan Rydon.[12] There were a couple of staff changes in the next few years – Doug McCallum shifted across to a lectureship in Philosophy, but remained a part-time teacher in Government, while Peter Westerway was promoted to fill his lecturing position. After a stellar undergraduate achievement of double University Medals in Philosophy and History, Peter Loveday also joined the staff.

In this period the university's attitude to staffing began to change. During the Bland period it was tacitly accepted that, except for Chairs, a large proportion of teaching positions would be filled by University of Sydney graduates; and if the professor knew a suitable candidate there was no need to advertise. Bland himself, Watts, Kewley, Wills, Westerway, McCallum, Loveday and Partridge were all Sydney graduates, although a number of them had studied in Britain. Even Henry Mayer, a Melbourne graduate, from a department where Partridge had briefly been head, fitted into the pattern of being hand picked. Only Spann was a complete outsider. In 1955 the Dean of Economics, Sid Butlin wrote to the Senate to make an argument for higher academic salaries. He saw that as an opportunity to get rid of a process that allowed for patronage and mediocrity:

> Permanent lectureships have in many cases been earned too easily; promotions to senior lectureships have sometimes been too easily won; there are grounds for disquiet in professorial appointments. The expedients of recent years have been more or less inescapable, but it would be disastrous if we now accepted permanently the standards of appointment and promotion of those years.[13]

From the end of the 1950s it became routine to advertise vacant establishment positions internationally, although it still remained the case that a resolute professor could give advantage to a local or preferred candidate, while direct recruitment by invitation rather than advertisement was still possible for many years. As late as 1970, for example, Michael Leigh was recruited to fill an urgent need for specialists in Southeast Asian studies; he had written from Cornell asking if there was a position available, and was accepted without fuss.[14]

One of the most influential of the new teachers was John Power, appointed to the department in 1963. With a Harvard doctorate he initially brought a different dimension to the study of public policy and administration from that developed by Dick Spann. He was a political activist in the Balmain Society during the 1960s when local community politics in Sydney was confronting policy decisions made according to conventionally party-political urban planning rules. This led to an interest in the sociological and anthropological aspects of politics which was a relatively new perspective in Australian political science, and which became one of the strengths of the department in future years. His concern for local politics was passed on to others in the department. He also helped to strengthen the Honours program, taking a leading role in the third year course design and becoming a popular supervisor of theses. He left the department to take up a chair at the University of Melbourne.

By the mid-1950s the Final Honours year was normally graduating about half a dozen students. Some of them would make notable contributions in their later life. In 1956, for example, two students from Arts and three from Economics made up the class. Topping the year was Dagmar Carboch, who was the first person to be awarded a University Medal in the department. She was a migrant/refugee from Czechoslovakia, who after graduation travelled to Oxford, where she held a research position at Nuffield College. There she met the American philosopher John Searle (UC Berkeley) whom she married before moving to California. She was a member of the California Bar and worked as a lawyer. Also receiving a First in 1956 was Dick Scotton who became a prominent health care economist in universities and the public service. He is best known for putting flesh on the Whitlam Government's plans for a national health system. Along with his Minister, Bill Hayden, and public service colleague, John Deeble, he was the creator of the first Medibank legislation that is still after many permutations the basis of Australia's health insurance scheme. Third on the list of 1956 graduates was Ken Turner, at the time a lecturer at Sydney Teachers' College, who would later become one of the pivotal members of the Government Department, and its head for seven years, during its years of expansion.

Ironically, the solution to the disjunction between requirements for the study of Government in the Faculties of Arts and Economics was not found initially by getting Government to amend its curriculum to be more acceptable to Arts. It came about because the Economics Faculty moved in 1957 to change from a four-year to a three-year degree. Spann was Dean at the time but it was not his initiative. There was considerable pressure within the university for the Faculty of Economics to make its degree structure compatible with Arts, especially by the imposition of a separate fourth year for an Honours degree. This suggestion encountered strong opposition from some members of the Faculty because it would reduce the compulsory content of Economics from four to three years, but also because it would reduce the choice of students to study a wide variety of courses in the different schools of the Faculty. The strongest argument in favour of the proposal was that the Faculty could change from a school devoted almost entirely to evening and part-time students to full-time students with mainly day lectures. As the submission of the Faculty to the Academic Board explained:

> All State and Commonwealth public servants are allowed time off to attend two courses per year; the same applies to employees of most banks, insurance companies and large businesses. Between them these institutions provide all but a small minority of Economics students.[15]

The implication for Government was that its three-year sequence would start in first year, and that Government would need to plan a special Honours year at the end of the sequence. The reduction of choice in the Faculty meant that there would be difficulties for students wanting a social science kind of Economics degree. Subjects like Government, Economic History and Industrial Relations were in competition (worsened by frequent timetable clashes) for the limited number of students who were not committed to a business-oriented degree based on Economics, Accounting, Commercial Law and Statistics. On the other hand, if Economics became a Faculty for full-time rather than evening students there was a possibility that a higher number would be available for Government. Despite disagreement in the Faculty the changes were approved with only one dissenting vote, by-laws drafted, and the new structure took effect from the beginning of 1959.

That year, 1959, thus marked a watershed for Government in its relationship with the Arts Faculty. If Government was to be a first year course for Economics students, with a separate fourth year for Honours, there was clear motivation to achieve something similar in Arts. Late in his life Dick Spann offered a summary of the reputation of his department in that Faculty:

> Government itself was thought to be vaguely disreputable as an academic discipline and only became a first year subject some years after my arrival, when various Arts departments grew too large for the comfort of their Professors, and they wanted to unload students.[16]

Apparently, then, the impetus for an accommodation came from the Arts Faculty, and for less than noble reasons.

The changed relationship with the Arts Faculty was already becoming obvious in the pattern of enrolments. In 1958 the number of Arts students in Government I doubled from 30 in the previous year to 60, while Economics students numbered only 25. Even more significantly, for the first time in 1959 four Arts students graduated with Honours, and not one from Economics. Moreover, it was already predictable that student support from within the Economics Faculty would decline further in the new three-year degree. Government would remain in the Faculty of Economics for nearly 40 more years, but its future student demand was overwhelmingly from Arts. Meanwhile students from the Economics Faculty from 1959 complicated matters by being governed by the new or the old by-laws. Only those under the new by-laws came into Government I as first year students – the first that the department had had to teach.

For the academic year of 1961 Government finally made a significant change to its curriculum that would make it more acceptable to the Arts Faculty. Government I remained a course on democratic political institutions, illustrated mainly with Australian examples; Government II had evolved into a course on comparative politics, with special attention to the UK and USA; a new Government III incorporated bits of the Mayer theory course, with discussion of the USSR and Marxism, plus bits of the old Bland-Kewley agenda, with the focus changed to public policy rather than public administration. During 1961 the Arts Faculty decided to accept the changed curriculum and list Government I as the beginning of a three-year sequence. The new by-laws came into effect in 1962, when Government I was available as a first year course.[17]

Since 1958 the numbers enrolling in Government courses had been rising steadily, with most of the increase from Arts. The total enrolment was 147 in 1953, which declined to a low point of 92 in 1957, then started on a regular climb to 542 in 1963. In those final six years student numbers had increased about six-fold, although from a fairly low base. There is a problem finding accurate enrolment numbers for these years. The figures used here, and in figure 3.1, are for actual numbers of students enrolled, not the measure of Equivalent Full-Time Students (EFTS) which became the normal measure for comparison in later years. In the late 1980s the results available in the university's annual published volumes of Statistics ceased trying to give actual numbers and relied completely on the weighted EFTS, or later the EFTSU. However, cross checking the numbers in the late 1950s and early 1960s with the students actually finishing their exams, as published in the *Sydney Morning Herald*, one finds some quite large discrepancies. The official university statistics are preferred here. If the discrepancy has any basis in fact, then the charts in Fig. 3.1 and 4.1 exaggerate the increase in numbers between 1957 and 1962, while underestimating the rise from 1963 to 1970.

Even a 600% increase over six years does not tell the whole story. The change was noticeable especially in two areas. There was an increase in the number of postgraduate students. By 1963 seven Masters and no PhD students had graduated. Yet more students were enrolled, as became clear in the graduations for following years. However, the increase in postgraduate students was not very significant in the overall figures. The same was not true of students in Government I. The baby boomers had not yet arrived in numbers, nor had there been a noticeable spike in community interest in politics, but much increase was almost certainly due to word of mouth communication among students whose overall numbers in the Arts Faculty were increasing strongly. This was helped by significant efforts in Orientation Week by teachers like Henry Mayer putting on a performance to attract students. Government I enrolled about 100 students in 1958. Once the number rose above that, then different arrangements needed to be made – to find larger lecture theatres, to decide whether to have repeat lectures, to hire more tutors, to think about whether curriculum changes would be appropriate. By 1963, with a total enrolment of 542, enrolments in Government I would have been a bit less than half of that, so about 250, although that was the figure at the cut off date at the beginning of Lent Term. The numbers presenting at the beginning of March would have been about 300, with the normal heavy proportion of transfers and drop-outs among the students. It was in Government I that the shock of rising numbers was felt first and with most urgency.

With the new arrangements the department could expect that the rising proportion of Arts students in the first two years would

Figure 3.1

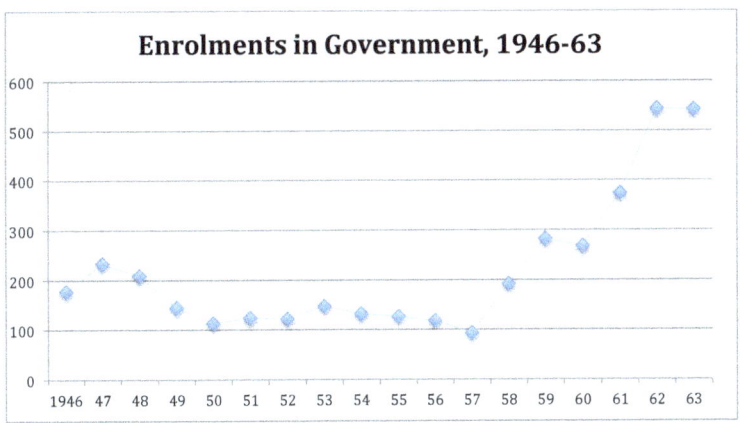

Source: Estimates from *SMH* (1946-52); Enrolment statistics, Planning and Information Office (1953-63)

flow through to Government III. In 1962 the department signalled a new direction for its curriculum with the appointment of Coral Bell, a specialist in international relations. Initially the only change in the course descriptions was the addition of a term of international relations to Government III, along with a term for Marxism and another term for public policy. It was certainly timely, because the early 1960s, with upheavals in Vietnam against the French colonial empire and then against American anti-communist involvement, put international relations questions onto the front pages of Australian newspapers.

By 1962 there were seven full-time teaching staff, (Spann, Kewley, Mayer, Bell, Loveday and Westerway, with Ken Turner as Senior Tutor) but that was expected to increase. There were also part-time tutors who brought the Equivalent Full-Time Staff number to eight. The curriculum had achieved a measure of development from first year to graduation that it had lacked 10 years previously. Government I surveyed the institutions of liberal democracy using Australia as an example. Government II introduced a comparative element, with attention to political systems in the USA, UK and USSR, along with a term of 19th and 20th century political and social theory. In Government III the three separate terms were devoted to public policy, international politics and public administration. There were some problems in delivering the same curriculum to evening and day students, and generally all teachers, including the professor, were expected to take their share of the heavy teaching in Government I. In Government I Arts students outnumbered Economics students by more than two to one, so part of the future was clear.

In the 15 years since the department had been established considerable progress had been made in most areas of teaching, research and publication, but there was one disappointing result. Postgraduate performance was not impressive. From 1948 till 1963 only seven students had graduated with Masters degrees (four from Arts and three from Economics), and none with Doctorates. There were mitigating circumstances, especially with the strong dependence on part-timers for teaching, but it should have been a concern.

There was no doubt that the members of the department knew that the changes to the Arts by-laws, and the acceptance of Government I as a first year course in both Arts and Economics, meant that enrolments were about to increase heavily. Government I was also accepted as an option in the Science and Agriculture Faculties, although there was no expectation of any heavy demand from those students. A reorganisation of the Department of Social Work would see some study of Government routine for its students, but, again, the numbers were not large. In 1962-3 Government I enrolled about 300 students. There was no indication of how rapid the increase might be, nor what staffing and curriculum changes would be needed. Was the comparison likely to be with a subject like Anthropology, where first year numbers were in the hundreds, or should one look at English and History for guidance, where numbers were well over the thousand? Probably most opinion in the department tended to the former comparison. Some shocks were about to be experienced.

Technology change

During the 1960s a major change was introduced into the whole teaching profession by the gradual rollout of the new technology of photocopying. Previously multiple copies of typescripts were available, first only through the use of carbon copies in a typewriter, then with spirit-based copiers such as the Fordigraph machines, followed by the almost universal adoption of the stencil technology of the Gestetner copiers, with the need to type the stencil (with correcting fluid for clumsy typists), mount it correctly onto the rollers, and hope that the ink flow was working properly. When the new photocopiers with the Xerographic photo technology came onto the market they replaced all previous copiers. There was no need to type the original, while the great improvement was that pages of books and articles could be copied directly from source. Frustrations for non-academic staff and other users did not disappear, as the technology has never managed to stay ahead of the huge volume of material put through the standard machines, but at least there was much less indelible ink spread onto hands and clothes as with earlier technologies. The first coin-operated photocopiers were accessible for staff and students in Fisher Library in the mid-1960s, while they became available in most departments a little after that.

The first impact was observable in Fisher Library, where articles and book chapters could be copied by library staff and placed in the "Closed Reserve" section (later called just "Reserve"). Students needed to find tutorial and essay readings by queuing and reading the material in the library. Within a short time teachers found that a more convenient method of putting readings into the hands of students (even if not free, as with Closed Reserve) was to produce photocopied books of readings that supplemented or even replaced textbooks. These were printed and sold either by the University Printing Office or by local commercial printers such as Kinko's. Only after the beginning of the new century did this process begin to give way to the availability of course readings online, and the virtually universal adoption of electronic teaching aides such as Blackboard. It would be an exaggeration to speak of the death of photocopying technology, but it has already been replaced by electronic resources as the fundamental tool of university teachers.

Publishing and entrepreneurial work

Henry Mayer had anticipated the demand for books of readings, especially important once tutorials began to take a central place in university teaching. In 1966 he edited the first version of *Australian Politics: A Reader*, which became a standard source for students of Australian politics in most Australian universities, although editors in other politics schools followed very quickly. The work went into five editions, from 1966 to 1980, trying to keep the readings up to date with changes in Australian government, parties and policies. From the Third Reader it was co-edited by Helen Nelson and was generally referred to simply as "Mayer and Nelson". The model gradually replaced standard textbooks on Australian politics, such as LF Crisp's *Parliamentary Government of the Commonwealth of Australia*, because of the need to incorporate the great changes to policy issues in the 1960s and 1970s. As Murray Goot commented: "Together, these volumes contain a substantial part of the discipline's contribution to the study of Australian politics in those years".[18] When Mayer turned to other interests, especially media politics, and then retired, the work was taken up by Rodney Smith, who edited *Politics in Australia*, first with Lex Watson and then alone, in three editions from 1989 to 1997. Seeking a more focused model of readings, rather than a general introduction to institutions and culture, Ariadne Vromen and Katharine Gelber edited *Powerscape: Contemporary Australian Theory and Practice*, while more recently Vromen also cooperated with Rodney Smith and Ian Cook to edit *Contemporary Politics in Australia : theories, practices and issues*.

As with photocopiers, the age of such books of readings or dedicated chapters is probably nearly over, although it would be impossible to overestimate their importance in the teaching of Australian politics in the last third of the 20th century.[19]

Mayer also realised that the commercial publications on Australian politics in the 1950 and 1960s were not keeping up with the work being done by researchers in the universities. (This was to change somewhat in later decades as politics became a more marketable publishing commodity.) He set the department up as a joint publisher for works, mainly by members of staff, that would not otherwise have found a publisher. The "Sydney Studies in Politics Series", as it was called, published five works in association with Cheshire, and three more in association with Sydney University Press. Towards the end of the 1960s another five books were published by the department alone, as "Occasional Monographs". Also published by the department at that time were two bibliographies – always a favoured project for Henry. The publishing venture was revived in the 1980s and 1990s with five more books published by the department, (two under the PARC title) and then, a little later, the first three volumes of *The People's Choice* NSW electoral studies published by the Parliament of NSW and the University of Sydney, explicitly building on the foundation of NSW electoral studies begun under Henry Mayer.[20]

With the infusion of extra staff, especially from America, in the early 1970s there was a realisation that the presence of so many researchers with expertise in areas studies around the world was a marketable commodity. Mayer encouraged and coordinated the formation of "Corpolplan", the trade name for "Corporate Political Planning" as a unit in the department that could act as a commercial consultancy. The major achievement was the preparation of a six-volume *Political Scenario for Qantas Airways Limited*, that attempted to provide an analysis of prospects and risks in international and regional areas serviced by Qantas for a 15-year period from 1974 till 1990.[21]

> **The Dick and Henry show**
>
> When I had completed my studies in law at the University of Sydney, I had come lately to the Byzantine world of student politics. To assure my political continuity and legitimacy, I embarked upon a third undergraduate degree, economics, thereby attracting Gareth Evans' comment that I had concentrated on quantity rather than quality in my academic preparation. I surprised myself by coming to like the discipline – and few lecturers more than Henry Mayer and Dick Spann in the courses in Government which I undertook. What a contrast they were. Truly an odd couple. Henry Mayer was provocative to the brink of the outrageous. Dick Spann was reticent, sceptical, reserved, rather unworldly – a kind of typical English god professor. But his topic was one of endless fascination – the deployment and control of administrative power.
>
> Michael Kirby, "RN Spann – Vision of Administrative Law – Have We Achieved It?", RN Spann Memorial Oration, Royal Institute of Public Administration Australia, 1996, p.2.

The work surveyed the likely reaction of the superpowers (USA, USSR, China) and regional powers (e.g., Britain, Germany, Japan, India, possibly Indonesia) to changes and challenges in Australia, Europe, North America and Asia, where Qantas flew, as well as in Africa and South America. In the third volume, for example, which discussed Asia, there were chapters discussing likely developments in Japan, Philippines, Malaysia, Singapore, North and South Vietnam, Cambodia, Laos, Thailand, North and South Korea, China, Burma, India, Bangladesh, Pakistan and Hong Kong. There were staff in the department who could manage each of those chapters. The idea of the consultancy was that it would provide a regular infusion of funds for the department that could be used for a variety of purposes. In the event, the authors of chapters needed to be paid for their contributions and there was little left over for the establishment of a significant fund, especially since no other clients emerged after the Qantas project.

In the 1990s another attempt at entrepreneurial activity began as an accounting mechanism to receive the money from various books published in the department about that time. PARC, or the Public

Affairs Research Centre, then developed as an extension of Ernie Chaples' course on quantitative research, and became an opinion polling agency, using mainly student labour and department offices and telephones in the evenings to conduct opinion polls. The main client was the Labor Party, and within a few years PARC was transformed into a private polling body, largely at the service of the NSW ALP.

Management style

In the small department of the 1960s there was little need for rigid management structures. Terry Irving remembers the teaching staff working with Spann in the late 1960s:

> It was very collegial. We would meet maybe monthly in Dick Spann's office and we would have tea and a discussion. And that was running the department. It was clear that Dick had the final say, but we were advisors, and that was very agreeable to me.[22]

As the department grew in the 1970s the meetings were held in the main department meeting room at the corner of the second level of the Merewether Building. By then Henry Mayer had been promoted to a Chair, so that his was probably the dominant voice in meetings, but even Henry was convinced of the value of informality and consensus. More formality, along with elected committees for things like curriculum, timetabling, finance, etc., was introduced along with the stormy events of the early 1970s that are discussed in Chapter 5. Yet, for all the growth and upheaval, as long as Dick Spann was alive, his was the assured hand on the tiller, even when he was not himself the head of department. The consensus culture became part of the pattern of management in the Department of Government at least until the end of the century.

1 Minutes of the University of Sydney Senate, 11 August 1952; 13 October 1952; 8 June 1953. Martin Krygier, "Obituary. RN Spann 1916-1981", *Quadrant*, September 1981, p. 42.

2 Ross Curnow, "Intellectual Stance: RN Spann", *Australian Journal of Public Administration*, Vol.39, (3-4), September 1980, pp. 283-292.

3 Martin Krygier, Obituary: "R.N. Spann 1916-1981", *Quadrant*, September 1981, p. 43.

4 Quoted in Peter Coleman, *Memoirs of a Slow Learner: An intimate and personal memoir*, Sydney, Angus & Robertson, 1994, p. 124. The original letter can be found in the *Observer*, 14 June 1958, p. 277.

5 Don Rawson, Obituary, Henry Mayer, Academy of the Social Sciences in Australia, webpage: http://www.assa.edu.au/fellowship/fellow/deceased/100085

6 ibid.

7 *Politics*, 20 (2), November 1985.

8 Jill Ker Conway, *The Road From Coorain*, New York, Alfred A Knopf & Random House, 1989, p. 220-1.

9 Elaine Thompson, "Henry Mayer as a Teacher", *Politics*, 20 (2), November 1985, p. 9.

10 Frank Bongiorno, "British to their boot heels too: Britishness and Australian radicalism", Trevor Reese Memorial Lecture 2006, London, Menzies Centre for Australian Studies, King's College London, 2006, fn, p. 34. http://www.kcl.ac.uk/artshums/ahri/centres/menzies/research/Publications/Reese2006Bongiorno.pdf

11 RN Spann, "Political Science in Australia", *AJPH*, Vol 1 No 1. 1955, pp. 86-97. See also "Political Studies: A Conference Report", *AJPH*, Vol 4 No 1, 1958, pp. 1-18.

12 Groenewegen, p. 71.

13 Minutes of the University of Sydney Senate, 21 March 1955.

14 Interview with Michael Leigh, 13 January 2014, University of Sydney Oral History Project.

15 Minutes of the University of Sydney Senate, 7 October 1958.

16 RN Spann, "Understanding public administration: reflections on an academic obituary – 'Alas, Poor Yorick' ", *Australian Journal of Public Administration*, Vol. 40, (3), September 1981, pp. 235-6.

17 *University of Sydney Calendar, 1962*, p. 133.

18 Murray Goot, "Henry Mayer (1919-1991), in Brian Gallagher & Winsome Roberts (eds.), *Oxford Companion to Australian Politics*, Oxford, OUP, 2007, pp. 334-5.

19 Henry Mayer (ed.), *Australian Politics: A Reader*, Melbourne, Cheshire, 1st & 2nd editions, 1966, 1969; Henry Mayer & Helen Nelson (eds.), *Australian Politics: a third reader*, Melbourne, Cheshire, 1973 (4th ed., 1976, 5th ed., 1980); Rodney Smith & Lex Watson (eds), *Politics in Australia*, Sydney, Allen & Unwin, 1989; Rodney Smith, *Politics in Australia*, Sydney, Allen & Unwin, 2nd and 3rd editions, 1993, 1997; Ariadne Vromen & Katharine Gelber, (eds.), *Powerscape: contemporary Australian political practice*,

Sydney, Allen & Unwin, 2005; Rodney Smith, Ariadne Vromen & Ian Cook (eds.), *Contemporary Politics in Australia: theories, practice and issues*, Melbourne, CUP, 2012.

20 The full list of department publications can be found in Michael Hogan & Kathy Dempsey (eds.), *Equity and Citizenship under Keating*, Sydney, PARC, University of Sydney, 1995, p. 203. Michael Hogan & David Clune (eds.), *The People's Choice: Electoral Politics in 20th Century New South Wales*, Sydney, Parliament of NSW and University of Sydney, 2001, 3 vols. The fourth volume, of elections in colonial NSW, was published in 2007 by Federation Press.

21 Corpolplan, Corporate Political Planning, a unit in the Department of Government University of Sydney, *Political Scenario for Qantas Airways Limited*, 3 vols. for private distribution, Sydney, 1973.

22 Terry Irving, Interview in the Department of Government Oral History Project, 24 July 2014.

4
The expanding department

At the beginning of the 1960s a number of factors came together to create a huge student demand for courses in politics. A deal with the Arts Faculty and a restructuring of the Economics Faculty meant that by 1962 for the first time students could enrol in Government I in the first year of their degree. Within a year or two the first children of the postwar baby boom would reach school leaving age and arrive at university.[1] By the 1960s, also, it was apparent that family expectations about the level of education for children had changed permanently. In the prewar years it was normal to leave school at 15 years old or even before that, with or without the Intermediate Certificate; by the 1960s children were normally expected to finish high school with the Leaving Certificate, and a growing proportion expected to proceed to university. This change of expectations was especially obvious for girls, so that the next few decades would see female completion rates both at high school and university surpass those of males. Sydney, which had been the home for one university for a century, would finish the 1960s with three.

These factors affected enrolments at the university as a whole, and especially the Arts Faculty. There was also increased community interest in politics that had direct consequences for the Department of Government. The international community awoke to an appreciation of the technological challenge to the West coming from the USSR and Communism after the launching of the Sputnik space satellite in 1957. The Cold War had taken on a world-wide dimension with the rapid collapse of the old colonial order in Africa and Asia. Although Britain was willing to withdraw from much of its empire in an orderly fashion, other imperial European powers were more reluctant. A more urgent disengagement was actively promoted by the Soviet Union and China, and its manifestations were close to Australia especially in Malaysia, Indonesia and Vietnam. At first France, then the United States and later Australia became involved in the civil war in Vietnam, leading to conscription in 1964 for young Australian men to fight in a foreign war. These issues became a cause of polarisation in the Australian community – especially for young people of university (and conscription) age.

Finally, even local Australian politics became interesting during the 1960s. The Menzies era had not been especially stimulating, but when John Gorton became Prime Minister in 1968, at a time when current affairs TV programs like *This Day Tonight* were developing a mass audience, Australian politics changed forever. Gorton was confronting a new Labor leader, Gough Whitlam, who was a breath of fresh air after many years of Labor stagnation under leaders like Arthur Calwell and HV Evatt. Television was to have an enormous impact on the conduct of politics and on popular perceptions of party competition and elections. The era of modern mass media communication that had begun with newspapers about the beginning of the 19th century, had moved up a gear with radio and movies from the 1920s, and now exploded into society with the idiot box and public opinion polls from the 1960s. After 1964, for the first time there was a national newspaper – *The Australian*. Henry Mayer was fascinated with the implications of such change.

Within the University of Sydney and the Arts Faculty the Government Department was almost the only place where these issues could find a place in the curriculum, especially for first year students.

The History Department did not take Australian history seriously except as a small part of a third year course, and even Australian literature was generally sidelined in the English Department until the late 1960s. For students interested in Australian politics, history and culture, Government was the obvious choice.

Government I challenges

One can see the impact of these factors on enrolments in Government in the years from 1963 to 1966. (See Figure 4.1) In four years the numbers more than doubled – from 542 to 1268 – and then levelled off in a slight rising trend until the mid-1970s. Each of those four years saw, on average, about 180 more students than the previous year. As in the earlier period of the late 1950s, the impact was felt first in Government I, flowing through not quite as strongly in successive years to Government II and III. By the 1970s this surge of numbers resulted in a radical revision of the curriculum for later year courses, discussed in a later chapter. That could happen only after the department had come to terms with how to react to a genuine crisis of resources caused by the sudden and seemingly relentless surge in numbers. The figures for enrolments in Government I are available only from 1966, but reasonable assumptions can be made for the few years before that. In 1966 the figure for first year enrolments at the beginning of the Trinity Term (about May) was 780. If one assumes that there had been a doubling since 1963, then the figure would have been in the order of about 400 in that year. Consequently the increase in Government I would have been about 100 extra each year. Moreover, the official figures underestimate the impact of the rise; in March the numbers are typically considerably higher than after the first Term, as many students drop out from university or transfer to other subjects because of timetable clashes and other factors. The director of Government I in 1966, Ken Turner, would have been confronted with a figure closer to 900 than 780 in the week before classes began, and he would have to make arrangements for accommodating them.

The department had been used to repeating classes at all levels during the 1950s because the Economics Faculty insisted on an evening class, while Arts students overwhelmingly preferred a daytime timetable. This had been a minor annoyance when numbers were small, but became a major issue for teachers as numbers rose. In 1954, when Dick Spann arrived, daytime classes for Government I were on Monday, Tuesday and Wednesday at 11 am, while the evening classes were at the awkward times of Monday at 5.15 pm and 7.15 pm, and Tuesday at 6.15 pm. When the Economics Faculty changed from a four-year to a three-year degree in 1959 there was less student demand for evening classes, but by then there was already a need for repeat daytime classes.

During the period of strongest expansion, from 1963 to 1966, Government I followed the previous model of a single course on liberal democracy illustrated by the study of Australian political institutions. As before, the course was co-taught by a variety of teachers – Ken Turner, Henry Mayer, Dick Spann, Peter Westerway and others as available. It was impossible to find a lecture room for nearly a thousand students at convenient times, so the only option was to repeat lectures, usually one in the morning, another mid-afternoon, and another late-afternoon. Most of this period predated the move to the Merewether Building, and any demand for extra lecturing space faced stiff competition from the other large departments in the Arts Faculty whose enrolment explosion had predated that of Government.

Ken Turner became one of the key members of the department in the years of expansion. He was an Honours graduate in Government (BEc Hons, 1956) who had pursued a first career as a high school teacher at Maitland and Newtown, before joining the staff of Sydney Teachers' College. While there he began taking occasional tutorials in Government, eventually accepting the offer of a job as Senior Tutor in 1961, with the task of managing Government I, with special attention to the tutorial program which was still in its early stages. With his interest in Australian politics and his teaching experience he was perfect for the job. He also had a down-to-earth personal style that allowed him to engage easily and productively with students and staff. He created an ever-evolving team of tutors (full-time and part-time) for whom he was mentor and friend, exchanging tips on good teaching and encouraging the development of their own interests in postgraduate study as well as in the occasional lecture or series of lectures. At a later period, by then an Associate Professor, his role as head of department in the 1970s was also pivotal for the department.

There were advantages for repeat lectures; it gave freer scope for students to avoid timetable clashes with other subjects, while teachers found that students in some time slots were more receptive than at others. For example, students who came to the late afternoon sessions tended to be more serious, and perhaps a bit older, than those who came in the mornings. Ken Turner tells how impressed he was with some guest lecturers – active politicians – who instinctively treated the morning group as a combative political rally, while in the afternoon session a more discursive and reflective approach was possible. Nevertheless, repeating lectures was a very tedious way to teach; sometimes the second lecture was an improvement on the first, but one could sense that for the third presentation even the lecturer was exhibiting boredom.

Students were expected to purchase textbooks to supplement the lecture material and to provide readings for tutorials. Modern students, used to a single textbook and/or a book of photocopied readings, or freely available online material, will be surprised at the extent of the costs involved. In 1967, for example, the course description in the *Economics Handbook* gave a list of 11 textbooks for Government I –

and "all textbooks must be bought". They included the first Mayer Reader on Australian politics, plus books by Crisp, Rawson, Sawer, Blondel, Dahl, Fried, Moodie, Sorauf, Stankiewicz and Wheare. Admittedly some were slim volumes, and many could be purchased second-hand from students in previous years, or in the second-hand bookshop on campus, but it still involved a considerable outlay of money. For tutorials, in addition, extra readings – single chapters or journal articles – were available only in the Closed Reserve section of Fisher Library, which involved queuing and often being disappointed when there were not enough copies for the demand.

Both Dick Spann and Henry Mayer were strong advocates of teaching through tutorials as a supplement for mass lectures. Until the early 1960s most departments in Arts and Economics subjects did not have compulsory tutorials, and assessment was almost exclusively dependent on performance in the end of year examination. Government was one of the earliest departments to make tutorials compulsory and to count essay and tutorial papers as part of the total assessment. This had an obvious effect on the shape of the teaching staff. Typically, from the 1960s to the 1980s, about a quarter of the full-time staff were non-tenured tutors (sometimes with the title of teaching fellow, assistant lecturer, or something similar) who taught mainly, but not exclusively in Government I. Such appointments were regarded by the department as apprenticeships for future academics, either in the department or in other universities. Tutors were encouraged to give small sets of lectures on areas of their special interest, and occasionally became the principal class lecturer when Government I was divided into a number of separate options by the beginning of the 1980s. There was a continuous exchange of insights between teachers – "This worked well. Why don't you try it?" Most ex-students of Government will recognise that the tutors were the frontline troops.

Among the responses of ex-students in the preparation of this book a significant number pointed out that Government was not a

Figure 4.1

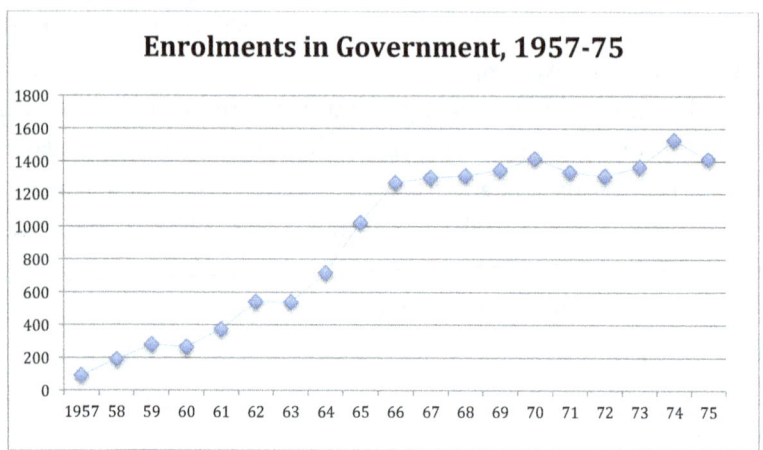

Source: Enrolment Statistics, Planning and Information Office,

first choice; rather it was chosen almost by accident and only then caught their attention and enthusiasm. For Ken Turner, Government had been not been a choice at all in his first degree (BA), and was only considered when he returned to do his BEc. Both lecturers and tutors were eager to engage their students and capture their interest – in a way that was not always obvious in a number of other large departments at the time. This was certainly the experience of the author as a student; I enrolled in English, History and Psychology, but dropped out of Psychology after a week to go looking for something else. I went to Anthropology, only to be told that it was full; there was always room in Government! For new students wondering about their mix of courses, word of mouth recommendations were clearly positive for the study of Government.

Internationalisation of staff

The department was fortunate that, during the time of its most rapid expansion, the university sector as a whole was also fairly well funded.

Consequently, the numbers of staff rose more or less in tune with those of students. When Dick Spann had arrived to start teaching in 1954 he found a department relatively well supplied with four teachers and an enrolment of 131 students. University statistics do not publish details of staff-student ratios based on Equivalent Full-Time Students (EFTS) and EFTStaff until 1970, but reasonable estimates can be made for earlier years. There is no recognised "fair" or equitable level for staff-student ratios, as some faculties and departments have traditionally warranted significantly higher levels of staffing than others. Throughout this book an indicative measure is used whereby in a non-scientific department like most in Arts and Economics Faculties a staff-student ratio below 20 means that staffing is relatively healthy, while above 20 significant problems start to appear. In 1955, with four established positions plus a few part-timers, a good guess would put the staff student ratio at about 1:11. By 1960 the established staff numbers had risen to six, giving an approximate ratio of 1:15. By 1965, with students pouring in and staff numbers rising only to 11, the situation had deteriorated to a ratio of 1:31. That was enough to send signals of the need for more staff, which were provided very quickly, so that by 1970 the official ratio was reasonable enough at 1:22. Between 1965 and 1970 staff numbers had doubled from 11+ to 22+. That marked a change from quite a small department to a relatively large one. Growth continued to 28.5 staff in 1975, peaking in 1976 before a period of hardship for Universities when positions were sometimes frozen. Nevertheless, for most of the 1970s and 1980s the staff-student ratio averaged about 1:16, which was very healthy.

It was not just numbers of staff that were significant, but their origins and their disposition in the teaching program. Most staff members in the early years of the department had been hand-picked by the professors and had usually been graduates of the University of Sydney. By the mid-1960s this was changing as stricter

Figure 4.2

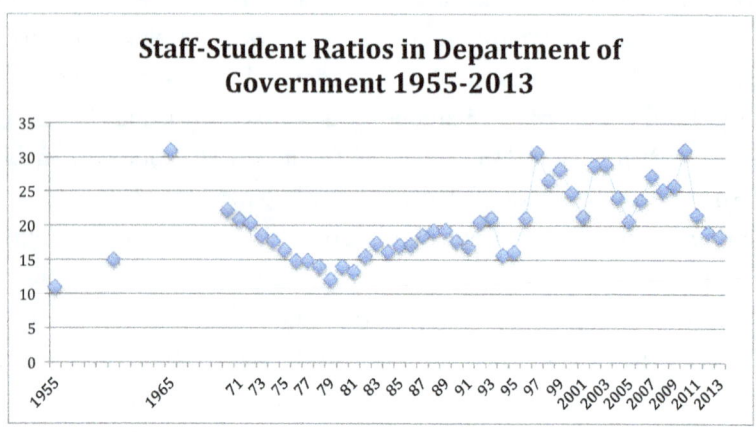

Source: Planning and Information Office. Estimated from 1955-1965; actual from 1970.

selection procedures were enforced throughout the university. From the beginning of the 1970s almost all establishment jobs were advertised, usually internationally, and selection committees included representatives of the Professorial Board and the Faculty, including members from cognate and non-cognate departments throughout the university. This does not mean that a determined professor could not influence the process – usually by setting the terms of the advertisement in such a fashion as to give an advantage to a preferred candidate – but generally the procedures guaranteed impartiality.

Most teachers appointed on establishment during the 1960s and 1970s had doctorates, often from American universities, although, even so, most were Australian-born. To the first four members of the Dick Spann's department (Spann, Mayer, Kewley and McCallum) the first significant additions during the 1950s were Peter Loveday and Peter Westerway, both graduates of the University of Sydney, plus Ross Martin who had a PhD from the ANU. By the mid-1960s John Power (PhD, Harvard) and Roger Scott (DPhil, Oxford) had joined the department, along with Trevor Matthews and Ken Turner, both graduates of the Sydney Faculty of Economics without higher degrees on appointment. Meanwhile, McCallum and Westerway had moved onto other positions. During the next five years (1965-70) there was strong growth, with the addition of: Ross Curnow (Cornell), Dennis Altman (MA, Cornell), Terry Irving (History, Sydney), Peter King (ANU), Michael Leigh (Cornell), Rex Mortimer (Monash), Bob Connell (Sydney), along with Jim Richardson (BA, Oxford), and Ian Grosart (BA, Melbourne) who was recruited from the Australian School of Pacific Administration, while Roger Scott had moved on.

Although a number of the staff members recruited in the 1960s had American higher degrees (why was Cornell so prominent?), most were Australian-born. The 1970s saw a significant Americanisation of the department with the arrival of Bob Taylor, Michael Jackson, Ernie Chaples, Fred Teiwes and Peter Nelson, along with the temporary appointment of Ed Cole in 1970-1. This surge is partly explained by the Australian salaries and tenured appointments that were attractive to academics in the United States at that time, and partly by a deliberate policy of advertising in the USA at the same time as American universities were recruiting. There were often also personal reasons that prompted a move to Sydney. Henry Mayer had hopes that the graduates of American universities would bring a stiffening

---

Here come the Yanks

The Department, led by Henry Mayer, was dynamic and relevant in the mid-1970s, full of young lecturers from the United States who had felt the hot breath of politics very personally as protestors against the Vietnam War. I loved Michael Jackson's "Ethics and Politics: Violence" class, in which we grappled with issues such as war crimes and the duty to dissent. I also enjoyed Ernie Chaples's in-the-real-world approach to gathering research by creating meaningful polls and crunching the resulting data. The Government Department was great preparation for my early career in journalism, and the questions that we argued over across those seminar tables continue to animate my fiction.

Geraldine Brooks, BA Hons, 1979 (Pulitzer Prize winning novelist)

of the "political science" credentials of the department. That was not immediately achieved, although Chaples eventually offered a very popular course on survey design and statistical analysis.

Decision-making style

There is no doubt that the arrival of these new teachers had a significant impact on the internal culture of the department, especially at a time of political upheaval within the university (see Chapter 5). The era of Professors Spann and Mayer presiding over a cosy, hand-picked family of scholars gave way to an open acceptance of conflicting interests that constantly needed to be resolved. While Dick Spann remained head of department problems were sorted by Spann consulting with colleagues, finding a solution that satisfied most, and getting approval from the Committee. However, when ill health caused Spann to step down from the headship in 1972, Henry Mayer, as the only other professor, was automatically confirmed as head. Mayer had not sought the job, and was not a natural administrator, but possessed enough of the "god professor" mindset to resent suggestions from the academic staff that his solutions might not be the best. When he was replaced as head by Ken Turner in 1975 staff demands for effective self-management could not be denied. Nor was it in Turner's plans to deny them.

Department meetings became battlegrounds where arguments that "this is how we have always done it" received short shrift or were often replaced by comments that "no other university in the world" does it that way. Attempts to find a consensus resolution of problems took up an inordinate amount of time and energy year after year. A good example was the difficulty in defining a standard workload for teachers. Each year there were complaints from some members of staff that the current formula discriminated against diligent researchers, or against teachers in Government I, or did not sufficiently recognise

> **The Jim Beam Club**
>
> *Named after Bob Taylor's favourite tipple, the Jim Beam Club had regular lunchtime meetings in one or other of the nearby Newtown pubs and sometimes more extended sessions late on Friday afternoons. It was not restricted to American members of staff; indeed, not all Americans were admitted, while Martin Painter, an expatriate Englishman, was a core member. Occasional Aussies were welcome if they were willing to observe the rules of the club, which were basically to pour scorn on the way the Department made its decisions, and on colleagues who had offended in that regard, as well as occasionally to recommend novels to be read, to play pool in the pub, or try to beat Michael Jackson at his portable desk hockey game. It was a clear pointer to the change in culture within the Department following the rapid growth and internationalization of teaching staff.*

membership of departmental or Faculty committees, or any of a dozen other factors. If research was subsequently given a greater weighting there would be a reaction from others who bore the greater workload in teaching; if a weighting was introduced to make first year teaching more attractive there were complaints that the really important teaching was done in later years or at Honours level; if administrative and committee tasks were compensated more liberally both the dedicated researchers and teachers would protest. Eventually the department, after extended committee consultation, came up with its "Ravenhill formula" that satisfied most interests and survived with minor amendments for most of the 1980s and 1990s. However, as new members were appointed to the department debate was likely to start all over again, with slogans from the past re-emerging to the hilarity of pre-existing staff members.

The sense that every problem faced by the department was the opportunity for debate meant, of course, that decision-making was difficult. In principle, it was accepted that majority support was sufficient for any departmental decision – no one ever envisaged the necessity for unanimity – so negotiation and compromise were strong characteristics of collegial management. Anxiety about a professorial veto, so much a feature of debate in the democratisation debates of the early 1970s (see Chapter 5), gave way to frustration about a universal veto, where any compromise acceptable to a majority of the Department Committee soon became a target of attack by members who had not been present at the relevant meeting or who were appointed at a later time. Professor Christopher Hood, who held the Chair from 1986 to 1989, found this culture of unattainable consensus particularly frustrating, as he was aware that hard decisions needed to be made, especially in the teaching program. He once compared the department's decision-making style – or rather, its non-decision-making – to the political immobility of between-wars Poland. Yet, for all its faults, collegial self-management enjoyed overwhelming support among staff, while helping to maintain morale.

Budgeting

Up until well into the 1980s there was a clearly understood pattern of funding for departments in the University of Sydney. The most expensive item was salaries for academic and general staff. Department heads and professors needed to negotiate with their Dean and perhaps with the Vice-Chancellor and his office to secure establishment positions. However, once that was accomplished the university took responsibility for salaries; as members of staff were promoted and moved into higher salary ranges the additional cost was automatically taken up by the centre. The annual salary bill was guaranteed, so that, for example, if a professor or senior lecturer arranged a secondment to another institution, as happened a number of times, that teacher's salary was available for the department. The money could go to replacing the absent teacher so that the teaching program could remain unchanged, or the decision could be made that the immediate teaching need that year was for two extra tutors who could be funded from the money. When Rex Mortimer was absent for three years to take up a chair at the University of Papua-New Guinea

Martin Indyk

Born in London, educated in Australia, and now a United States citizen, Martin Indyk graduated BEc in 1973, with First Class Honours in Government, completing a thesis on US foreign policy towards Israel. After postgraduate study at the ANU, he moved to the United States, where he became US Ambassador to Israel under the Clinton administration (1995-7; 2000-1), and Assistant Secretary of State for Near Eastern Affairs. He has taught and written widely on issues of national security and diplomacy. He was founding Director of the Washington Institute for Near Eastern Policy, and later became Vice President and Director of Foreign Policy for the Brooking's Institution in Washington. In 2013 he served as US Special Envoy for Israeli-Palestinian Relations.

from 1974 to 1976, that was exactly the arrangement. Effectively, the head of department did not need to worry about salaries, except when a new position was sought.

There were standard expectations about other items in the department's budget. While it had two professors, Government could expect two positions of professorial secretaries, as well as at least one other non-academic staff member to attend the department office. At appointment professors were normally guaranteed a full-time research assistant; this could be supplemented by additional research assistance for targeted projects by negotiation with the Vice-Chancellor's office. Such salaries were handled in the same way as academic salaries, so that when general staff resigned or retired there was normally no difficulty in advertising to fill the position. Both Spann and Mayer were generous in making their allocated support staff available for the needs of the department, although it was clearly understood that the demands of the professor came first.

Other items on the departmental budget needed to be negotiated year by year with the Faculty – money for part-time teaching, which was always a large amount; money for stationery and equipment, which increased substantially in the 1980s when desktop computers were needed and had constantly to be updated and provided with appropriate software – although there was normally an expectation that such allocations would be automatically renewed, perhaps with a small increment. The head could sign off on items under the appropriate heading until that budget ran out for the year. When Ken Turner became head he realised the limitations of having to budget in this fashion because there was often an urgent need for spending under one heading that was already virtually exhausted, while money still remained unspent under another heading. He found that, by consultation with officers in the university's accounting and budgetary section, there were often ways around that problem known only to accountants. The reality was that each department had considerable autonomy in its budgeting, especially once salary costs were accepted as a problem for the centre.

After Dick and Henry

Dick Spann died suddenly in July 1981, just as he was about to retire. A few years later, at the end of 1984, Henry Mayer retired from the department, serving as a visiting professor at the University of New South Wales and Macquarie University until his own death in 1991. The loss of two such men who had dominated the department for nearly 30 years marked a change in the culture of the department and left a leadership vacuum. Since the mid-1970s administrative control had passed to a non-professorial head – Ken Turner was the first of a succession of associate professor heads – but there was general agreement that the department needed the academic clout that only a talented and vigorous professor could give. Although there was support for a candidate with Spann's expertise in public policy there was general agreement that the chair should be advertised in the widest terms so as to find the best possible candidate. Since the headship was not automatically tied to the chair the department

Lester Cashen

A graduate in pharmacy at the University of Sydney, Les Cashen later studied for the priesthood, being ordained for the Catholic Archdiocese of Sydney in 1958. After work in various Sydney parishes he became Vice-Rector (1969-73), then Rector (1980-91) of St John's College in the University. While Vice-Rector, he did a major in Government as part of his Arts degree (BA, 1978).  Throughout his life he was politically active, founding the National Association of Pharmaceutical Students in 1947, then becoming first president of the national association (NAPSA) and helping to establish the international federation (IPSF). He also gained a national profile for his leadership within the Australian Catholic Church, being a founding member of the National Council of Priests and of the Sydney Archdiocesan Senate. He was awarded an honorary Master of Philosophy degree by the University of Sydney in December 1991, and honoured with the Medal of the Order of Australia (OAM) in 2003. In his later years he was parish priest of Pyrmont and Forest Lodge, where he died peacefully in 2003.

was prepared to wait until outstanding candidates were available. In retrospect the lack of urgency was surprising, but the late 1980s saw the beginnings of economic stringency in the university as a whole, and perhaps the department believed that the money should be better spent on additional lecturers and tutors. Perhaps, also, there was a wariness about the possibility of a new, strong minded, professor upsetting the pattern of self management that had developed in the department.

The first new professorial appointment came in 1984 when Gianfranco Poggi arrived from the sociology department at Edinburgh University. Poggi took the position on trial and lasted only a year before returning to Edinburgh and then moving to the University of Virginia. It was an unusual appointment since it brought a touch of European political theory and sociology to the department (although Poggi had achieved his doctorate at Berkeley, so he was well acquainted with American political science). He could be seen as a replacement for Henry Mayer rather than Dick Spann.

In the event his stay was too brief for him to have any long-term impact on the culture of the department.

In 1986 the appointment of Christopher Hood was welcomed by staff members, especially the public policy/public administration people who saw him as a worthy successor to Dick Spann. He was recruited from Hong Kong, having written important books on public administration such as *The Limits of Administration* (1976) and *The Tools of Government* (1983). He worked hard to persuade the department to undertake a serious review of teaching and research priorities but was frustrated by the consensus culture he encountered in the Department Committee. Unlike most of the Americans he never became "Australianised", so the pull of home must have been strong. After four years Hood returned to Britain where he has held senior positions at the LSE and Oxford. As an anonymous editorialist in the department's occasional newsletter commented when regretting his departure: "we suspect that our rating of him would be higher than his of us".[2]

Hood was replaced in 1989 by Alastair Davidson, a sociologist and theorist best known as an historian of the Australian Communist Party, although his central interest was probably in the nature of citizenship. Even more than Christopher Hood, Davidson had plans for a reorientation of the department that were resisted by staff. There was some friction between Davidson and the head of department at that time, Michael Leigh. Davidson lasted only four years before moving on to further challenges.

When Dick Spann had been appointed to the Chair there was no doubt that academic matters at the department level were firmly in the hands of the professor, who was normally head of department unless there was more than one professor. At the Faculty level professors were dominant, and at the Professorial Board they had exclusive rights. By the 1970s, however, this situation was beginning to change in the University of Sydney as the Professorial Board was replaced

> **Not the cricket team**
>
> Michael Leigh (Wicketkeeper; bats at no.11)
>
> *It is apparent that the wicketkeeper has a difficult yet crucial role in this team. A number of the bowlers are capable of deceiving both batsman and keeper with flight, swing and turn. Leigh is fearless and draws admiration from the crowd when he occasionally stands up to the stumps to bowlers of the class of Davidson and Springborg. Inevitably he misgloves a few, but it makes for an exciting spectacle. If he has a fault it is that he is reluctant to return the ball to the bowler or even to show it to the other fielders. Even his companions in the slips cordon sometimes have not been amused when he impishly slips the ball into his back pocket and pretends to look for it at silly point. As a batsman Leigh has a respectable record but refuses to practise his strokeplay. Some of his teammates would like to see him elevated in the batting line up, but he seems content to be a tail ender.*
>
> Anon., "The First Eleven", *Beyond the Cringe*, (Newsletter of the Department of Government), September 1990.

by an Academic Board where non-professorial members were a significant proportion. Moreover, as non-professorial heads became more common – at first in small schools when the professor was absent, then more commonly in larger units – university regulations recognised more and more that administrative decisions were the preserve of the head. Of course professors were still very influential, so that conflict between a professor and a non-professorial head was a recipe for disaster, while many departments recognised that their interests could be better protected by a professorial head, able to be taken seriously at every level of the university.

The first non-professorial head of the Department of Government (except for brief acting appointments when Dick Spann was on leave) was Ken Turner, appointed after Henry Mayer was persuaded to step down from the position. He was a friend and admirer of Spann and Mayer, and was under no illusions that an associate professor could have the same impact as a respected professor who could solve problems by having a quiet word in the ear of the highest university officers. Fortunately both professors had a similar respect for Turner. During his seven-year tenure Turner oversaw a gradual loosening of the professorial grasp on established research assistant positions, which became more explicitly departmental resources (although previously both professors had been generous in making those resources available for worthwhile projects of other staff members). The two professors retained their secretaries, but, again, there was no problem from the professors in making them available for departmental work. Turner had only one agenda as head – to work for the welfare of the department and its academic and general staff members. At a crucial stage in the evolution of the Department of Government, Turner was the right man at the right time and was universally respected and admired. One of his junior colleagues at the time has commented:

> I think Ken was successful because he was a decent bloke (in the best sense of the word); seemed not to play games (I don't know whether he did or not) after Henry, who was seen to play games when he probably wasn't; fair minded; good unionist; pragmatic; problem solver.[3]

He was assiduous in university committees to ensure promotion or tenure for staff members or the appointment of extra staff, as he networked successfully with faculty and university administration officers to achieve favourable treatment for his department. His contacts with senior academics on the Academic Board or various faculties were often inaugurated with social meetings in the University Staff Club (now, sadly, no more). Otherwise his intention was that things should continue as normally as possible as in the past. In fact this helped entrench the culture of consensus decision-making that most members of the department wished to continue, but which made rapid adjustment difficult for problems still to be faced.

Until the end of the century Ken Turner was followed as head by a series of associate professors – Terry Irving, Trevor Matthews,

> **Sue Wills**
> Sue graduated from the University of Sydney with a BA (1967), BEc Hons (1971), PhD (1982) and Dip Law (2002). During most of her undergraduate and postgraduate time in the Department of Government she was an activist in feminist, as well as gay and lesbian, political issues. She has continued those interests, helping to write the history of local developments in the Gay Pride History group. She was a tutor in the Department of Government, then later lecturer in politics courses at Ku-ring-gai CAE and then at Macquarie University. She was Equal Education Officer at Macquarie University from 1984 till 1994. She then returned to academic life, convening the Master of Politics and Public Policy at Macquarie University until her retirement in 2007. Since then she has been engaged, amongst other things, in writing a history of the Sydney Women's Liberation Movement, 1969-1980.

Michael Leigh, Helen Nelson, Rod Tiffen, Michael Jackson, J Ramesh. The usual appointment was for two years, which could be extended for another term with some collegial arm twisting. It was certainly not a task to aspire to, even though it had implications for academic promotion. There was always a culture of criticism from the backbench of the Department Board, as any decision or non-decision was greeted with scorn. At one meeting of the department to discuss who should be next, Helen Nelson volunteered that since she had been so critical of previous incumbents she should be prepared to put her money where her mouth was and do the job herself! Her offer was accepted. Most did the task assiduously, according to their different personalities and talents, defending the department against threatened job cuts and financial stringencies, assisting staff applying for promotion, and cajoling reluctant staff into teaching in Government I, while experiencing frustrations in trying to implement reforms in a department culture of consensus. By the turn of the century, when the department became just one discipline in the social sciences school of the Faculty of Economics and Business, the role of head of discipline became even more frustrating because of the loss of autonomy, while most significant decisions were made by the head of school.

The Merewether Building

In 1966 the Merewether Building opposite the City Road gates of the university was officially opened by Senator John Gorton, Commonwealth Minister for Education. It had been designed and built for the use of the Economics Faculty, which moved over from the Mills Building occupied since 1951. The Government Department was allocated space on Level 2, along the southern and western sides of a pleasant green quadrangle. The space included two large rooms for general staff, two professorial offices, a meeting room at the corner of the two corridors, and a variety of smaller rooms for storage and clerical use (although the uses for these have changed many times over the years). The building contained two large lecture theatres and

Entrance to the Merewether Building (Photo by MH)

three smaller ones, plus a large number of tutorial and small teaching rooms on Level 1. It must have seemed like heaven for staff after the limited space in the Mills Building.

One of the problems encountered in the early years in the Merewether Building was the shortage of telephones. Professors and their secretaries, along with the Department Office, had phones, but initially most other members of staff did not. They had to go to the central office to make calls out, but the main problems were with incoming calls. Office staff had to answer, then try to find the teacher, which was often impossible. Much time was wasted. Ross Curnow tells how he was constantly frustrated that calls from colleagues in the Commonwealth Public Service were missed, leading to him drafting a fierce letter of complaint to the administration (which Dick Spann amended diplomatically and supported).[4] By the 1970s all offices had a telephone, but for most of that decade two teachers had to share a line, leading to highly variable levels of cooperation (or lack thereof) in passing on messages. By the 1980s the university had upgraded its systems so that such problems were a thing of the past.

If it was a clear improvement on previous accommodation, the building has not gained universal approval from its occupants over the years since then. The offices for academic staff are of a comfortable size – larger than the tiny cells that have become the norm in many modern Australian university buildings. Yet many teachers have noted that if the offices had been designed to be about 20% larger they could have been used for tutorials (as is the case in many traditional offices in the Old Quad of the main University Building). Conversely, the purpose-built tutorial rooms downstairs were rather larger than necessary, more suitable for small classes than intimate tutorials. Merewether was designed with hard floors, making for a noisy environment; it was not till about 30 years later that this problem was resolved with the provision of carpet throughout the corridors and offices.

Probably the greatest problem has been that of noise in many of the teaching rooms. This has mainly affected the smaller lecture rooms on Level 2 and the original set of tutorial rooms on Level 1 – both ranged along the Butlin Avenue side of the building. It is a busy road, used by many commercial and heavy vehicles. That constant problem was exacerbated because the road was constantly being dug up in the latter part of the 20th century (probably to constantly update wiring connections between the Computer Centre and the main university campus). Especially at the beginning of the academic year, when the weather is still hot, teachers had to choose whether to leave the windows open – and be deafened – or to close them – and to suffocate. Another kind of suffocation is mentioned by one of the Government students: "I didn't like the Merewether Building as I always felt intimidated by the hordes of commerce and business students mulling around with their yuppie identities."[5]

One of the attractive features of the new building was the space on Level 1 for the Wolstenholme Library. This provided books, journals and a reference section for the use of the various disciplines in the Faculty. Many of these were duplicates of material held in Fisher Library, but the convenience for academic staff doing research for teaching or publication to be able to spend 10 minutes finding an article in Wolstenholme and returning upstairs was inestimable. Sadly, when Fisher Library underwent a rationalisation of its resources and secondary library centres in the 1990s Wolstenholme disappeared, to be replaced by a study centre for students.

Over time, especially by the 1990s, demand for space outgrew Merewether, so that a new building, mainly for the business-related departments, was constructed opposite the university swimming pool. That provided only temporary relief as a huge increase in academic and non-academic staff in the Faculty meant that by the end of the 20th century severe space pressures were being experienced by the Department of Government. At different times some space was

Merewether Quadrangle. Through the leafy space to the Department of Government (Photo by MH)

found for visitors, postgraduates and honorary staff in the Institute Building next door, or in university-owned terrace buildings in the street behind, but there was always more demand for space than supply. As the business disciplines of the short-lived Faculty of Economics and Business expanded rapidly at the beginning of the new century, more and more non-academic staff officers from the faculty were accommodated in Merewether; their preference was for Level 2 which put them close to the faculty student information centre on that level. Staff in the Government Department were relocated wherever space could be found temporarily, often on Level 4. This meant that the older pattern of the department occupying two corridors on Level 2 was seriously eroded, with an obvious negative impact on collegiality.

More recently, the Faculty, now renamed the School of Business, is to expand to another building under construction in the "Abercrombie Precinct". Meanwhile, now that most residents of Merewether

(Departments of Government, Economics, and Political Economy) have been transferred to the Faculty of Arts and Social Sciences, there have been constant promises of new accommodation that is now in the planning stage. Occupants of the Merewether Building are under notice that the whole precinct is be redeveloped and will need to be vacated in the interim. A recent university communiqué mentioned that a new building adjacent to the RD Watt Building (near the Ross Street gates of the university and the Wallace lecture theatre) would eventually accommodate the social science school. Promises of new and better permanent accommodation for the School of Social and Political Sciences are scheduled to be fulfilled "soon", although department staff during 2014 saw little need for urgency in preparing for the move.

A community of scholars?

With the influx of new teachers, including graduates of American universities, there was a clear change of institutional culture in the Department of Government. The development from a tiny department when Dick Spann arrived in the 1950s to the large group of teachers of the 1970s would have been enough to have caused most of that change. Nevertheless, a strong endeavour, led by Dick Spann and Ken Turner, ensured that professional and personal relationships within the department remained cooperative. Although there were members of staff who were politically and socially conservative, alongside others who were neither, disagreements were handled with tolerance by virtually all. As has been mentioned, the downside of such tolerance of difference was that tough decisions tended to be postponed. Few members of the department would have preferred a more authoritarian and more proactive regime.

Part of the reason for the maintenance of civility was that almost all members of staff, senior and very junior, shared the same work space along two corridors of Level 2 of the Merewether Building. Most teachers until the 1990s came into the office at least four out of five days in the week; a high proportion left the doors of their office open when possible; there was constant contact in the corridors and the department office. (Most of this was before personal computers created radical changes in work culture of the academic environment.) During the 1970s the faculty coffee room on Level 3 of the building was an important meeting point for members of the department; at mid-morning there were usually a dozen or so teachers occupying a couple of tables in the corner that was known as the "Government" spot. Dick Spann and Henry Mayer were regulars, so that the coffee room was a good place to get up to date with the academic rumour mill – and also to have a chat with members of other departments. Other opportunities for social interaction were regular evening parties, weekend barbeques and occasional games of cricket. The pay-off from the ensuing sense of community was seen most obviously in the early 1970s when severe stresses were imposed by the political upheavals discussed in Chapter 5. The department was able to survive intense ideological division and personal disagreement without a breakdown of courtesy and mutual accommodation.

It would certainly be an exaggeration to describe the department of the 1960s to the 1980s as one big happy family. There were personal animosities and even a few staff members who did not hide their contempt for others. Yet there is a sense in which an almost compulsory social interaction complemented the more professional relationships seen in committee meetings or staff seminars. In following decades a few members of staff tried to encourage continued participation in forums like the coffee room, but it was a losing battle against the atomisation of direct relationships being imposed by a computer-bound environment. There is still contact in the corridors, and some staff members welcome an interruption in their offices when they are there, but in the new century it is difficult to describe the department as a "community" in any but a formal academic fashion. On the other hand, there are strong pressures – from within the university, as from external funding agencies such as the ARC – for scholars to reach out beyond their own department to other cognate departments and to other universities in Australia and overseas. In the world of political science Australia, and in particular the Department of Government, is becoming more and more part of a wider international academic community. This was only occasionally evident in the earlier period, and is to be welcomed in the present.

---

1 If we assume that the baby boom became undeniable in 1947, then children turning 17 (the normal age for finishing the Leaving Certificate in five years of secondary schooling) would surge into university from about 1964, although it would have made an impression in the couple of years before that.

2 "Government Capers", *Beyond the Cringe*, Vol.2, No.1, Winter 1989, p. 1.

3 Sue Wills to Michael Hogan, 17 March 2014.

4 Interview with Ross Curnow, 24 February 2014, in Department of Government Oral History Project.

5 Thomas Moore to Michael Hogan, 20 July 2013.

5
Real politics in the 1970s

Young Australians in the 21st century are often told by their parents or grandparents about the stimulating period of the 1960s and 1970s – a time supposedly of positive social change, the acceptance of multiculturalism as a desirable national characteristic, giant steps forward in sexual liberation, and the arrival of great pop music. Younger generations are right to be sceptical about such claims, yet for the Government Department those years were certainly a time when political struggle seemed a worthwhile enterprise. For staff and students political activity was very much part of the university experience.

The great issue that mobilised Australian youth into political activity in the 1960s was the Vietnam War and the associated controversy over the conscription by ballot of young men to fight in the war. Universities were battlegrounds for student activists, but most influences on student politics came from outside academia. For the Department of Government there is no doubt that course enrolments were pushed up by the heightened interest in politics, but the department as a separate entity had little impact on events. Certainly many teachers had determined views on the war and conscription; classes by Peter King, Terry Irving, Dennis Altman or Rex Mortimer would have sent unambiguous messages to students. Peter King spent considerable energy advising draft resisters and in 1965 he was on the executive of

> **The nuclear threat**
>
> *I was always aware, it's really the main focus of my life, my main personal response to the 20th century, that the nuclear situation was completely unacceptable and that any life on earth should acknowledge that this is the main issue confronting mankind and that political science departments typically didn't make an adequate response to this, and I don't think that Sydney did, or at least I tried my best to do it. The thing I did in particular was to join with the Social Work Department and others to set up CPACS, the Centre for Peace and Conflict Studies, started in 1988.*
>
> Peter King on nuclear deterrence, Oral History interview, 6 February 2014.

the "Sydney University Staff-Student Committee on Vietnam" which organised a petition against Australia's involvement in Vietnam. *Honi Soit* mentions as signatories from the Government Department to various petitions opposing conscription: Terry Irving, Peter King, John Power, Henry Mayer, Dennis Altman, with tutors Juliet Richter and Bill Waters.[1]

During this time of ferment the Australian security organisation, ASIO, took a keen interest in political activists critical of government foreign policy, so that the ASIO records of persons of interest contain almost a who's who of Australian political science and political history of the period. During the 1970s files were collected for a number of members of the department – certainly for Dennis Altman, Des Ball, Terry Irving, Henry Mayer, Rex Mortimer and Lex Watson, and perhaps more.[2] Other contemporary members of staff, looking at that list, might wonder why they were ignored. That number would not have been unusual for most large or medium sized schools of politics in the country. In an earlier period, wartime security agencies had kept an eye on Percy Partridge and Neville Wills.[3] Likewise, a significant number of graduates of the Government Department for that period came to the attention of ASIO. It is also highly likely that seats in the lecture halls would have contained regular ASIO informants.

Jim Spigelman

Spigelman made his mark at the University of Sydney, graduating in Arts (1967) and Law (1971), with Honours in Economics, Government and Law – a medallist in Law and a First in Government. He was also a very busy student politician, being president of the SRC in 1969 and a student member of the University Senate (1969-71). He took a leading role in the Freedom Ride of 1965 to highlight Aboriginal disadvantage. (When did he get time to sleep?) His subsequent career was no less stellar. From 1972 till 1975 he was Principal Private Secretary and Senior Advisor to Prime Minister EG Whitlam. He was briefly the Secretary of the Department of the Media in 1975. He then progressed to his legal career, serving in the Australian Law Reform Commission and appointed Queen's Counsel in 1986. From 1998 till 2011 he was a distinguished Chief Justice of NSW and Lieutenant Governor of that State. Also a member and chair of numerous community and arts boards, and recipient of many awards, his appointment as chair of the ABC in 2012 was widely welcomed.

The Moratorium campaigns of 1970-1 brought onto the streets large sections of the community, of all ages and occupations, so that members of the department staff who took part were absorbed into those huge numbers. In the university it was a student fight that had an impact on the university, while the university contributed little more than the environment where students met, organised and demonstrated. Hundreds of students of Government must have been activists – mostly against the war, but some in opposition to the protests. In 1969 Dick Spann was a member of the University Proctorial Board, which spent much of that year dealing with militant students disrupting events, especially after a number of students were called to appear after the Governor of New South Wales, Sir Roden Cutler, was pelted with tomatoes while visiting the University. On that occasion the Proctorial Board itself was condemned by student protests led by a few radical members of the Department of Philosophy.[4] The Government Department was virtually the only place at the University of Sydney where students could find focused

> **Meredith Burgmann**
>
> Grand-daughter of a notable Anglican bishop, Meredith Burgmann's social conscience pushed her to militant political activity, especially in opposition to South African apartheid. During the 1971 Springbok Rugby tour she was arrested a number of times for confronting the police and "disturbing the peace". Her photograph is from her ASIO file. Meanwhile, she gained a BA (1969) and an MA (1974) in Government. Her Masters thesis assessed postwar Australian foreign policy attitudes towards the Soviet Union. She later earned a PhD at Macquarie University (1981), where she went on to teach industrial relations and politics. An involved member of the Labor Party and the trade union movement for many years, she was elected to the NSW Legislative Council in 1991, and from 1999 to 2007 she was President of the Legislative Council – the longest serving female presiding officer in Australia. She was one of the founders of the annual Ernie Awards – highlighting conspicuous examples of media comments belittling women, especially by male (and occasionally female) politicians. She comments about her experience at university: "When I enrolled in Government I in 1966 I had no idea what to expect. I just needed a third subject for first year Arts. However it was part of the wonderful 1960s experience that changed my life. My lecturers, who included Henry Mayer, Peter King and Lex Watson, started me thinking about Vietnam, apartheid, and the rest of the world. I think I started off wanting to be a novelist and I ended up teaching and being involved in politics."

discussion of contemporary social and political issues. Just one name from that era is Jim Spigelman (BA Hons, 1967), who was President of the SRC in 1969, a sometime part-time tutor in Government, and one of the most determined of student politicians.

Other issues that had an impact on students in the 1960s included Aboriginal affairs (Spigelman, with many others, joined the Freedom Ride of 1965), and disputes over apartheid in South Africa. At least one Government graduate, Meredith Burgmann (BA Hons, 1969; MA, 1973), became notorious for invading the football field during the Springbok tour of 1971. She was arrested 21 times and spent time in prison for her activities. Peter King was active opposing the terms of the nuclear non-proliferation treaty, which has been a lifelong concern for him. However, as with conscription, the University and the Department of Government contributed mainly by providing a place where students met, debated and organised.

The important point was that the 1960s saw students politically interested and involved in great numbers. Among those numbers a significant proportion was attracted to the more militant political tendencies directed by Marxists in the Communist Party and by various radical splinter groups such as the "Trots", who took inspiration from Trotsky's theories of permanent revolution. With more conservative students also organising to oppose such groups there was always the likelihood that protests by university students would degenerate to minor physical violence. By the 1970s, once Australia withdrew from the war, many of these students were available to be mobilised for other issues.

The Political Economy dispute

There is a sense in which the Department of Government had no choice but to be involved in the politics associated with the political economy dispute. The Faculty of Economics was quite small (compared, for example, with Arts), while Government was one of its largest departments. Moreover, very many students of political economy (PE) courses were also students of Government. Individual staff members of Government ranged from very conservative to quite politically radical, but in general almost all would have preferred not to get directly involved. The dominant reaction was that if Government could accommodate a full spectrum of political ideology among its staff without constant warfare, why couldn't Economics? In July 1974 Jim Richardson, chair of the Department Committee, probably expressed the reservations of many staff members, arguing:

> ... that the Department should tread carefully in the matter given the adverse reaction to the perceived role that the

> Department was seen to have played in Faculty's earlier decision in favor of Political Economy. He also stressed the dangers of one Department arguing in favor of another Department being split.[5]

When the matter was again raised in the Department Committee in 1975, Ken Turner, recently appointed head of department, expressed similar reservations, arguing that it was a matter for individual, not departmental, decision:

> K Turner summed up by saying that the Committee would be setting a bad precedent by endorsing political economy as a department position and would be inviting further intervention into its own business by others.[6]

One can understand the underlying fear. Government was a potential target both for some conservative academics and for some radical students. Much effort had been expended within the Government Department over the years in maintaining good professional relationships in a united department, and that effort would continue into the future.

The origins of the dispute in Economics can be summarised only by oversimplifying them, but an attempt has to be made here. Divisions in the Department of Economics started to open up in the late 1960s when two new Professors, Warren Hogan and Colin Simkin, moved to stiffen the professionally-oriented and econometric nature of the curriculum by enforcing a neo-liberal interpretation of the discipline that had become dominant in the Anglo-Saxon academic world. This was a significant change from the undergraduate Economics curriculum that had evolved under the old four-year degree, where the history of economic thought, descriptive economics, economic history and competing economic theories had been central. The complete emphasis on economic modelling and statistics was also a style of economics that Dick Spann, for example, would scarcely have recognised from his Oxford PPE degree.

A significant group of teachers in the Economics Department resisted the consequent sidelining of their interest in courses that expressed criticism of that neo-liberal model. The dissidents borrowed the newly invented phrase of Thomas Kuhn – "paradigm shift" – to explain that, for them, neo-classical economics was a classic paradigm that resisted any fundamental criticism by regarding it as unthinkable.[7] The promoters of a new paradigm were denounced as Marxists by supporters of the two professors who insisted that the critics were intent upon depriving Economics students of the skills needed in the modern business world. There were members of the political economy faction who would have accepted a Marxist tag, but it by no means defined the group, who promoted principles espoused by classical political economists such as Adam Smith, David Ricardo and JM Keynes, as well as contemporary scholars such as JK Galbraith, Joan Robinson, Paulo Freire and feminist theorists. A number of members of the political economy group were, moreover, skilled in the mathematical and statistical aspects of modern economics, but did not regard those as defining an adequate study of the discipline.

The rapid development of a division in the Economics Department into a full crisis is documented in the chronology presented in *Political Economy Now!*[8] By 1970 there were demands from the dissenters for an independent inquiry into the department – dismissed by Vice-Chancellor Bruce Williams, who was firmly on the side of Professors Hogan and Simkin. At the end of that year two tutors who were members of the group, David Hill and Bill Waters, had their contracts terminated, which led to student protests in the following year. These protests continued with greater vigour in 1974, with a "Day of Protest" and a later "Day of Outrage" when classes were boycotted.

In the Faculty, which had elected as Dean Geelum Simpson-Lee, a member of the dissident group, an inquiry into the department recommended a separate department for PE, and a full sequence of PE courses. This was accepted by the Faculty and the Professorial

Board but ignored by the Vice-Chancellor. At the end of that year two more PE tutors, Paul Roberts and Jock Collins, were informed that their employment would be terminated. Nevertheless, the first course in Economics I (P) was introduced in 1975. When Ted Wheelwright, one of the leaders of the group, was overlooked for appointment to a third chair in Economics, student protests intensified, including an occupation of the Vice-Chancellor's office.

Despite continuing unrest, PE courses at second and third year level were introduced, but not an Honours program. Some autonomy was granted by the new Vice-Chancellor, John Ward, who appointed Associate Professor Frank Stilwell as the Director of "P" courses within the department in 1983. However, the group faced another threat almost immediately, when a restructuring of the Bachelor of Economics into a Commerce-style degree left no room for "P" courses. That restructuring went ahead, but a compromise was accepted by Faculty and the university which saw the establishment of a new degree – Bachelor of Economics (Social Sciences) – giving mainstream Economics courses and "P" courses equal weight. That degree began in 1987, seeming to ensure the future of the critical group in Economics teaching, especially once it was recognised as a separate discipline (as departments were named when the new Faculty of Economics and Business set up a structure of two schools in 1999). However, within the newly named faculty new threats emerged for the group as the Dean moved the faculty closer to an eventual School of Business. The Departments of Political Economy, Government and International Relations, then later Economics, were repositioned in the Faculty of Arts and Social Sciences.

Students in the Department of Government who were also enrolled in "P" courses had been prominent in political agitation on behalf of the PE issues through most of the dispute. Leading roles were taken, for example, by Kathi Peterson and Rick Kuhn, while Anthony Albanese gained some of his earliest political experience in the dispute. Days of protest inevitably affected classes in Government. During the 1970s and early 1980s the main contribution of the staff of the Department of Government was as a moderating voice in the Faculty, the Professorial (later Academic) Board, and on University committees, especially for academic promotions where members of the PE group faced a virtual veto from the Economics professors.

Dick Spann was a moderating influence in the Faculty and the Professorial Board during the 1970s. He had little sympathy with the professors in the Economics Department, but even less for the militants of the PE group. Explaining later why there was so little cooperation between Economics and Government (cooperation that might have been useful, particularly in areas of public policy that were of interest to him) he wrote:

> At Sydney we have of course some rather bloody-minded senior economists, and now most political scientists and public administrationists are economically illiterate, and most economists politically and administratively illiterate, so it is becoming harder and harder to bring them together.[9]

Spann's frustration with the issue, which he believed was destroying the Faculty and the Department of Economics, concentrated on his belief that the central issue was one of separation, which he opposed vigorously, although for most of the PE activists a separate department was only a second-best option; most would have been happier with one department where both conventional and critical Economics could be taught. Spann partly blamed members of his own department for the intransigence of both sides. When a vote in Faculty on curriculum saw a professorial proposal defeated by the narrowest majority, Spann drafted a handwritten speech for a rescission motion:

> Finally, where do these people come from? I want now to say something which distresses me, and which certainly

> isn't calculated to make me popular in my own department. A good deal of the trouble in Economics rises from the behaviour of members of the Department of Government. ... These are people who in the past showed the slightest interest in Faculty meetings – the department has a very bad record as Faculty attenders. Reason is simple. Most of them know very little about Economics and care less.[10]

A subsequent, typed, draft of the speech omitted directing blame at his colleagues in the department, instead arguing that the professors were trying to achieve a reasoned compromise.

In the Faculty the voice of Government was particularly influential in those years (despite Spann's slighting reference to lack of attendance) because of the willingness of Government Department members to undertake leadership positions, with Rex Mortimer and Ken Turner serving briefly as Dean, while the role of Undergraduate and Postgraduate Sub-Dean was almost a Government Department preserve (Helen Nelson, Michael Hogan, Graeme Gill, Martin Painter, Michael Jackson, Ken Turner). This role was very important in decisions of the Faculty in 1974, which approved "P" courses separate from the neo-liberal mainstream courses. Despite the expressed caution about getting involved, noted above, the intransigence of the professors in Economics in the face of reasonable compromise proposals impelled the Department of Government to get involved. At the 1974 meeting of the Department Committee where Jim Richardson had expressed his reservations, the meeting unanimously decided that PE courses should be expanded and:

> ... that unless such courses can be provided within the framework of the Department of Economics, this meeting supports the creation of a separate Department of Political Economy in 1975.[11]

The same meeting then, again unanimously, instructed the Chair of the meeting to inform the Dean of Economics, the head of the

Economics Department, the chair of the Professorial Board, and the Vice-Chancellor, of the department's concerns in the matter, and to arrange a delegation of staff and students to the chair of the Professorial Board. Richardson reported back to the next meeting of the Department Committee that Professor George, chair of the Professorial Board, had received the delegation and "accepted that a legitimate claim was being pressed by students and staff in relation to the economics department dispute".[12]

The role of the department was also pivotal in 1985, when the survival of the PE program was guaranteed with the establishment of a new degree in Economics (Social Sciences). This latter decision was by no means a foregone conclusion. The then Dean, Stephen Salsbury, was determined that the main Economics degree would be remodelled to suit the demands of business and commerce, although he was prepared to allow the design of a new social science oriented degree if the Faculty would support it. He set up a committee to design an alternative degree, expecting it to fail.

> The committee to consider the latter degree comprised Associate Professor Michael Hogan (no relation to the professor of Economics) from the Department of Government, Ron Callus from Industrial Relations, and Eric Kiernan and Frank Stilwell from Economics. Michael Hogan, who chaired the committee [as Sub-Dean], took a strong leadership role and ensured that a broadly based degree was recommended.[13]

The role of the Government Department in this final decision was mixed. The author, as Sub-Dean, had previously appealed to the department to help put an end to the PE dispute by presenting a united vote in Faculty in support of the new social sciences degree. However, the then head of department, himself a Sydney Economics graduate, supported by other senior members, rejected that. Some satisfaction was gained on the floor of the Faculty meeting when a successful vote was ensured by the support of a majority of members of the large Accounting Department, who, while generally favoring the reform of the degree structure, were convinced that supporting the social science degree was the only way to secure a peaceful resolution of all the issues. This decision was also a major step forward in the university's process of giving due systematic attention to the teaching of social sciences.

Women's movement

One of the dominant social movements in western developed nations during the late 1960s and the 1970s was the demand to have feminist issues placed firmly on the political agenda. Feminism was nothing new, of course; Australia had experienced a successful wave of pressure at the turn of the century to have women given equal rights with men to vote in democratic elections. Yet the third quarter of the 20th century brought an extra dimension. Some of the new factors emerging in the 1960s were: the increasing proportion of females finishing high school and proceeding to university; the availability of a convenient form of contraception in the new birth control pill; the changes in mass media brought about by the introduction of television; a strong focus in Australian politics with the problems of youth, obvious in the two major issues of the 1960s – in home affairs with education and state aid so dominant, and in foreign affairs with the war in Vietnam and the dispute about conscription of youth; and, of course, important writing and organisation by women themselves trying to counter the conservative "feminine mystique" of contented housewives and mothers. Why should a woman who wanted a different kind of life need to stay at home to be truly feminine?

In 1970 all 14 tenured staff members of the Department of Government were male; of the full-time tutors three were female and two were male. (One early female appointee, Coral Bell, had left by than.) Clearly there was work to be done if the values of feminism were to be taken seriously. By 1980 the department had grown to 21 tenured staff, but only three women. By this test the department could not boast of its feminist credentials during the 1970s. One would like to think that the next generation of women was being educated in the department to take its rightful place, but that also would be a hard argument to make. Of the 34 Honours graduates in the department between 1970 and 1980 who secured First Class Honours, only eight were female. Twenty years later, in the staff list of 2000, of the 23 teaching staff, still only six were female. Of the Honours graduates in that same year a clear majority (19 of 28) were female, while the numbers receiving First Class Honours was equal (seven of 14). Perhaps one should look to the generation after next?

Those figures do not paint the whole picture. A number of women in the department during the 1970s – staff and students – played important roles in the development of feminist organisation and in consciousness raising among women. The major ground-breaking book written by an Australian on these issues was Germaine Greer's *The Female Eunuch*, published in Australia in 1972 and promoting vigorous media debate that many Australians of the time (male and female) found confronting. Greer had a background at the University of Sydney, but not in the Department of Government. It was up to Greer's successors to build on the controversy to ensure that feminist ideals and values became more generally accepted in the Australian community. Anne Summers was one of the founding members of the Women's Liberation Movement (WLM) in Adelaide in 1970. Soon afterwards she came to Sydney where she gained a scholarship to study for a PhD. After a brief attendance at the University of New South Wales she chose to enrol in the Government Department at Sydney and to have Henry Mayer as her supervisor. It was a fruitful partnership which built on an idea that had already gained her a contract for a book with Penguin publishers. Her research was

Anne Summers

Anne Summers was one of the founders of the Women's Liberation Movement in Australia, which had its first national conference in Melbourne in 1970. Moving from Adelaide to Sydney, she was also one of the founders of the Elsie Women's Refuge in Glebe. The thesis project for her PhD in the Department of Government at Sydney, supervised by Henry Mayer, was published commercially in 1975 as *Damned Whores and God's Police: the colonization of women in Australia*, four years before she was awarded her doctorate. She has impeccable credentials as one of Australia's leading feminists, which led to her appointment by Prime Minister Keating to head the Office of the Status of Women (1991-3). She works as a journalist and writer. In her autobiography, *Ducks on the Pond* (p.374), she writes of her introduction to the Department of Government: "Henry Mayer made me feel very welcome and immediately arranged for us to meet weekly. The other professor in the Department of Government was Dick Spann, a courtly man of about 60 who taught Public Administration and English Political Theory, and whose ineffable courtesy enabled him to conceal whatever distaste he may have felt for the new notions of women's liberation that I so enthusiastically espoused. Henry, on the other hand, had embraced them with an excitement that at first I found startling."

published in 1975 as *Damned Whores and God's Police: the colonization of women in Australia* – a study of contrasting images of women in colonial Australia that highlighted the central question for the feminist movement of the derivation of female stereotypes. Publishing the material before completing her doctorate seemed to have threatened her graduation. However, with Mayer making a strong case on her behalf, the University accepted the published book as her thesis and awarded her a PhD in 1980. There are very few examples of a thesis being published five years before the degree has been awarded, but Summers was convinced, almost certainly correctly, that the research would be of greater value to the movement in the mid-1970s, when the issues were still quite strongly on the public agenda, than in the early 1980s when national politics in the post-Whitlam era had taken on a very different complexion. In 1980 Summers, in cooperation with Margaret Bettison, emphasised the importance of women writers with the publication of *Her Story: Australian Women in Print 1788-1975*. She later worked as a journalist, published a number of other important contributions to the national debate over feminism, and was recruited by Prime Minister Paul Keating to take charge of the Office for the Status of Women from 1991 till 1993.[14]

Political theorist, Carole Pateman, was appointed to the staff of the Government Department in 1972, after publishing a book in 1970, to international acclaim, on alternatives to existing models of popular participation in politics – *Participation and Democratic Theory*. The central argument of that book was not about the participation of women in politics, but by 1972 it was obvious that its relevance to that fundamental theme of feminism was direct. Most of her publications making that link date from the 1980s and 1990s – for example, *The Disorder of Women: Democracy, Feminism and Political Theory* (1989) – but in her lectures on political theory Pateman became one of the important sources of intellectual ammunition for her students in the Government Department, and in the University as a whole, from the time she arrived.[15]

Another doctoral candidate, also supervised by Henry Mayer, was Sue Wills, who had graduated with Honours in the department after completing both Arts and Economics degrees. In 1981 she completed her PhD thesis, "The politics of sexual liberation", which used the experience of the Australian women's and gay movements in the early 1970s to examine the ability of contrasting political science models to explain the data. Not surprisingly, given that Wills and Summers were both working on related topics under the same supervisor, her thesis also highlights the issue of how images and stereotypes of women and homosexuals are created and exploited. A rapid survey of thesis titles from the 1970s in the thesis library of the department (which is, sadly, by no means a complete collection) reveals that Government students were encouraged to examine feminist issues also at undergraduate and Masters levels. Some of the titles are: "The Women's Suffrage Movement in New South Wales"; "Sydney Women's Liberation and the Problem of Revolutionary Praxis"; "A Preliminary Sketch of the Role of Women in the NSW Branch of the ALP".[16]

Sue Wills' thesis provides a wealth of information about the formation and role of feminist political organisations in early 1970s Sydney. Sydney University students (and some junior staff members) contributed strongly. The "Glebe Group" that Wills claims had a dominant position in the movement in the early 1970s, had strong representation from the local Communist Party and the "Trots", as well as from Sydney University. Members of the Department of Government working actively in the formative years of the Sydney Women's Liberation included Barbara Levy, Jean Brick and Sue Wills (all, incidentally, from the 1970 Final Honours year), Anne Summers, Caroline Graham and Warren Osmond (mostly tutors and postgraduate students) – although the influence of men in the movement, and specifically of Osmond, was controversial.[17]

In 1970, (before the publication of Greer's *Female Eunuch*) the Government Department had organised a colloquium on Women's Liberation. This was mainly an initiative of Henry Mayer, who was a strong supporter of the involvement of his students in the movement. One of his research assistants at that time, Judith Keene, was encouraged to participate in feminist groups and published one of the earliest defences of the movement against its critics. In 1972 members of a number of departments at the University (Government, History, Philosophy, Psychology, among others) formed a collective to publish the feminist journal *Refractory Girl*. Ann Summers was an important promoter of that enterprise. In 1973 Summers and Liz Fell, at Mayer's invitation, taught an Honours seminar course on "Politics and Family Structure" that addressed feminist issues (without the publicity or the controversy of the attempt to get a feminist course in the Philosophy Department in the same year). In 1974 the

Departments of Government and Fine Arts, with leadership from the Political Economy unit, mounted an interdisciplinary course on "The Political Economy of Women", which attracted large numbers of students.[18]

The introduction of such courses, while not controversial within the department, was seen by some external critics as just one more manifestation of the influence of Marxist ideologues within the university. The militantly conservative president of the Students Representative Council at the time (later to become Prime Minister), Tony Abbott, was dismissive:

> There's an awful lot of courses here which can only be described as so much nonsense. In the Government Department, for instance, you have things like feminism and the political exploitation of women and what have you. And, quite frankly, I think that these courses are trivial.[19]

Even conservatives on the staff of the department recognised that the time was long overdue for the role of women to have a firm place in any political science curriculum. Moreover, an emphasis on feminism was likely to be suspect for many Marxists for whom the issue was a distraction from the class struggle.

There is no argument here that the Department of Government was a central part of Sydney Women's Liberation. It was merely one of dozens of environments where cells of concerned women could meet, argue and organise. Rather, the argument here is that the development of the women's movement in Sydney in the 1970s had a major impact on the Department of Government. All its students – female and male – were forced to come to terms with the ideas of sexual liberation, whether to agree or reject. Among the teaching staff virtually all female members during the 1970s (as few as there were) accepted the need for a reorganisation of society and politics away from the current paternalist values. Most of the male staff also accepted that there were serious problems identified by the women's movement – even if they might not agree on what should be done about them.

One way in which the women's movement affected the Government Department and the university was through the formation of the department's "Women's Collective", mainly non-tenured academic and non-academic staff and postgraduate students. One of the objectives of that group was to improve the relationship between academic and general staff by blocking any attempts at exploitation of the general staff by some male academics who could see only a task that they wanted done. The non-academic staff members in the 1970s department – professorial secretaries, typists, research assistants – were no shrinking violets, but a united front gave even professors pause for thought. When the Collective pointed out that there were more male than female toilets in the Merewether Building they were able to liberate at least one staff toilet on Level 2 which became available for women. Another victory claimed by the Collective was the safety bus provided by the University that still shuttles students from Redfern Station to and around the University. It was initiated after a campus murder/rape, but only after frustrated discussions with the security service for better protection of women on campus.

Women in the non-academic staff also organised through the trade union – the Sydney University branch of the Health and Research Employees' Union. During this period executive positions on the union were held by Sue Scott, Jackie Walter and Sylvia Krietsch, while the formidable Betty Johnson went a step further by becoming a staff representative on the University Senate. The primary purpose of this involvement was to try to achieve equal pay for equal value. According to Sue Scott (Irving) this involved strong negotiations with the Registrar and eventual strike action.[20]

There is one final matter that demands attention in this issue of feminism and its place in the academic environment. By the late 1980s

Geraldine Brooks

Born and educated in Sydney, Geraldine Brooks graduated with an Honours degree in Government (Arts, 1979), writing a thesis on middle class political activists. She achieved distinction as a journalist in Australia and America, winning awards for foreign correspondent reporting, before turning to writing historical fiction. She won the American Pulitzer Prize for Fiction for her novel, *March* (2006), imagining the Civil War historical context for the classic *Little Women* story of Louisa Alcott. Other bestsellers include her first novel, *Year of Wonders* (2001), set in a 17th Century English village devastated by bubonic plague, *People of the Book* (2008) about Jewish citizens suffering in the breakup of the old Yugoslavia, and *Caleb's Crossing* (2011) about a native American Indian who graduated from Harvard. She comments about her study in the Department of Government: "I arrived at Sydney Uni thinking I would be an English literature person. I took Government on a whim, as my fourth course, a throw-in to fill out my schedule. By the end of my first year I'd dropped English and was determined to do honors in Government instead. ... The Government Department was great preparation for my early career in journalism, and the questions that we argued over across those seminar tables continue to animate my fiction."

Carole Pateman had been promoted to the position of Reader in the department – a senior rank emphasising research and publication, with a lesser weighting to teaching and administration. It recognised the strong international reputation that Pateman had achieved in political theory generally and in women's studies in particular. When she applied for the advertised chair of the department, a male Reader in the department opposed her promotion:

> Okay there's Carole, she had this big reputation, she was pretty much lionised for the political participation book and another one on that theme. I read them both and I thought they were very thin, and I thought in the context of the time her fame was due to the lefty atmosphere around the academic community. I just didn't think there was anything there worthy of a Chair, and when my turn came to speak at the appropriate meeting I said it.[21]

Of course, one of the tasks of any academic is to evaluate the research of others, so it would be very hard to criticise any academic for giving a frank assessment at such a committee meeting. However, the assessment was contrary to a very strong international reputation for Carole's work, and its worth must be judged by the academic values of a very strong empiricist evaluating the work of a scholar whose work was theoretical, speculative and normative. The intervention had special force when used by a man against a woman, and against a woman who wrote on feminist issues. Among other senior members of the department there were some reservations, not about Pateman's research record, but about her potential administrative role.[22] Pateman was refused promotion and almost immediately accepted a chair in the University of California, Los Angeles (UCLA), shaking the dust of Sydney from her shoes in 1990. Appointment to a chair is not within the gift of any department; it is a highly competitive process where very few candidates are successful. Nevertheless, any candidate who is presented to the University Committee without the unanimous support of her department's senior members will almost certainly be rejected. This was not one of the finest moments for the Department of Government.

Gay and lesbian politics

An interest in the rights of homosexuals came relatively late to Australia, and came initially from outside the gay community. During the 1950s and 1960s significant publicity had been given in the media to developments in British law reform circles towards decriminalising homosexual (especially male homosexual) activity among adults. The Wolfenden Report in Britain of 1957 and the later British legislation had been the main points of reference for reformers. Eventually similar aims arrived in Australia promoted by civil libertarian and "small-l liberal" law reform proponents, so that it was fairly unsurprising when Liberal Party Attorney-General Tom

Hughes announced in May 1970 that homosexual law reform was on the political agenda. The political context in Australia for such an initiative at that time was probably the heightened community concern for civil rights, following the 1960s campaigns for human rights in the United States, the willingness of important politicians such as John Gorton and Don Chipp to promote a debate on censorship and sexuality, and the fascination of the mass media with elements of the counter culture. One early group along these lines – mainly about rather than by homosexuals – was the ACT Homosexual Law Reform Society (Canberra, 1969). Lex Watson claims that he was alerted to its existence by one of Henry Mayer's weekly columns in *The Australian*, which publicised the ACT group and its rationale.[23]

In Sydney in July 1970 two University of Sydney homosexuals, John Ware and Christabel Poll, founded CAMP – an acronym with its own connotations of a homosexual stereotype, and spelled out as "Campaign Against Moral Persecution". Support was forthcoming from the Council for Civil Liberties and the Humanist Society. Unlike the organisations promoting women's liberation, there was little interest at that stage from the left of the Labor Party, let alone the Communist Party. CAMP, sometimes called CAMP Inc, along with its journal, *Camp Ink*, had various functions, including providing social opportunities for meeting people, encouraging homosexuals to "come out" by publicly acknowledging their sexual orientation, educating about issues of relevance to homosexuals, and political campaigning. Few members were interested in political action.

From the Department of Government, one early member of CAMP in 1970 was a tutor, Lex Watson. He had a strong interest in the possibilities of CAMP for political mobilisation.[24] Within the Faculty of Economics support came from humanists or members of the Council of Civil Liberties such as Ken Buckley in Economic History and Dorothy Symons, a research assistant in Accounting.

For the first year or more the organisation had a low visibility. The spark to make it newsworthy came from the publication of a book by Dennis Altman.

Altman had joined the Department of Government at the beginning of 1969 after postgraduate study at Cornell University and a couple of years teaching at Monash University. He returned to the United States in 1970, using the time to investigate the American gay movement. In 1971 he published *Homosexual: oppression and liberation*, the first major work on the issue by an Australian.[25] Originally published in America, its public launch in Sydney in July 1972 became a media event that gave celebrity status to Altman and, for a time, to the issue of gay liberation. The book may not have provided a theoretical guide or agenda for gay politics in Australia, but it certainly acted as a catalyst to help put gay liberation on the general political agenda – along with feminism, environmental concern, and Aboriginal rights as a firm part of the "new left" in Australian politics. Altman used the media attention to promote a national body – Gay Liberation. The Sydney branch of Gay Liberation split from CAMP in 1972, reflecting constant tensions in the general movement about aims and tactics.

From 1972 the corridors of the Government Department at Sydney became one of the main Australian centres of political agitation on gay issues. Watson and Altman were joined by postgraduate student, Sue Wills, becoming the first point of reference for media journalists and commentators. Another tutor, Craig Johnston, joined them a little later. Altman began his long career as a public intellectual on political issues generally with a regular column in the *National Times* and frequent participation on Radio Double J. Watson organised a staff colloquium at which he, Sue Wills and Dennis Altman formally "came out". There was also a forum in the Wallace Theatre of the university where Germaine Greer, Dennis Altman and anthropology student Gillian Leahy discussed issues of sexual liberation politics. Watson and Wills became joint presidents of CAMP in 1972 and were also among the most regular writers in *Camp Ink*, either under their own names or using pseudonyms, insisting that CAMP should consider itself as primarily a political organisation. Some of their earliest political activity was a campaign against the use of aversion therapy to attempt a "cure" for homosexuality that was promoted by Professor McConaghy from the Department of Psychiatry at the University of NSW. Watson also helped set up the Gay Union of Tertiary Staffs (GUTS) to try to spread gay activism from Government to other departments.

The presence of Altman, Watson, Wills and Johnston in the Government Department made it an important focus for Sydney gay and lesbian politics in the 1970s. Heterosexual staff members tended to be generally supportive of the political activity, even when they may have been bewildered by some of the campaigning style and ambivalent on some of the issues. Henry Mayer and Dick Spann had encouraged Altman to write his book, while Mayer was strongly supportive of political activity for sexual liberation. The role of the Government group was strengthened by a close relationship with like-minded activists in the nearby Department of Economic History, especially Garry Wotherspoon and Robert Aldrich, with Ken Buckley in support. For a number of years the Merewether Building was "gay and lesbian central". Although there were disagreements even among such close colleagues they performed a number of important functions in the Sydney movement. They constantly reminded their fellows of the political nature of the movement, and they were an important factor in moderating tensions among gay and lesbian movement activists.

The Philosophy Department dispute

A split had been emerging in the Philosophy Department since the end of the 1960s. Initial divisions concerned the teaching of Marxism, where senior professors were concerned about teachers proselytising for communist political ideas. This Cold War mentality gained little support in the Government Department, where Professors Spann and Mayer, themselves associated with anti-communist organisations, had no difficulty giving active support to courses and research highlighting Marxist critiques of capitalism, politics and society. Although Philosophy courses on Marxism were subsequently approved, a more insistent division emerged in 1973 over courses in feminist philosophy. When approval was reluctantly given for a course on "Philosophical aspects of feminist thought" to go ahead, the immediate problem was: who should teach it? The only teachers in the department available and eager were two tutors, Liz Jacka and Jean Curthoys. This was not acceptable to the head, Professor Campbell, nor subsequently to the Professorial Board, with the result that a major conflict broke out across most disciplines in the Faculty of Arts in June/July 1973. An indefinite strike was called by students and staff in the Philosophy Department, which was supported by the SRC and staff members in a number of other departments. A majority of staff in the Government Department voted to join the strike. The strike continued for several weeks until eventually a compromise was reached that enabled the course to proceed. The conflict made the survival of a workable Philosophy Department impossible, so that both supporters and opponents of the professors promoted the division of the department into two separate units – "Traditional and Modern Philosophy" for the conservatives and "General Philosophy" for its critics. That came into effect in 1974.

Within the Government Department the decision of a majority of staff to strike in support of the course on feminism placed great stress on all concerned. Conservatives in the Government Department had little sympathy with the intransigence of the professors in Philosophy, yet disagreed with the strike, while those staff members who voted to strike were very ambivalent about being associated with some of the extreme ideological positions underpinning the rebellion in the Philosophy Department. A document circulated by six staff members entitled "On Strike But ..." expressed the reservations of many more:

> Thus we are on strike in the sense that we support the strikers and donate our salaries for strike purposes. We will continue to teach classes for those who believe (rightly or wrongly) that they would be severely disadvantaged by discontinuance of such learning activities.[26]

There was also another small group who expressed their ambivalence by being "Not On Strike But ...". A total of 20 staff members joined the protest, although half of those were not tenured. In a similar spirit there was no attempt to enforce the strike on teachers who did not support it. The high proportion of extremely vulnerable non-tenured teachers who put their jobs at risk was one reason for some senior staff members, such as Ken Turner, to express their solidarity despite strong reservations.

The major contribution of Government Department members to the conflict was endeavouring to find an acceptable compromise solution. Following a Government Department resolution condemning the refusal of the Professorial Board to support decisions approved in the Department of Philosophy and the Faculty of Arts, a fundamental intervention was made when a delegation of Anne Summers, Terry Irving and Peter King met with the Acting Vice-Chancellor, Professor Bill O'Neil, on 28 June.[27] Indeed, Peter King had previously had a number of meetings with O'Neil, and claims to have taken effective leadership of the Strike Committee.[28] A direct result of that meeting, and a subsequent meeting of Professor O'Neil with Liz Jacka and Jean Curthoys, was the so-called "O'Neil formula" for resolution of the issues. The essence of the compromise was that John Burnheim, a tenured member of that department just returned from leave, would supervise the course to be taught by Jacka and Curthoys – unwritten was the assumption that he would supervise but not interfere.

Compromise was not something that gained universal approval among the supporters of the protests. A strong and vocal section of the strike committee would clearly have preferred a symbolic defeat to a compromise victory. On the other side, Professor Armstrong in the Philosophy Department was also unwilling to accept the compromise. The interest of Government Department strikers was to get the compromise accepted. Peter King and Terry Irving moved a series of motions in the Arts Faculty on 11 July 1973, aimed at getting Faculty support.[29] Members of the Government Department also attended meetings of the strike committee, attempting the unpopular task of recommending moderation. Peter King, Dennis Altman and Ken Turner were prominent in that endeavour.

The longer the dispute continued the more apparent it became that the most vocal members of the strike committee were intent on broadening the issues to mount a direct confrontation on the university power structure. The feminist issue was still present, but even many women active in the Philosophy Department felt that it had been relegated to a minor role compared with the Trotskyite agenda of revolution. Some students of Government were part of that endeavour, but among the staff the sole objective of the strike was to gain approval for the proposed course on the philosophical issues in feminist thought. Eventually the compromise was accepted and the strike called off. However, the wider agenda of university governance was still alive. The Philosophy Department strike committee had made this explicit early in the dispute, immediately after Government Department members had voted to join the strike:

> The strike has now changed from being solely an act of withdrawing staff and student labour to a positive contribution to alternative education. We as strikers are beginning to realize the potential of mass student/staff

action. The strike action in its origins was aimed at smashing the sexist decision of the Professorial Board, it still is and will be, but self-determination is now taking grip as an important secondary issue. We are effectively taking over the determination of our philosophical and political education by planning alternative courses.[30]

Democratisation in the department

Student demands for greater participation in decision-making in the Department of Government had been emerging even before the Philosophy dispute, and continued to escalate during the three weeks of the strike on that issue. One of the factors contributing to the emergence of the issue was the retirement of Dick Spann as head in 1972 due to ill health, and the automatic appointment of the other professor, Henry Mayer, as head. It is very doubtful that Mayer wanted the job. He was admired as a teacher and public intellectual, but his personal relations style was fairly aggressive – very different from the urbane style of Spann – with the result that there were rumblings of discontent among both staff and students. In 1972, when Mayer was succeeding Spann as head, Rex Mortimer and Terry Irving circularised a memo entitled "Charter for a Departmental Decision Making Structure", which called for a Departmental Conference, to meet monthly, with representatives from academic staff, general staff and students – with equal representation of academic staff and students.[31]

The following year, in April 1973, the issue of student participation in the management of the department surfaced more seriously. Again, there had certainly been consultation between teachers and students. The Minutes of the Department Committee noted:

> Three students (Mark Piddington et. al.) were invited to present and answer questions, on the Petition of 540 (student count – 521 HM count) students calling for student/staff self-management in the Government Department. (Since

Friday 27th April this petition has been signed by a further 34 students. By the end of the Friday meeting 16 staff members – out of 22 present – had also signed the petition, 6-7 with "qualifications", both specified and unspecified). There was some discussion of the student proposals and it was agreed that "dialogue" should continue further before decisions were made.

HM [Henry Mayer] offered to write a paper on his views "as an intellectual" ie. not in his professorial capacity, on student/staff "self management".[32]

Debate did continue. During early 1973 the Department of Philosophy had experienced some forms of self management (although without the cooperation of its professors) and other departments such as Fine Arts were experimenting with mechanisms of consultation between staff and students.

As he had promised earlier, Henry Mayer produced his reasons for disagreeing with the proposals for student staff participation. In fact there were two versions – the longer version on six foolscap pages, and a summary on just over one page. Again, as promised, it was written as by a political theorist rather than as professorial-head. The argument was pure "Henry", emphasising the likely unexpected consequences of formal arrangements and pointing out hidden paradoxes: "Participation need not reduce elitism and hierarchy, on the contrary it may foster it."

> Why not trust the students not to abuse their formal power? That's a very strange view in a department of Government. It assumes that self restraint is the one thing needed. Over any length of time institutionalized limits are needed for all – including professors.[33]

One of the most significant meetings was held in early June 1973, just before the Philosophy dispute escalated to a strike. A student-staff workshop was held on 8 June, with Professors Spann and Mayer present. The meeting was chaired confidently by Bernard Carey, a postgraduate student. Beginning with a statement by Henry Mayer, opposing formal student involvement in management, speeches opposed to the democratisation proposals followed from Dick Spann, and students Martin Krygier, Cliff Fogarty and Klaus Cordeus. Speeches supporting the proposals came from staff members Dennis Altman, Craig Johnston, Carole Pateman, Peter King, Rex Mortimer, Michael Hogan and Juliet Richter, and students Peter Wertheim, Peter King (sic), David McKnight, Philip Ascot, Chips Mackinolty, Michael Hurley, Ian Davis and Bob Boughton. No votes were taken. Most contributions were reasoned and concerned with principles and desired educational outcomes. A number of student interventions, however, became personal and unfair attacks on Henry Mayer, rejecting his written arguments as specious, while accusing him of hypocrisy and being concerned only for his own privileges. That set the tone for some of the later memos.[34]

Clearly these events put great stress on the relationship between colleagues among the teaching staff in the department. Ross Curnow sent out a circular suggesting that he shared many of the ideals of reformers and trusting that he would not be thought "intransigent or reactionary", while he hoped that "the situation does not arise where there is variance and animosity, and where one speaks only of colleagues, never of friends".[35] The only clear breakdown of communication among the staff at this time came between Henry Mayer and one of the tutors, Terry Metherell. There was a spectacular and public yelling exchange between the two of them in the corridor outside the department office and, at the end of June, Metherell sent round a circular to his colleagues apologising for his behaviour at a recent meeting.

> Inevitably there will be a strong difference of opinion. But if I have given the impression that I harbour any animosity toward individual members of staff I would like to apologise and assure you all that such is NOT the case. I am particularly

grateful to those of you who have felt moved to take this matter up with me privately ...³⁶

Otherwise virtually all academic and general staff members were very diligent in maintaining business as usual both in professional and personal relationships. No one wanted the poisonous personal relationships evident in both the Philosophy and Economics Departments.

The atmosphere within the department was not helped by the outbreak of university-wide confrontation over the Philosophy Department and the consequent strike. A memo signed by 13 Government staff members tried to play down the connection between the two issues of the women's courses and student power (which was being made by some students on the strike committee).

> It has been said that the staff of the Government Department are really on strike about the issue of democratization in the Department.
>
> On the contrary, we have high hopes of resolving the current debate over the structure of the Government Department in agreement with its Head.
>
> Our going on strike was in response to the frustration of the decision of the Philosophy Department and the Arts Faculty in approving the Women's Studies course.³⁷

Indeed, Henry Mayer was still debating and putting out memos of his own hoping to get a resolution of the democratisation issue.

Discussion in the following period was directed towards achieving a draft constitution for the Department Committee that reflected the level of consensus between supporters of formal student involvement in department management. One draft released in July 1973 embodied called for abolishing the "professorial veto", while making "the course assembly ... the basic unit of staff-student participation".³⁸ This resulted in a memo from Dennis Altman, announcing that he had changed his mind and that he could "no longer accept the granting of absolute decision-making power to general meetings". He explained how his experience in such meetings had been very disillusioning – minimising rational discussion and maximising pressure on individuals to conform.

> There is a further factor that has influenced this reversal, I do not want to work in a department as bitterly and personally divided as Philosophy (nor do I think such a department could long survive).[39]

Terry Irving also agreed that the more radical model was unworkable. Both Altman and Irving were condemned as traitors by radical students. One reaction was an anonymous and bitterly sarcastic circular from "Your humble servants, the nasty radicals. P.S. Fuck the lotta yez!"[40] Thereafter the consensus between student and staff supporters was directed at achieving parity of representation of students in the Department Committee.

By the end of 1973 a "Committee on Committees", set up by the department to produce a constitution, reported with detailed recommendations on student representation on the Department Committee and on its internal committees. At the first meeting of the Department Committee in March 1974, where some students were present, Peter King moved to bring the matter forward:

> Peter King recommended that the meeting resolve in favour of student representation as such. This could then be discussed by the students as a concrete proposition.
>
> Chips Mackinolty spoke against the present meeting of the staff adopting the principle of representation. Rather, the issue should be discussed by a general meeting of students and staff.[41]

By October 1974 a decision still had not been made. At a special meeting calling for parity of student and staff representation, Henry

Mayer asked for a document of his own to be inserted into the minutes. It repeated some of his earlier arguments preferring informal arrangements over rigid institutionalised ones. Significantly, however, the document finished with an implied threat. He was clearly losing patience with the level of personal invective in arguments from students.

> It is absurd and unfair to suggest that all that is at stake in my own position is personal and some kind of game. I have no desire whatsoever of having to conform more closely to my official role. If I have to do this and be compelled to withdraw from the Departmental Committee and act, where I differ from it, on my own, it would not be of my own doing.[42]

At the beginning of 1975 elections were held in the different year levels for student delegates, according to principles worked out in the Committee on Committees. The Department Meeting of 17 April proceeded to elect student and staff representatives on all the standing committees (assessment, teaching, planning etc.) and to conduct business with parity of representation. The University of Sydney Archives contains a fairly full set of minutes for the Department Committee during 1975. Generally, meetings were drawn-out to a full two hours, with extended and generally courteous discussion. Student concerns tended to be matters of assessment in particular courses (with unsuccessful demands to be allowed to attend examiners' meetings), the choice of options available, especially at Honours level and in the final Honours year. For example, demands for a new course on Marxism in 1976 were frustrated by the fact that all staff interested in teaching such a course had other commitments for that year.

The arrangements continued for 1976. As in the previous year the full Department Committee with parity of representation was shadowed by much shorter meetings of the Staff Committee, which discussed questions such as appointments or study leave arrangements. The Department Committee received minutes of those other meetings. However, towards the end of the year student apathy set in. The October Department Meeting had to be abandoned for lack of a quorum (nine students were present while 17 were absent). The November meeting was abandoned for lack of interest. That was the end of democratisation in the department. One explanation for the failed experiment was provided by a student member to *Honi Soit*:

> When students tried, earlier this year, to bring an important motion concerning assessment to the Committee, they were told by staff that the Committee was only advisory and its decision would have no effect within the Department. The "progressive" Government staff had been finally drawn to admit to the fact that they had been deceiving students over the issue of democratisation. After this a few students began to boycott meetings until it was found that the Departmental Committee was unable to function for lack of a quorum.[43]

Meetings of the Department Committee in 1977 were conducted without student representatives, even though some staff members had tried to help organise elections in classes. In later years it became normal for student representatives to attend department meetings, but there was never any question of parity or democratisation.

The issue was also important because it accentuated a perceived estrangement between the two professors and many of the senior staff members. Dick Spann refused to attend Department Committee meetings. When this led to a move to give voting strength only to "active" members of the Department Committee, Spann protested. The secretary of the Committee, Ernie Chaples, wrote to Spann to reassure him that such an amendment to the rules would not happen:

>   5. We want you to participate. I personally consider the fact that you do not attend to be a great loss to the Committee. I think we need your wisdom and experience, and I think you would be very influential if you did attend, just as you are in the Staff Committee. I also think you would find the students elected this year to be a more serious and responsible lot as a whole compared to last year. I also think you would find that our new procedures lead to much more careful and reasoned consideration of the major issues before the Committee. So please come when you can, give us a chance, and see what you think.[44]

The reasons for the end of the experiment were many. Demands by the "Trots" and other radical students for a central role for a mass meeting of students and staff had failed, leaving more moderate students to participate. They found meetings boring and bureaucratic, and most of their demands were frustrated by arrangements that were beyond the control of the department. On the other hand, some of the aims of the student movement had been met. The Professorial Board became the Academic Board in 1975, allowing room for representatives of faculties and elected delegates who were not professors. The "professorial veto" that had been such a central issue was seen to be largely mythical.

One interesting consequence of student participation – concern over assessment inconsistencies – was the decision of the department to appoint one member of staff as an Ombudsman. The main task was to review the grading of essays where the student believed that the mark or the comments were unfair. The normal expectation was that essays of that kind would be reviewed within any course, but where that still did not satisfy the student the Ombudsman would arrange for another teacher with competence in the essay topic to conduct a new assessment, with an unmarked essay, and without any indication of the original mark or commentary. There were usually between a dozen and 20 such reviews each year. It was a good indication of consistency within the department that very few grades were changed as a result of the review. Occasionally teachers abused the system by trying to avoid their own responsibility to give a second opinion on disputed work, and it was interesting to see which teachers figured most frequently in student demands for a review (usually because of perfunctory or unhelpful feedback). The role of the Ombudsman lasted until the 1990s when the university instituted a compete set of protocols for disputed assessment, supervised at faculty level.

Student involvement in politics was at a high point in the early 1970s, as was indicated also by the large membership of student politics societies. Such cooperative endeavours have always had a difficult task to keep going – from recruitment during orientation week to problems over too weak (or too strong) leadership, to the perennial problem of the short period of student presence before graduation. Such groups occasionally found a burst of health in future years, sometimes resulting in the involvement of students in departmental decisions. In fact, with help from the department's External Advisory Committee, their current activity is quite strong, although drawing on only a tiny proportion of potential students' involvement. In 2014, for example, besides the Politics Society, there is also an International and Global Studies Society and the *Sydney Globalist* journal, as well as the Sydney University United Nations Society all of which sponsor talks and events, with occasional publications.

An elected head?

There was still the issue of the election of the head of department. Professor RS Parker of the ANU (a friend and colleague of Dick Spann) had recognised the problem just a few years previously in an article on "Departments and God Professors":

12. Departmental headship is at present, so far as the rules go, perfectly autocratic, and this is due to the head's unique status as the only professor, as well as to his specific powers; it is also due to his powers as professor, in other reaches of the university, as much as to his powers within the department.[45]

Parker went on to give cautious approval for some form of rotating headship, but only within a context of substantial redefinition of competencies. Dick Spann had allowed – even encouraged – rotating headship of the Department Committee (later Department Board), which became a fundamental part of the department's own political culture. However, that was very different from having a rotating executive headship of the department.

In the abovementioned 1972 "Charter for a Departmental Decision Making Structure", signed by Rex Mortimer and Terry Irving, there was an explicit call for an elected head:

> The Conference shall elect a Head of Department from the academic staff, annually, who shall act as responsible executive officer of the Department and Chairman of the Conference.[46]

It should be noted that this initiative had come primarily from the academic staff, although there had no doubt been previous conversations with students. The context was not only the appointment of a head of department without consultation with the staff, but also continuing disputes in the Economics Department, where the powers of professors, heads of department, faculties and Professorial Board seemed to deny any genuine participation from staff, let alone from students. One of the reasons for the involvement of people like Irving, Mortimer and Connell in this issue was their previous enthusiastic involvement in the Free University experiment that envisaged a completely different model of academic teaching and learning, where student demand had a central role and where

> **The influence of teachers**
>
> *The staff in Government were also a great influence. Professor Henry Mayer was a caustic and perceptive intellectual who taught us much about how to construct an argument and pull a piece of writing apart. I met Raewyn (then Bob) Connell for the first time when she/he was lecturing in the Government Department then and participating in the Open [Free] University project. She has been a long-term influence, for someone who, like me, moved from Government into Sociology.*
>
> Dr Terry Leahy, *Sydney Alumni Magazine*, October 2013, p.31.

the curriculum was explicitly and politically radical. The Sydney Free University faded away at the end of the 1960s, but there were many defenders of its values.

At the end of 1974 a petition, signed by 18 members of staff, including some who would normally be on the conservative side of most disputes, was presented to the two professors, calling on them to "establish the right of a staff committee to elect the head of department". The University Archives contain a draft response by Dick Spann, somewhat along the lines of Parker's article, in which he claimed he had "no decided views on the subject". He did, however, signal that he would not allow any non-professorial head to have rights over the use of his secretary who had acted as de facto department officer – "new arrangements would need to be made".[47] (In fact, when a non-professorial head was appointed, Spann was much more cooperative in allowing departmental use of his professorial resources and privileges.)

In mid-1975 a delegation of senior members of the department – Bob Connell, Michael Leigh and Terry Irving – approached Henry Mayer with the urgent request that he step aside and allow an elected head. This had apparently been discussed at the previous department meeting. According to Michael Leigh the primary issue was the democratic principle, but it would be naïve to suggest that such a principle could be separated from a protest against the idiosyncratic personal style of Henry Mayer, which had been the target of considerable student and staff criticism.[48] (It is difficult to imagine the same delegation making similar demands of Dick Spann, if he had still been head, for example.) According to Terry Irving the issues of principle and personality were almost inseparable. The Mayer style of consultation was to talk to individuals without any previous knowledge of an agenda, and to make instant decisions which often clashed with established policy, instead of putting controversial matters to the Department Board.

> Henry and I were always friends, and so later on he used to ask me: "What did I do wrong, Terry?" And I could never tell him. I tried to – and I could say things like inconsistent decisions and things like that – but I think that the real problem was that we felt betrayed. Here was this unconventional and wonderful figure, a man of intellectual power, who suddenly turned out to have feet of clay. We just felt disappointed and betrayed.[49]

Mayer was deeply hurt by this action of his colleagues, but he did as he was asked, recommending that Ken Turner, newly promoted Associate Professor, be appointed head in his place. There was no election, but there is also no doubt that Turner had virtually complete support in the department; he would not have accepted the appointment without it. The temperature of potential conflict was lowered immediately. As for the election of the head, time was to show that the real problem was not having an election but persuading one of the professors or associate professors to do the increasingly more difficult task.

Tensions might well have accompanied the change of head, especially as it was not clear at that time what were the appropriate administrative powers and responsibilities of a head without full professorial status. Ken Turner reflected later that both Mayer and Spann could not have been more cooperative in the new situation throughout his seven-year tenure of office. These smooth working

Henry Mayer at home in retirement (Photo courtesy of Terry Irving)

arrangements also owed much to the effectiveness of the talented administrative staff led by professorial secretaries Mary Pollard, Sue Scott and later Betty Johnson.[50] If the author may be allowed a personal observation here, during the years 1973-77, when I was a junior untenured member of staff, Henry was my doctoral supervisor, and I have only praise for his diligence in commenting on drafts, along with his friendship and enthusiasm for my project.

Aftermath

By the end of the 1970s a brief period of political activism in the department was largely over, except for individuals in the politics of sexual discrimination. And, even there, much of the agenda of the beginning of the decade was well under way. In the wider Australian context the enthusiasm for progressive causes had declined with the fall of Whitlam and the imposition of a conservative hegemony of Malcolm Fraser, reflecting Thatcherism and Reaganism dominant among Australia's allies.

In the discussion above there is clearly a problem of distinguishing between tactical decisions of the Department of Government as an institution and the political activity of some of its members. At times the two areas intersect well, as in the issue of democratisation in the department. At other times, especially in the two areas of sexual liberation politics, there is quite an obvious distinction. However, in all the matters discussed, even when the initiative was clearly taken by a minority, virtually all staff members (and often many students) were affected, debated the issues, and took sides.

By the end of the 1970s informal meetings of staff in the corridors or the tea room mused over the campaigns of the previous years and generally agreed that they were better teachers and researchers than political activists. That was true, but perhaps a little harsh. All political activists, even or especially professionals, make errors of judgement, are diverted from their original goals, and even, in some notable cases, finish their political careers on the opposite side of the political spectrum from where they started. If the Government Department staff were to evaluate their own political performance as if they were grading an academic essay, the result would be a reasonable Credit mark. They helped resolve some important problems and they conducted their politics without violence and with a general attention to courtesy.

There was also a significant contribution of staff members to the academic analysis of Australian politics during this period of political upheaval. Not only were there new issues – the so-called "new social issues" of gender politics, peace issues, the environment, Aboriginal affairs, awareness of urban dysfunctions and more – but the nature of party politics and allegiances, so obviously transformed in the new century, was just starting to break away from what had seemed to be a rigid two-sided contest. Bob Connell's groundbreaking work on how children get their political and party values and identifications, *The Child's Construction of Politics* (1971), was published precisely when Australians were beginning to question why they should accept the values of a previous generation. The book of documents and commentary by Connell and Terry Irving, *Class Structure in Australian History* (1980), became a fundamental textbook introducing students to ways in which class affected the conduct of Australian public life, and how changes in Marxist notions of class were pushing political reform in new directions. Henry Mayer opened the door to the study of the mass media, which have revolutionised the conduct of politics in the modern world. And, of course, the changing content of the Mayer and Nelson readers from the 1960s to the 1980s can be used as a marker of changes in the Australian political agenda over that period.[51]

---

1 "Joint Staff-Student Action", *Honi Soit*, 23 June 1965. *Honi Soit*, 16 July 1968; 4 July 1969.

2 National Archives of Australia, ASIO records, name search.

3 Ibid.

4 See the folder "Proctorial Board" in Box 46 of the Spann Papers, University of Sydney Archives.

5 Minutes of the Government Department Committee, 9 July 1974, File "1971-4", Box #1, University of Sydney Archives.

6 Minutes of the Government Department Committee, 8 May 1975, File 1975, Box #1, Archives, University of Sydney.

7 Thomas Kuhn, *The Structure of Scientific Revolutions*, London, University of Chicago Press, 1962.

8 Gavan Butler, Evan Jones & Frank Stilwell, *Political Economy Now! The struggle for alternative economics at the University of Sydney*, Sydney, Darlington Press, 2009, pp. 193-205.

9 RN Spann, "Reflections on an Academic Obituary: 'Alas, Poor Yorick'" *AJPH*, 40(3), 1981, p. 238.

10 Draft speech of RN Spann [1976?], in Spann Papers, Box 44, University of Sydney Archives.
11 Minutes of the Government Department Committee, 9 July 1974, File 1971-4, Box #1, Archives, University of Sydney.
12 Minutes of the Government Department Committee, 6 August 1974, File 1971-4, Box #1, Archives, University of Sydney.
13 *Political Economy Now!*, p. 79.
14 Germaine Greer, *The Female Eunuch*, London, McKibbon & Kee, 1970. Anne Summers, *Damned Whores and God's Police: the colonization of women in Australia*, Ringwood Vic., Penguin, 1975. Anne Summers and Margaret Bettison, *Her Story: Australian Women in Print 1788-1975*, Sydney, Hale & Iremonger, 1980.
15 Carole Pateman, *Participation and Democratic Theory*, Cambridge, CUP, 1970; *The Disorder of Women: Democracy, Feminism and Political Theory*, Cambridge, Polity Press, 1989.
16 Sue Wills, "The politics of sexual liberation", unpublished PhD thesis, University of Sydney, 1981. Sue Wills, Eva Cox and Gaby Antolovich, *Attitudes to Sexuality*, Sydney, Canberra, AGPS, 1977. RG Cooper, "The Women's Suffrage Movement in New South Wales", MA, 1970. D Hollingsworth, "Sydney Women's Liberation and the Problem of Revolutionary Praxis", Final Honours, 1971. Pam Allen, "A Preliminary Sketch of the Role of Women in the NSW Branch of the ALP", Final Honours, 1974.
17 Sue Wills, "The Politics of Sexual Liberation", unpublished PhD thesis, University of Sydney, 1981, pp. 13-60.
18 Sue Wills to Michael Hogan, 20 July 2013.
19 Interview with Tony Abbott, reproduced in "Radical Economics: the political economy dispute at Sydney University", ABC Radio National, 1 September 2013.
20 Interview with Sue Irving, 24 July 2014, transcript in the Department of Government Oral History Project.
21 Interview with Fred Teiwes, 13 March 2014, Transcript in Department of Government Oral History Project.
22 Interview with Graeme Gill, 23 April 2014, transcript in the Department of Government Oral History Project.
23 Sue Wills, "The Politics of Sexual Liberation", unpublished PhD thesis, University of Sydney, 1981, pp. 61-3. Lex Watson to Michael Hogan, 6 August 2013.
24 For a summary of Watson's activity in support of gay causes, see his obituary by Robert French, "Lex Watson, leading gay activist and trailblazer", *Sydney Morning Herald*, 28 May 2014.
25 Dennis Altman, *Homosexual: oppression and liberation*, New York, Outerbridge & Dienstfrey, 1971. Published by Angus & Robinson in 1972, and by Penguin Australia in 1973.
26 Undated circular, "On Strike But ...", signed by Michael Leigh, Fran Hausfeld, Julie Richter, Jeff Hilliker, Lex Watson and Trevor Matthews. Hogan personal papers.
27 "Motions Passed at an Extraordinary Meeting of the Government Department Teaching Staff, called at short notice on Wednesday, 27 June at 4.30 p.m.", signed by Peter King, Convenor. "Notes on the Deputation of Three Striking Government

Department Staff (Anne Summers, Terry Irving and Peter King) to the Acting Vice-Chancellor", 28 June 1973, signed by Peter King and Terry Irving. Both documents in Hogan personal papers.

28 Interview with Peter King, 6 February 2014, transcript in the Department of Government Oral History Project.

29 "Motions for the Special Meeting of the Arts Faculty, 2 pm, 11 July 1973", signed by Peter King and Terry Irving. Hogan personal papers.

30 "Strike Bulletin No.5, Thursday 27/6". Hogan personal papers.

31 "Charter for a Departmental Decision Making Structure", memo distributed to Government Department, 1972 (no more precise dating), signed by RM and TI, in papers of the Department of Government, Box #1, Sydney University Archives.

32 Department Committee, 27 April 1973, in papers of the Department of Government, Box #1, Sydney University Archives.

33 "A Comment on the Petition – Full Version", six page memo signed by Henry Mayer; "Discussion on the Petition – June 8, 1973. Comment by Henry Mayer. Summary", one and a half page memo signed by Henry Mayer. In Hogan personal papers.

34 "Student-Staff Workshop (Government): 8 June 1973", Minutes of meeting in Hogan personal papers. For one personal attack on Mayer, see "Politics, Pluralism and Professors", two-page memo distributed to Government Department staff, undated [July 1973], signed by Michael Hurley. In Hogan personal papers.

35 "To all Staff", memo of 3 July 1973, signed by Ross Curnow, in Hogan personal papers.

36 "To all my colleagues", memo of 29 June 1973, signed by Terry M, in Hogan personal papers.

37 "Statement by Striking Government Department Staff, 5 July 1973" memo signed by 13 staff members (RM, DA, CP, PK, TM, TI, JR, KT, ET, TM, ML, JW, DW), in Hogan personal papers.

38 "Draft Constitution", July 1973, signed by Chris Hingerty, Michael Hurley, Peter King, Chips Mackinolty, Monica Murray, Carole Pateman and David Wells, in Hogan personal papers.

39 "Of Participation & Mass Meetings", undated circular signed by DA, in Hogan personal papers.

40 "To the Staff", unsigned and undated circular [July 1973], in Hogan personal papers.

41 Department Committee, 4 March 1974, in papers of the Department of Government, Box #1, Sydney University Archives.

42 Minutes of Department Committee, 18 October 1974, in papers of the Department of Government, Box #1, Sydney University Archives.

43 Garry Bennett, "Toilet Lid Closes", *Honi Soit*, 19 October 1976, p. 26.

44 Memo from Ernie Chaples to Dick Spann, 7 May 1975, in Spann Papers, University of Sydney Archives, Box 44, Folder "1973-79".

45 RS Parker, "Departments and God Professors: some suggestions", *Vestes*, March 1965, vol.8 (1), p. 21.

46 "Charter for a Departmental Decision Making Structure", memo distributed to Government Department, 1972 (no more precise dating), signed by RM and TI, in papers of the Department of Government, Box #1, Sydney University Archives.
47 Petition of 5 December 1974 on Elective Headship, in Folder "1973-79", Box 45, Spann Papers, University of Sydney Archives.
48 Interview with Michael Leigh, 13 January 2014, transcript in the Department of Government Oral History Project.
49 Interview with Terry Irving, 24 July 2014, transcript in the Department of Government Oral History Project.
50 Ken Turner to Michael Hogan, comments on draft chapter, 24 July 2013.
51 RW Connell, *The child's construction of politics*, Melbourne, MUP, 1971. RW Connell and TH Irving, *Class Structure in Australian history: documents, narrative and argument*, Melbourne, Longman Cheshire, 1980.

Dick Spann in praise of Mary Pollard

Most photos reproduced here come from a farewell meal for Mary Pollard in November 1977, after a period as secretary to Dick Spann and also to the Department. The meal brought together most of the academic and non-academic staff of the 1970s, along with some postgraduate students. The photographer for most photos was Warren Osmond. The photos are, unless otherwise stated, courtesy of Mary Pollard.

Liz Kirby

Ernie Chaples

Kate Barlow, Amanda Thornton, Bernard Carey, Michael Jackson, Helen Nelson

Sue Coleby, Michael Leigh

Warwick Richards

Lex Watson, Bob Taylor, Carole Pateman, Peter Nelson

Sandra Gibbons, Margaret McAllister, Bernard Carey

Bob Taylor, Ross Curnow

Fred Teiwes, Mary Ann O'Loughlin

Terry Irving, Henry Mayer, Sue Irving (Scott). Photo courtesy of Terry Irving

Ian Grosart, Bob Howard, Sue Coleby, Judy Walker

The power group: Lyn Freedman, Kate Barlow, Mary Pollard, Sue Scott

Judy Walker, Sue Wills, Michael Hogan

A serious discussion: Dick Spann, Terry Irving, Ken Turner

Ken Turner with post-prandial glow

Bruce Coram

Mary Pollard, Ken Turner, Lyn Freedman, Martin Painter

Peter King

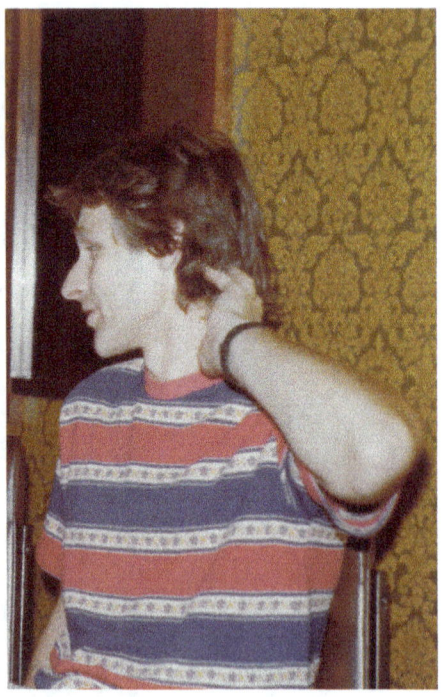

Warren Osmond

6

Redesigning the Curriculum

By the mid-1960s the teaching resources of the department were under great stress. Most teachers were expected to contribute to courses that were not their primary academic concern: Dick Spann taught the political philosophy strand in Government II, which was a genuine interest for him; Henry Mayer performed to mass classes of Government I on Australian politics, with his Hawaiian shirt barely hiding an ample belly; Ken Turner worked up some ideas on Southeast Asia (informed, as he later claimed facetiously, by flying over the region on the way to Europe) and even published on the topic. Some newer members of staff felt that their special talents and interests were not being recognised in the teaching program – leaving a clear disjunction between teaching and published research.

The most urgent problem was in Government I, where the great growth in student numbers made its immediate impact, but the same factors pressed for a reform of the second and third year courses and the Honours stream. A major restructuring of curriculum began to take shape in 1972. By then the department had acquired a substantial and talented set of teachers – 14 tenured positions, along with seven full-time tutors (including an Assistant Lecturer and a Teaching Fellow), as well as a small platoon of part-time tutors. The basic content of terms one and two remained similar to previous years. There were issues of timetabling and finding convenient classrooms, but in the 1970s most of those problems could be solved. (Such logistical problems became more critical towards the end of the century.)

There is a problem of terminology when writing of "courses" at the University of Sydney. The term had been used to describe full courses and half courses for many years up till the 1970s. Yet the word had a number of references. To ask a student "what course are you doing?" might get the response "Government", or "Government I", or perhaps, "Japanese Politics" or "Government Honours". To avoid such ambiguities the University introduced the term "Unit of Study" ("UoS" or just "unit") to describe any freestanding assessable teaching program of whatever size and at whatever level. In the discussion below that is the terminology employed (although many students still use the word "course").

Redesigning Government I

On his arrival, Dick Spann had taken a year or two to organise a curriculum for his department that took best advantage of his staff's talents and conformed to a growing consensus among Australian political scientists about the appropriate content for a major sequence in politics. Spann had taken a central role in two important colloquia on that topic, published in the *Australian Journal of Politics and History*.[1] From the mid-1950s until the early 1970s a student enrolled in Government completed a very similar program. Government I was an introduction to the institutions and ideology of liberal democratic states through the example of Australian politics. Government II introduced a comparative element by studying the political systems of countries like the USA, UK, USSR, France and Germany, plus an introduction to political theory through a review of major political philosophers. In Government III students studied public policy and administration, were introduced to basic concepts current in the international relations literature, and, increasingly as time went on, studied the politics of new states, especially in Southeast Asia. The particular content and weighting in the three years was in constant flux, but the general outline remained recognisable. Changes reflected the arrival of new teachers with specialised interests and the absence on leave of other teachers. The growing interest in Southeast Asia of course also reflected student concerns about the involvement of Australian conscripts in Vietnam.

First year was taught by a circus of teaching staff – supervised and led by Ken Turner, but with significant slabs of lectures taken by Henry Mayer, Dick Spann, Peter Westerway and whoever else was available, plus occasional visiting lecturers. Huge numbers of students in first year meant that each lecturer had to present a class three times on the same day to large classes of Government I. With three lectures on three days per week one needed a soothing drink at the *Lalla Rookh* pub across the road at the end of the day. (Sadly, the hotel disappeared with the redevelopment of the new Wentworth Union building.) Three groups would mean an average size of about 300 students, but there was always one time slot that was overcrowded and others that were less popular. A squad of about five full-time tutors, plus up to 20 part-timers took care of the tutorial program. Once the initial enrolment reached over 900 students that meant about 80 tutorial groups would need teachers (with an average size of about 13 students each). A normal workload for a full-time tutor in the 1960s and 1970s was nine hours of face-to-face teaching (although this increased over time), plus the grading of tutorial papers, essays and exam scripts. Changes in Government I were driven primarily by the great surge in the number of students, and could not be avoided, although various directions of change were available.

The direction of curriculum reform was foreshadowed in 1972. It began by exploiting the capabilities of the three-term academic year to introduce some extra choices for students. The established pattern of circus teaching and repeat lectures continued in Government I, but only in the first two terms. The innovation was that students had a choice in third term (Michaelmas) from a number of themes: class structure in Australia; current policy issues in Australia; democratic theory; and aspects of modern political thought.[2]

By 1974 the choice had been made to abandon the teaching model that demanded repeat classes. Also, the experiment with third term options was short lived; later year units were moving to a semester arrangement, so that Government I also used semesters in following years to provide additional choice, although students still enrolled in year-long units of study. In 1974 there was a choice of three distinct Government I units, all based on Australia as an example of a liberal democracy: Australian Politics, Liberal Democracy: Australia; and

David Band

David graduated BEc with Honours in Government in 1971, then progressed to achieve a PhD from the ANU. He taught for some years in the Department of Political Science at the ANU before serving for three years in government as Chief of Staff to two Ministers. He then moved into business, working for three different global consulting firms. In mid-life he branched out on his own, becoming an investor in start-ups or new ventures, and a board member of organisations in Australia, New Zealand and the USA. He also teaches in MBA programs in three countries. His profile on the UTS website refers to him as a "serial investor and entrepreneur" who enjoys giving back to students some benefits from what he has learned. Of his undergraduate career in the Department of Government he writes: "My overwhelming memory of the Department in the late '60s is of the fundamental decency of so many of the staff. Ross Curnow, Terry Irving (my Honours supervisor), Trevor Matthews, Jim Richardson, Ken Turner, Helen Nelson and above all Dick Spann were unfailingly helpful, challenging in the best possible way, and seemingly focused on pushing the student to new levels of achievement. Each had their own way of doing this, of course, but each gave me lasting insights – not only into good teaching practice but also into how to behave towards others. I welcome this chance to express my lasting gratitude."

The Australian Political System. These were taught by different teams, with a supervising lecturer, sometimes assisted by others for slabs of lectures, and a salaried tutor-in-charge, assisted by part-time tutors. Australianists like Ken Turner or Lex Watson were likely to serve in a number of teams. The units had different emphases, depending on the staff teaching them, but clearly in terms of curriculum they covered much of the same territory.

By 1975 the first year offerings had increased to five, although in any year only four were likely to be offered. Some study of Australia was present in each unit, although two had an explicitly comparative perspective: Liberal Democracy and the Third World; and A Critique of Liberal Democracy: Australia and USA. Another adjustment came in 1980, when the number of offerings increased to seven, with only six normally being taught in any one year. That continued to be the pattern for the remainder of the 1980s, with some units having distinct content and teachers – the first semester usually (but not always) Australian politics, and the second semester providing a "thematic option". In 1989, for example, the choices for students in first year were: Australian Politics; International Politics; Politics and Society; Comparative Politics; Public Policy and Administration; and Rights, Justice and Democracy; (a seventh option, Introduction to the Study of Politics, was not offered that year).

When the university changed its calendar from a three-term year to that of two semesters in 1990, the Department of Government had already been using semesters for short units in the second and third year of the sequence for a number of years, and it was a logical step to bring Government I into line, with completely separate Junior semester units followed by Intermediate and Senior units. From that time students have normally enrolled in semester units at all levels of the undergraduate and postgraduate programs. The other significant change at that time was to structure Government I so that all students would be introduced to one option that introduced them to aspects

> **From student essays**
>
> *Outer ministers are placed in the libidious position of being unaware of what conclusions are made in cabinet.*
>
> *The changes in the Soviet Union will affect the Middle East and other countries which share boarders.*
>
> *Specific purpose grants are given for a specific purpose, say e.g. given to the department of education specifically to fund teachers' strikes.*
>
> *Government is administered by men and women who are prone to human nature.*
>
> *Those who stand for election in the USSR other than as a representative of the communist party will probably lose their jobs, be unable to get others, find their male interfered with, and so on.*
>
> Beyond the Cringe, occasional newsletter of the Department of Government, various pages.

of Australian politics and another that gave an introduction to international politics. There was some attempt to provide a first year that provided an introduction to concepts and theories that would be explicitly prerequisite knowledge for later year courses, especially in international relations and public policy. However, teachers in the department have never been able to agree on what the detailed items of such prerequisite knowledge might be, so that the policy remained a wish rather than a firm reality.

By the end of the 1990s it was clear that an attempt to provide a curriculum that would build on concepts learned in Junior units to be developed later in Intermediate, then Senior units, was seriously flawed in practice. The reason was primarily the market of student demand in an environment where an increasing proportion of students were from overseas and with little interest in Australian politics, social issues or public policy. International and regional politics were much more strongly favoured. In 2000, for example, first year students in the first semester were offered a choice from Australian Politics; World Politics; and Change in Modern World Politics, while in the second semester there were Australian Politics;

World Politics; Global Politics and the Environment; and Ethnicity, Nationalism and Citizenship. The expectation that each student would do an Australian unit in one semester and an international relations unit in the other was still available, but it was not enforced. Many students chose to do two courses in aspects of international relations, which meant that later year courses in, for example, public policy, could not assume that students had been introduced to the basics of institutional politics at a national level. This pattern of curriculum, along with priorities in recruitment of staff, reflected a significant change in the nature of the department – a boost to the international relations emphasis, and a softening in the concentration on Australian politics, public policy and social issues. This change was connected with developments in the Faculty of Economics, which changed its name to Faculty of Economics and Business (and a few years later to School of Business). It was also reflected in the related change of name of the department itself – from "Government and Public Administration" to "Government and International Relations". There were good reasons of student demand why international relations had supplanted public policy and administration at the heart of the department, but Professors Spann and Bland must have turned in their graves.

Short units for second and third year

During 1972 the use of Michaelmas Term to provide variety and choice was exploited in Government II/III as it was in Government I. In Government II, separate options were promised on specific matters of comparative politics arising out of the study of the USA, USSR and Eastern Europe done in the first two terms; Government III offered greater choice, asking students to choose two out of the following courses for the first two terms: Public Policy and Administration; Southeast Asian Politics; International Politics; and Approaches to the Study of Power.[3]

> **Not the cricket team**
>
> Lex Watson (L/H bats no.8)
>
> *Considering his effectiveness with the bat, Watson has been disappointed that he has not been elevated in the batting order. He has often had to occupy the crease for long intervals when the higher order batting has collapsed. His natural style is aggressive and he is often tempted to flash at the rising ball outside the off stump or to sweep against the spin, but he can play the straight bat defensive game when it is required. He is a superb fieldsman in any position, but especially in the covers where his returns to the wicket are fast, accurate and deadly.*
>
> Anon., "The first Eleven", Beyond the Cringe, (Newsletter of the Department of Government) September 1990.

It very soon became clear to the staff that the use of the third term did not give sufficient opportunity for legitimate freestanding units of study. The eight or nine weeks of a normal term's teaching barely gave time for an introduction to any topic before examination preparation was required. Teachers with American experience naturally thought of using a semester system, but that seemed difficult in a university still clinging to the British three-term arrangement. However, there was an opportunity for change already existing in the by-laws of the Economics and Arts Faculties – the "half course". Even in the time of Professor Bland the Public Administration strand had used half courses, which then meant that a unit would be taught for the full academic year, but with fewer weekly teaching hours. It was fairly easy to convince the faculties and the Academic Board to vary that existing arrangement, especially as a number of other departments were becoming interested in using semesters. The only problem in 1972 was that it would be another 18 years before the university abandoned the three-term arrangement, which had implications for the spacing of mid-term, instead of mid-semester, vacations.

There is considerable lead-time between thinking of a new unit of study description and actually presenting it to students. This was probably less in the 1970s than in more recent times, but it still entailed getting the approval of the department (after canvassing staff for suggestions of desired options), getting approval from the various faculties (which involved frequent objections of conflict of interest from other cognate departments), waiting for the usually routine approval of the Academic Board, and meeting the long deadline for publication of the department's offerings for next year's Faculty Handbooks. For a new unit to be offered to students in 1973, for example, planning within the department would normally have had to start in 1971.

In 1974 the department offered 19 Intermediate and Senior units for second and third year students – 11 in the first semester and eight in the second. In principle, Senior courses required an Intermediate course as a pre-requisite or co-requisite, but in practice there were very few such demands and students were allowed to dip into the pool of options almost at will. In 1974 there was a division of semester units into Group A (the majority of offerings) and Group B (five units which were generally interdisciplinary or interdepartmental, such as The Political Economy of Women). Within Group A, units were listed under five headings: political theory, Australian politics, public policy, international politics, and comparative politics. The influence of staff preference became obvious in that year when each of the first four strands presented two offerings – one for each semester – while there were six offerings for comparative politics. There were few constraints on student choice; they could concentrate on one field of

---

From an essay in Soviet politics

There were three conditions for the Terror: personal dictatorship, environmental factors and erogenous conditions.

Graeme Gill suggested, tongue in cheek, that: "perhaps we need this combination in order to achieve curriculum reform".

Beyond the Cringe, (Newsletter of the Department of Government) November 1986.

study or they could diversify. By 1975 the Group B courses were reclassified into the five strands, which remained the basis of planning until the new century, although there were occasional name changes. For example, with few offerings in Australian politics beyond first year, that strand became Political Sociology for some time.

In most years only about 20 or 25 units were actually offered. However, the offerings differed from year to year as some staff were on study leave, on secondment, or had moved on to other universities, retired or died. Meanwhile, new staff were appointed who usually had strong views about what courses they would like to teach, so that new titles were added to the list. Consequently the pool of Intermediate and Senior units gradually increased to about 40. In the early period Faculty Handbooks tended to list all courses, with a note indicating which were scheduled for that year, but this led to some student frustration that a particularly desirable listed unit was not being offered. Consequently, the usual practice became to list only those courses that would actually be taught in that year. Nevertheless, administrators were not happy with an ever-expanding list of options, requesting, usually unsuccessfully, that unit titles which had not been used for some years should be abandoned. Eventually, when the Faculty of Economics was re-branded to become a Faculty of Economics and Business, a rationalisation was enforced, along with an attempt to redirect the Government Department curriculum to be more compatible with a business education.

Individual unit titles were not meant to remain the preserve of individual teachers (although some, in fact, were). The hope was that options such as Classical Political Theory, Environmental Issues and Policies, Public Policy I, Theory of International Politics, or American Politics (and most others) could all be taught by more than one teacher, so that individual teachers would not become locked into one area of the curriculum. Thus the five "strands" mentioned above became the focus of curriculum planning in the department. Every member of the teaching staff was self-nominated into one or more strand committees, depending on a willingness to teach units in international politics, Australian politics, public policy, political theory and comparative politics. Each strand tried to get commitments from its members to teach a minimum offering for the following year, at all levels of departmental teaching, usually with a priority on staffing any units that were regarded as central to the interests of the strand. Normally the department curriculum committee and the head of department would merely rubber-stamp the combined decisions coming from the strands, unless there were glaring gaps at some level of the undergraduate or postgraduate program that necessitated further negotiation.

One of the elements of curriculum reform that emerged along with semesterisation was a reduction in teaching hours. During the 1970s the previous pattern of each unit of study comprising three lecture hours and one for tutorials began to break down. A semester unit made some experimentation in teaching style considerably easier to arrange; with units of a small size there was little difference between a lecture and a tutorial, while some units preferred slabs of two hours, rather than one, in order to have a more concentrated presentation for teachers and students. The standard pattern became two hours of lectures per week rather than three. For larger classes, especially in Government I, teachers convinced themselves that the questionable educational value of mass lectures justified reducing their number. It would be remiss to fail to point out that this period was one when perhaps the major continuing issue within meetings of the Department Committee was that of teaching workloads.

In a similar fashion semesters, which started out as comprising 13 teaching weeks, soon adjusted to a normal 12 weeks, partly to allow a more significant gap between the end of the first semester and the beginning of the second, but also because of a marked fall in student enthusiasm late in most units of study. The University of Sydney adopted a semester system, with appropriate vacation breaks, only in 1990. Before that, a 13-week semester unit starting at the beginning of the first term took teaching up to mid-June, while the next semester course would need to start at the beginning of July to complete before the November examination period. In the first semester this entailed a rush to complete classes, sit and mark examinations, and be ready to start new units – all in a period of two or three weeks. One of the solutions to the problem was to reduce the semester length to 12 teaching weeks, which is what most course supervisors did. Moreover, the term vacation periods were at inconvenient stages of the semester. In the first semester often students were still drifting in and out of courses when the Easter break intervened. At least that break could be used for assignments and essays. In the second semester, teachers found that, once the September break took students away, many of them never returned to lectures and tutorials, preferring to prepare for exams in their various subjects. Once the university adopted a semester timetable, vacation periods were adjusted to minimise these problems, although some difficulties remained.

An Honours program

From the time the department was formally established in the late 1940s the desirable shape of an Honours degree was regarded as a four-year degree in which some extra work was done by aspiring students in second and third year before the completion of a small thesis in fourth year, along with one or two specially designed fourth year seminar units. It took a few years for the by-laws of the Arts and Economics Faculties to be harmonised before the older three-year Honours degree disappeared. Even within the Arts Faculty there were different expectations about what the extra work in second and third year entailed. In the Government Department this usually involved

> **Jeff Angel**
>
>
>
> One of Australia's leading actors in environmental politics, Jeff Angel is Executive Director of the Total Environment Centre (TEC), which campaigns on issues such as forest and coastal protection, waste and recycling, air pollution, clean energy, climate change, threatened species and sustainable cities. He is a prominent media spokesman on environmental issues, as well as a skilled negotiator with business and government leaders. The subject for his Final Honours thesis (BEc Hons, 1975) was: "Environmental Politics in Australia: A General Survey and an Interest Group". Of his time at university he writes: "I came to the Government course in my second year at Sydney University having opted out of English – and it was the best academic decision I could have made as it eventually brought me into contact with the environment movement and a future career as an environmental campaigner. The course was far more in touch with political reality and the process of social change. There was a lot going on in the 1970s and I became more and more interested in how change could be made to advance environmental sustainability. That's not to say the Government Department and courses had much to say on the environment but their perspective on the workings of politics, government structures, society and community movements laid an essential basis for understanding how change can happen and why it often takes many years."

a separate half course in both years. After the reorganisation of the whole curriculum in the early 1970s this became a semester-length unit in both years.

In the 1960s the unit in second year was usually taught by Henry Mayer, who confronted students with a highly critical review of contemporary social and political theory. This was confronting both because very few students had any previous acquaintance with theory, and also because part of Henry's agenda was to get rid of students from the Honours stream who would not try to keep up with him. In third year the seminar (by then a smaller group) usually addressed contentious issues in public policy and administration, usually taught by Dick Spann, Ross Curnow or John Power, although John Power also taught a seminar on politics and literature.

By the 1970s, with many new teachers arriving, and Mayer involved more with media studies and the headship of the department, this pattern began to break down, to be replaced by whatever individual teachers who were available to teach those units believed would be useful. There were even strong arguments in the Department Committee – promoted especially by Dennis Altman – that Honours units in second and third year should be abandoned. Altman recalls the issue:

> I remember exactly why: I thought culling students out of first year would penalise those who might improve during their U/G years, and would create an unnecessary divide between those students seen as honours material and the rest.[4]

This did not gain strong support among either teachers or students.

By the end of the 1970s the department decided that the second year Honours unit should be dedicated to a review of "power", and that has continued to the present. However, it has been taught by a variety of staff members, and the department has never specified anything about the content. There has generally been a concern with theoretical perspectives on power, while some issues of methodology were drawn into discussion, but the constant theme was an attempt to give students an appreciation of the centrality of the concept of power to the study of politics. The third year Honours unit came to be oriented to the approaching task of writing a thesis in fourth year – again with different emphases depending on the teacher's preferences. Issues of appropriate theoretical perspective and methodology tended to be frequent themes, although without any set form.

Over the years the academic standard of the department's Honours graduates has been very high. This has been due to the excellence of most teachers and to the intelligence and enthusiasm of the students themselves. A fairly permissive attitude of the department towards general curriculum design, and also about how much supervision

> **Not the cricket team**
>
> Peter King (R/H leg-spin bowler; bats no.9)
>
> *Old time supporters of the game will remember with delight the great bowling performances with Chaples at one end and King at the other – a combination which left opposing teams in compete disarray. King's control of direction and length has never been his strength, but his ability to surprise the batsman with the ball that turns sharply form an unexpected direction keeps him in the team. He is an enthusiastic batsman – more suited to the slash-and-run style of limited over matches than for test matches but he has a small but devoted following among aficionados of the game.*
>
> Anon., "The first Eleven", Beyond the Cringe, (Newsletter of the Department of Government) September 1990

is required for the completion of a thesis, may have left some gaps in the students' academic armoury, and perhaps resulted in some completed theses that have not come up to expectation, but there is no certainty that a more directive approach to curriculum, or a more hand-in-hand approach to thesis supervision would not have produced other problems. Nevertheless, some Honours graduates from the department moving to other universities to do postgraduate study, especially in the United States or Britain, must have encountered supervisors mystified at the strange gaps in their political education.

A postgraduate program

A similar eclectic and permissive attitude has governed the attitude to postgraduate research. From the beginning of the department in the 1940s the major emphasis in research for Masters degrees or the PhD has been on self-motivated work by the student. Some of the earliest research graduates explained that, while they had a formal supervisor, consultation was largely voluntary and sometimes almost non-existent.[5] For many years this continued to be the dominant pattern, with occasional seminars given by students to mark some level of progress in the writing up of chapters. Some supervisors, such as Henry Mayer, were extremely industrious in pushing ideas and suggestions to postgraduate students. Indeed, for some of his students the level of help was occasionally more bewildering than comforting. For other supervisors the attitude was that they were available if the student wanted help, and otherwise they were content to watch from a distance.

From the 1970s faculty officers began to demand that evidence be produced annually of progress – and pressure was exerted to terminate the candidacy of students who had been unproductive candidates over a period of many years, as had become quite common. The department customarily appointed one teacher as a Director of Postgraduate Studies (or some similar title). Rod Tiffen claims responsibility for stiffening the expectations of student progress and consultation.[6] It was also helpful that in the late 1980s the Economics Faculty found space in the neighbouring Institute Building for postgraduate students to work at dedicated carrels and so become closer to the university and department community. It became normal for postgraduates to meet and discuss their progress with one another, and for consultation with supervisors to be more institutionalised. However, there was great variety in the direction given by such Directors, and there was little supervision of policy by the Department Committee. Very rarely was any coursework prescribed, other than a suggestion that "you might like to audit" this or that course in this or another department. A candidate could be left hanging loose when a teacher went on extended study leave or secondment. Some supervisors took their tasks very seriously; others less so. The progress of a student depended heavily on this variable. The Department of Government was not alone in this haphazard approach to postgraduate research supervision; it was common fault in most Australian universities at the time.

There was also considerable variety over the years about how diligently the department promoted its postgraduate program. In the early years (in accordance with the attitude of both the Arts and Economics Faculties) doctoral programs were regarded as something more suitable for scientific disciplines. Part-time candidates were accepted at one time and rejected at another. Candidates were welcomed at times before an appropriate supervisor was chosen; at other times, after an approach from a student directly to a potential supervisor who was enthusiastic, the candidate was rejected. One of the principal factors in recruitment of candidates was the very limited number of Commonwealth funded postgraduate scholarships. Universities were in competition for the best students. By the 1990s, when funding levels were linked to various performance indicators, the economic implications of any department having an extensive graduate program persuaded Government to enter the marketplace for graduate students with greater vigour and rigour.

Political science methodology

The question of appropriate methodology is related to any planned curriculum reform. Again, there is much to be said in favour of a rather messy approach; there are many methodological approaches used in the social sciences, and why should political science deny itself the use of any of them? In effect, students in Government I have been introduced to a methodology most appropriate for history – the proper use and interpretation of secondary and primary written sources – and it is hard to argue that this is not a necessary introduction for any student of politics. Students quickly become aware that other methodological approaches – interpretation of time-series statistics and public opinion polls, questionnaire surveys, in-depth interviews, participant observation, discourse analysis and many more – are valuable resources cited in the literature. Yet there is very little direct attention to a critical approach to methodology except for Honours students, and even for them it is minimal.

Granted that a large proportion of the political science discipline worldwide is committed to a behavioural and statistical methodology, and that many of the highest rated academic journals give preference to it, it should be a required part of the armoury of all political science graduates that at least they can read the literature from such sources with some critical capability. When the department was recruiting new teachers during the 1960s and 1970s Henry Mayer was very aware of this gap in the curriculum and he expected that new teachers with doctoral training in the United States would be willing to pass on their acquired knowledge. They resisted successfully. One made a joke of it by covering his office door with a "dump" of unintelligible computer babble from a failed attempt at programming during his doctoral education. Mayer had written to Dick Spann in 1970, putting his point of view. After getting support from Bob Connell, Ross Curnow and Ed Cole, he asked:

> Have you got any ideas re the crux ie. making some kind of quantitative thing required for 1st Hons year? The fact that I'd fail it, does, I must admit, weigh heavily if irrationally with me; the fact that it's done in both psych and ecs at pass level, the fact that looking at last 4 APSR something like 60% of papers at least require this to be understood, the fact that in so far as we're training people for academia and/or as a sideline have a vocational spin off in Public Service, parties etc. all seem to argue decisively for making it compulsory at present for 1ˢᵗ Hons level.[7]

A young American academic on a mainly research appointment for two years to Sydney, Ed Cole, taught a Final Honours seminar in 1970 on statistical analysis. In that period before personal computers were generally available students learned to calculate measures of association and significance with slide rules and printed tables. The seminar did not give the training necessary for a student to be confident in independent survey design or statistical analysis, but it did give a *sensus dubitandi* – an awareness of one's level of ignorance and an acquaintance with the main terms likely to be used in the literature, along with the knowledge of how easy it is to cheat with numbers if the reader is not vigilant.

A year or two later, in 1974, the Department of Economic Statistics was persuaded to offer a short unit, available for Government students, in Elementary Sample Survey Design and Execution. It was meant for students from the Economics Faculty who had already completed the first year of Economic Statistics. Very few students took advantage of it. Few Arts students had the prerequisite, while few Economics students who were attracted to Government wanted to do more econometrics than was absolutely necessary. After two years the unit was withdrawn, both because the Department of Economic Statistics did not want to waste its teaching resources on a course with little student interest, and because the Department of Government had found something better to take its place.

In 1976 Ernie Chaples first offered his short unit, An Introduction to Field Studies in Political Behaviour. This was very much a hands-on style of learning, as can be seen from the prospectus:

> All students will participate as a group in joint formulation and execution of a cooperative field project, and every participant will prepare and analyse some segment of the data collected by the group as a whole. Students will be introduced to the use of a comprehensive statistical computer package and must be willing to spend time doing field work, meeting with others for cooperative work and learning how to use computers.

By that time workstations were available in the Computer Centre, slide rules had been consigned to museums, and powerful statistical packages such as SPSS were becoming standard tools. Chaples conducted survey research into elements of Australian politics and public opinion that were available to students in Sydney. In later years one fruit of his unit was the establishment of a commercial venture to conduct opinion polls, at first as a body within the department (the Public Affairs Research Centre, or PARC), and then later as an independent small business unit specialising in research for the Labor Party.

The Field Studies unit was always popular with students, so that Chaples usually had to restrict enrolments if hands-on tuition was to be possible. There were limits on what could be learned in 12 or 13 weeks, but a basic appreciation of the methodology could be achieved. Nevertheless, most students of Government did not do the unit. Nor was it regarded as in any way indicative for Honours students, who could graduate with virtually no acquaintance with such matters. Nor, when Ernie retired in the mid-1990s, was it replaced with something similar. In the new century there is no regular instruction available for students within the department, except in passing, on behavioural methodology, although Government students also doing subjects like economics, psychology, sociology or the physical sciences will have had to confront similar issues. There are suggestions that the Faculty of Arts and Social Sciences might move towards introducing some core method units for its Social Sciences degrees. However, at present this is merely optional. The Faculty has on its list a unit of study entitled "Quantitative Methods for Social Science" (SCLG3606) designed for students in the BA Advanced stream. As the *Faculty Handbook* for 2013 mentions: "It is also available for PE and GIR students". It was not taught in 2013 or 2014.

The narrowing of the department's teaching focus during the time of its membership in the Faculty of Economics of Business, and then the opportunity for a more comprehensive cross-disciplinary approach since moving to the Faculty of Arts and Social Sciences have provided an opportunity and motivation for a completely new attempt to reform the curriculum. No doubt the process will take some years to come to fruition.

Curriculum reform?

The changes made to the curriculum in the 1970s were in response primarily to pressures from student numbers, and then from student and staff demand for more flexibility and attention to a new political agenda – the so-called "new social issues" of feminism, sexual liberation, the environment, along with issues of peace, race and civil rights. There is no question that the new curriculum was welcomed by an overwhelming proportion of both students and teachers in the department. Government continued to be a popular choice with many students, who were introduced to a wide range of issues and theoretical perspectives that hopefully enriched their lives and prepared them for life beyond the university. In these senses the changes of the 1970s can be regarded not just as change but as reform. As Michael Leigh, a head of department in the early 1990s, commented:

> I think my philosophical starting point with teaching is if you can capture a student's interest, then they can fly, and there are various ways to capture people's interest, but the critical thing is to have the teachers excited by what they're teaching and, to me, to let staff teach fundamentally what they're most excited by – will get better outcomes for students than forcing them to teach material that they're really not interested in and I was fortunate in never having been forced to teach the things that I just would have read up in the textbook and regurgitate. ... So I wouldn't take the view that you must cover this part of the curriculum and this part and this part in order to be a political scientist.[8]

Yet there was a price to pay. Until the 1970s the undergraduate curriculum was designed to give students an introduction to the wide range of material that generally covered the field of modern political science – political institutions in a contemporary liberal democratic state, some comparative perspective of other liberal democracies and authoritarian states, the beginnings of a study of public policy,

> **A reaction to curriculum reform**
>
> *I suppose my reaction was a little bit conservative. To be worried about developing a Department that had no coherence, that bits and pieces would be taught that didn't come together, and a student would come out with a package of courses with no continuity or no great depth. But I was persuaded that this wasn't the case and that it wasn't a serious enough risk to resist the move. First of all I was impressed by the fact that it was so popular among students. Second, staff had a range of expertise for this to be done at such an outstanding level. Third I came to realise that it would resolve a lot of the problems even in first year like repeating the same old stuff three times or four times. You couldn't keep doing that.*
>
> Ken Turner, Oral History interview, 3 February 2014.

an abbreviated look at the history of political philosophy and more modern political theory, a taste of the complex study of international relations, war, peace and international organisation, and some political sociology by examining divisions in society on the basis of class, gender, religion, ethnicity and conflicting value systems. A student with a three-year pass major in Government could expect to have covered the field. And a student with a four-year Honours degree could expect to have an understanding of basic issues of research method relevant to writing a small thesis, and a depthed knowledge of at least one of the central parts of the field of political science. After the 1970s that was much less the case.

At different times since the 1970s the department has tried to build into its program some restriction on choice so that students would need to have faced at least two of the major areas in the field, but both at Government I level and for the Intermediate and Senior courses such restrictions have been easy to evade. In fact most students would have achieved some diversity – but one can ask how satisfied the department should be that a graduate of the department has done no political theory, or no international relations, or no public policy? Or even to have no systematic knowledge of Australian politics?

The new curriculum is effectively a smorgasbord of courses. Some students will make a healthy meal of it while others will not.

At the core of the curriculum question is the fact that the discipline of political science normally in Australia, and certainly in Sydney, is seen as an eclectic mixture of insights and aspects of the study of power. Unlike other social sciences there is no strong consensus about either the content or the methodology most appropriate for political science. A discipline like history has little sense of what should be central **content** of courses, but insists that there is a firm agreement about historical **method** that can be applied to almost any aspect of the study of society. In sociology, likewise, there is a dominant consensus that a behavioural methodology is a necessary tool for any graduate in the subject. In economics, statistical analysis is central to the methodology, while their students are normally introduced to the subject matter through an introduction to macro- and microeconomics. It has to be pointed out that there is strong dissent in almost all disciplines about appropriate content and methodology. And that is certainly true of political science, where an American tradition places a heavy emphasis on behavioural methodology, while a strong European influence places social theory at the heart of the subject. For most of its history the Department of Government at the University of Sydney has resisted all attempts to nail its colours to any such mast.

In effect, the result has been that students in a Government major have been encouraged either to spread their interests over the wide field of content matter, or to concentrate on one or two parts of the discipline. To spread too widely – to feast greedily at the smorgasbord – brings the danger of losing all connection between disparate courses and finishing with little appreciation of the nature of power in society. On the other hand, there is much to be said for concentrating one's attention on one field – so, for example, subfields of the discipline like industrial relations, public policy, and international relations have become entirely reputable independent studies in some universities.

Clearly many students over the years have chosen to specialise, concentrating on international relations, political theory or public policy, but the organisation of the curriculum in the Government Department does not maximise the advantages of that approach. Staff and students have resisted attempts to impose any but the most basic prerequisites, so that it is very difficult for a student to progress through Junior, Intermediate and Senior courses where each level provides a basis which then becomes assumed knowledge for the next. (Some strands, like public policy, have done better at this than others, but the generalisation stands.) Teachers in a Senior course of international relations, Australian politics or political sociology can assume almost nothing about what students have covered and mastered in earlier years. Some students will already have a good basic understanding of, for example, contrasting theoretical approaches to peace and war, while to others the whole set of questions will be something new. Pity the teacher and the more advanced students!

There were some members of the teaching staff who believed that the smorgasbord of courses was just too anarchic to serve as a proper introduction to the study of politics. This came to a head in the late 1980s, when Christopher Hood was the professor. Although Hood could see the attraction of the current arrangement for staff and students, he was convinced that some stiffening was needed at least in the first years of an undergraduate degree. The department set up a committee to survey the curriculum and to recommend how it could be improved. After considerable consultation and debate the committee recommended that a greater weight be given to the teaching of theory in the first three semesters of a Government major. This was designed to ensure that Australian politics, public policy, international relations and the history of political thought should have a firm basis upon which to build in later year courses. It was a source of considerable frustration to Professor Hood and Terry Irving (who was a leading member of the committee) that newly arrived members of the teaching staff refused to support the plan in the Department Board.[9] Nothing came of it.

Any arrangement of curriculum will have pluses and minuses. Choices made by the Government Department over the years have placed a high value on good teaching that stimulates students to learn for themselves and provide a basis for a lifelong critical approach to the politics and everything else that surrounds them in everyday life. There may be deficiencies in providing an appreciation of what makes political science distinctive as one discipline among the many social sciences – as well as in training practitioners of the craft of that discipline. Yet, there is an argument – supported by current policies in funding for research by the ARC – that more attention should be given to breaking down the barriers between separate disciplines than building them up. Scholars are encouraged to cooperate more with colleagues in other disciplines, universities and countries to bring about new perspectives on old problems. There is certainly room for further curriculum reform in the Government Department in the years ahead, but the pride of the department's history lies in the generations of students who have been stimulated by the questions asked and given the intellectual tools to examine such questions with a critical and unprejudiced attitude.

---

1 RN Spann, "Political Science in Australia", *AJPH*, Vol 1 No 1. 1955, pp. 86-97. See also "Political Studies: A Conference Report", *AJPH*, Vol 4 No 1, 1958, pp. 1-18.

2 Details of changes to the Government I curriculum in this section have been taken from the Economics Faculty Handbooks for the various years.

3 Details of curriculum in *University of Sydney Calendar, 1973_1*, p. 502.

4 Dennis Altman to Michael Hogan, 8 September 2014.

5 See interviews with Ken Turner, 3 February 2014, and Ross Curnow, 24 February 2014, Department of Government Oral History Project.

6 Interview with Rodney Tiffen, 29 April 2014, Department of Government Oral History Project.

7 Henry Mayer to Dick Spann, 4 March 1970, in Spann Papers, Box 45, Folder "1970-72", University of Sydney Archives.
8 Interview with Michael Leigh, 13 January 2014, Department of Government Oral History Project.
9 Interview with Terry Irving, 24 July 2014, Department of Government Oral History Project.

7

The corporate university

Towards the end of the 1980s the university sector of Australian education underwent a fundamental transformation that, coinciding with the arrival of computer technology and the internet, became almost revolutionary in the speed and nature of change. It was introduced at the initiative of the Commonwealth Minister responsible for education in the Hawke Government, John Dawkins (1987-91), and was reflected in the change of the Ministry's name from "Education" to "Employment, Education and Training". For universities, the most urgent problem at that time was funding. There had previously been an almost complete dependence on public money, mostly from the Commonwealth, but with some contributions from the States – even though the richer universities like Sydney had considerable capital resources from foundations and donations. The problem had been exacerbated by the decision of the earlier Whitlam Government to provide free university education in a world economic environment where costs were rising rapidly, student demand for university places was expanding, and scope for increased university funding was declining. Dawkins abolished free tuition and introduced the Higher Education Contribution Scheme (HECS) of student loans. He also abolished the second level of tertiary education, Colleges of Advanced Education (CAEs), whose existing institutions were forced either to become genuine universities, merge with existing universities, or to lower their sights so as to become traditional technical colleges. In 1988 the Australian Research Council (ARC) replaced the earlier Australian Research Grants Committee (ARGC) in a way that transformed the pattern of research funding, while withdrawing much of the autonomy of individual universities in that matter. The ARC gained its present state of independence under legislation in 2001.

The rationale behind the changes (other than reducing the dependence of universities on direct Commonwealth funding) was to introduce an explicit element of competition into the university sector – competition for students, prestige, public monies, research funds and private donations. Private universities were encouraged to enter the education market, universities were free to adjust staff salaries and overseas student fees according to market forces, while increases in government funding depended upon rankings according to various performance indicators, but were fundamentally tied to the fees that student numbers could bring in. Universities were expected to become efficient businesses, generating their own funds and managing their own affairs. Legislation in 1989 established a "Unified National System" for universities that demanded "strong managerial modes of operation", "streamlined decision making processes" and a "minimal time lag between making and implementing decisions".[1] Very soon the elite universities established their own "Group of Eight" to protect their interests, while all universities were forced to adopt management models based on big commercial companies. Vice-Chancellors effectively became typical company CEOs, with inflated salaries to match, collegial decision-making was replaced by line management, elected Deans were replaced by appointed executives, management consultants introduced their knee-jerk mechanisms of re-branding, cost cutting and tougher industrial relations, along with "mission statements" and "corporate strategic plans" that needed constant review. Welcome to the corporate world.

Not all these changes were completely novel. Universities have always been constrained by concern over finances and competition for the best students. One could make an argument that the colleges of Oxford and Cambridge had perfected their own corporate model soon after their medieval origins, while American universities have always operated in a very competitive environment. Nevertheless, the Australian experience was a shock. Some changes in management style were probably inevitable, but much of the adoption of the commercial model was uncritical and inefficient, which in retrospect is not surprising given the failures of that model for so many large companies in a series of worldwide economic crises at the end of the 20th century and the beginning of the 21st century. Former Vice-Chancellor, Bruce Williams, points out, for example, that the reconstitution of the Academic Board, making it easier for management to ignore, was one example of this: "The Board had not become an effective general policy body by 2000, and might not become so".[2] In fact, the old Professorial Board, which had been one of the principal mechanisms of collegial management at the University of Sydney for well over a century, became a body which simply rubber-stamped decisions made by university line managers, either from the Vice-Chancellor's office or from the faculties.[3]

At the University of Sydney the new era began with the appointment of Don McNicol as Vice-Chancellor in 1990, replacing John M Ward, a master of traditional consensus and collegial administration. McNicol embraced the corporate model with enthusiasm, while his successors have continued along a similar path, although perhaps not with the same delight.

One of the first areas affecting subsidiary units of the university such as departments was the withdrawal of the remnants of budgetary autonomy. When budgetary matters were concentrated at the centre the new process was defended as a rational measure that would allow academics to concentrate on teaching and research, not needing to

> **The corporate university**
>
> *I'm winding up my career at a time when I don't think it's a happy time for universities. We've fallen into a culture of hyper-competitiveness where universities are regarded by their managers and governments essentially as competitive firms, competing against each other for resources, rather than what's the reality, which is a knowledge system based on cooperation and sharing.*
>
> Professor Raewin Connell, *Sydney Alumni Magazine*, July 2014, p.23.

concern themselves with financial matters. Instead, it transformed departments into beggars at the door of Deans, who themselves had to compete annually for a fair share of funding from the centre. Meanwhile, the rationality of the new process was undermined by a spectacular demonstration of Parkinson's Law in action – where bureaucracies expand irrespective of the work to be done. With finance centralised, of course more staff would be required at the centre.

However, this did not mean, as promised, that there would be fewer management staff at the periphery. Instead, finance officers have become more necessary at faculty, school and department level, partly to implement the new protocols set in place from the centre, and partly to handle the increased reporting responsibilities coming from Canberra. In the 1970s, for example, budgeting was handled at faculty level by the Dean and the head of the Dean's office, while a similar situation prevailed at the department level for the head and the graduate assistant or department secretary. New positions were demanded by the changed circumstances. An IT unit was created to serve needs that were unknown in an earlier era, while a competitive academic environment demanded positions such as Marketing Manager, Client Services Manager, Staff Planning and Development Manager, Student Administration Manager, Faculty Events Coordinator, and a host of Student Advisors. In the *Faculty Handbook* for 2005, just the Dean's

Unit in the Faculty of Economics and Business listed 43 managerial positions, not counting the Associate Dean roles exercised by academic staff. Then there were the support staff in the two schools that took the place of the professorial secretaries and departmental typists of the old days. When Mary Pollard was secretary to the Dean in the 1980s her staff consisted of three assistants in one large room in the Merewether Building. The explosion of non-academic staff positions was designed to attract and service more fee-paying students, but more directly it took resources that in an earlier period would have been devoted to more academic staff.

During the 1990s one development of line management was the appointment of Rebecca Simmons, not as "department secretary" or some such title, but as Department Manager, responsible primarily to the university through the Dean. She continued the great tradition of superb non-academic staff, and was especially valuable in inducting successive heads of department into the mysteries of university administration, while maintaining the close personal professional relationship between academic and non-academic staff. When the Faculty of Economics was rebranded as the Faculty of Economics and Business at the turn of the century, Government lost its own

---

Not the cricket team

Betty Johnson (R/H off-spin bowler; bats no.10)

It is always a delight for lovers of the game to watch a true professional in action. Johnson's control of direction and length is immaculate and the record books indicate the success of this approach. She can be relied upon for long spells at the crease, and even when the wicket offers no assistance she gives little away. When the wicket starts to turn then even the most accomplished batsman knows that classic defensive technique will not be enough to keep her out. She bats well down the order, but loves nothing better than to slog fast bowlers back over their heads to the boundary.

Anon., "The first Eleven", *Beyond the Cringe*, (Newsletter of the Department of Government) September 1990.

manager. The role is now spread between two departments; Jane Borton manages administrative matters for the Department of Government as well as for Political Economy. At the beginning of 2015 an administrative restructuring will provide even less autonomy in this area for Government.

For the Department of Government one of the developments of the new environment was the disappearance of full-time tutors. From the 1960s to the 1980s, approximately a quarter of the full-time teachers in the department were non-tenured but full-time salaried tutors, senior tutors, teaching fellows, or assistant lecturers. (In an earlier period the position of Senior Tutor, held by Henry Mayer, Ken Turner and then Lex Watson, was a tenured rank.) From the 1990s the demands of managerial efficiency forced the department to rely much more directly on its established tenured staff, supplemented with a limited budget for part-time teachers, either lecturing or tutoring, being paid sessional rates rather than a salary. In Government I and larger later year units, tutors had been the frontline troops in teaching for many years – and their skills had helped to establish the reputation of the department for teaching excellence. Moreover, senior members of the department had regarded the shape of the department as reflecting their responsibility to help develop the teaching and research skills of the next generation of political science teachers.

It was not just the absence of salaried tutors, but the nature of tutorials that changed. In the 1970s the size of tutorials was customarily in the order of 10 to 15 students in each group. With increased demands on the time of tenured teachers, and continual cutbacks in the budget for part-timers, by the 1990s there was an insistence that larger classes should be scheduled, so that the normal size of tutorials became 20 to 25. That size brought about a marked change in the internal dynamic of tutorials. A dedicated and innovative teacher could still manage to encourage good cross communication between students directed towards uncovering interesting questions and alternative responses from the material presented in the unit, but with overworked lecturers and underpaid casual tutors that was less and less likely.

One development that helped the department face the new environment was that in 1990 an internal candidate, Graeme Gill, was appointed to the Chair of Government and Public Administration, which he held till retirement at the end of 2014. Gill's primary expertise is as a scholar of Soviet and Russian studies. Like Dick Spann, Gill has strengths across the whole spectrum of professorial responsibilities – he is a scholar of international reputation, a dedicated and popular teacher, and a master of university politics and administration. He was an ideal person to take a senior role in the department as it was about to enter a period of serious and confronting challenges arising from the new corporate university culture and the transformation of the Faculty of Economics into a School of Business. He was head of department or head of school a number of times, as well as serving as Chair of the Academic Forum and Deputy Chair of the Academic Board, while for brief period he was Acting Pro-Vice Chancellor (Research). From the 1990s the department gained other professors, either by promotion or by appointment, so that by 2014 of the 39 members of staff listed in the faculty handbook 10 were professors. They number some outstanding scholars, yet none has had an influence on the fortunes of the department to compare with Graeme Gill's.

Among the support staff in the Faculty was a Director of Teaching and Learning, along with an Undergraduate Teaching Quality Fellow and a handful of student advisors. It would be hard to argue that this was a waste of resources, although the University Office of Teaching and Learning had been very useful over a number of years before the Faculty office was established. Besides the help given to students who were struggling, assistance to newly appointed lecturers and tutors was an advance on the haphazard apprenticeship system of teacher education in an earlier era. Moreover, an emphasis given to teaching by regular awards for gifted or assiduous teachers has been a welcome innovation at national, university and faculty level. However, one would be more impressed with these advances had they not been accompanied by the loss of full-time tutors, the blowing out of the size of tutorials, the exploitation of sessional teachers, and the overworking of tenured teaching staff that were significant developments over the same period.

Some coping mechanisms

The university, pushed into a more openly competitive environment, turned to its alumni in an endeavour to find a continuing source of extra funding and to foster a community pride in the achievements of the university. In an ever changing organisational structure where the continuation of departments was not a given, when the Department of Government moved to the Faculty of Arts and Social Sciences, the time was right to find allies and supporters in the local community, primarily for support, rather than funding. Its External Advisory Committee (EAC) was created in September 2008. Most, but not all, its members are alumni. At its most general, the purpose of the EAC has been to affirm the profile of the department among its key communities, which in turn enhances its profile within the university. Members of the EAC have hosted interns in public and private sector organisations, cooperated in research projects and provided time and expertise to the department. The committee helped gain affiliation for the department in the Association of Professional Schools of International Affairs to which many world-ranked universities belong. Members have also contributed substantially to the creation of an HSC enrichment course on World Politics offered in Summer School to lift the profile of the department among high school counsellors, teachers and principals. Its major achievement has been the "Best and Brightest" showcase for Final Honours student research held at Parliament House. More recently, it has embarked on a campaign to bring the department into closer association with think tanks in the Sydney area.

One noticeable reaction within the department to a competitive environment for postgraduate students has been an inflation of marks and grades given to students, especially at the Final Honours level. Since the 1990s, examiners' meetings of staff have been constantly reminded by colleagues that if the top levels of grades are not more generously available, then Government students will be disadvantaged in the fierce competition for postgraduate scholarships – in comparison with other, especially scientific, departments, where marks close to 100% are habitually given out, and with political science schools in other universities. There are many pedagogical reasons why it is desirable to use the full range of marks, especially in the context of continuous assessment where few students can perform at the highest level in all work assessed, but it is certainly true that in earlier times teachers were reluctant to consider any piece of work as nearly perfect. During the 1970s, for example, a quick survey of Final Honours results indicates that, of the 165 Honours graduates from 1970 to 1979, 7% were awarded a University Medal, 19% received Firsts, 35% received upper Second Class Honours, 32% received lower Second Class Honours, while 7% received Third Class Honours. As a marked contrast, in the 2000 graduation class, of 28 students there were four medallists (14%), 14 Firsts (50%), 10 upper Seconds (36%), four lower Seconds (14%), and no Thirds. To have half the large class receiving a First would have been unheard of in an earlier era. Perhaps the students of that year really were extraordinary. If so, the next cohort was much better. In the following graduation year of 2001, of the 17 students, 13 (that is, more than three-quarters) received Firsts and there were no lower level Seconds or Thirds. In succeeding years results were not so extreme but still consistently higher than in the earlier period.

> **Not the Cricket Team**
>
> Lynne Thomson (Masseur and Trainer)
>
> *Corked muscle? Bruised ego? Thomson can fix it. Lost your pads? Thomson can find a spare set. Forgotten the score? Thomson will know. Batsmen and bowlers depend upon the Thomson assistance to perform at their peak. Other teams have now recognized the role she plays in the success of the team and have been making offers for her services. The prospect of having to manage their own bruises or carry their own kit strikes dread into the hearts of most of the team. She is also a handy bowler at the nets and has occasionally been persuaded to have a bat in minor games.*
>
> Anon., "The first Eleven", *Beyond the Cringe*, (Newsletter of the Department of Government) September 1990.

Some inflation of grades and marks at Final Honours level was common to virtually all political science schools at that time, because they were all subject to the same competitive pressures. In 2003, perhaps because of the results of the previous few years noted above, the department asked Dr Michael Crozier, the Honours Coordinator at the Melbourne University Department of Political Science, to prepare a benchmarking report of standards at the two university schools of politics. He reviewed the examiners' reports and marks for a sample of 10 recent theses. He found some disagreement at the border between a First and a high Second, suggesting that he would have lowered one Sydney grade and raised another, but overall it was clear that standards in Sydney and Melbourne were very similar.[4]

Postgraduate coursework degrees

Now that universities were engaged in direct competition and constrained by the decline of public funding, they found that the opportunities for finding extra continuing sources of funds were very limited. The most obvious source that could be expanded was overseas students, who could be charged full fees. Sydney, like most other Australian universities, marketed its courses aggressively, especially in Asia. Within the Faculty of Economics, and later the Faculty of Economics and Business, overseas students were more than welcome in the undergraduate programs, but the most aggressive expansion designed to attract overseas and full fee-paying students was in the area of coursework postgraduate degrees. Because of the funding formula being implemented for departments and schools at the time a large proportion of such moneys went directly to those lower teaching units. Such funds, needless to say, were also heavily taxed by the faculties and the centre.

Up till the 1980s the postgraduate offerings in the Faculty of Economics were very simple; a PhD program based on a substantial research dissertation was supplemented by a Master of Economics program, either at Honours level (mainly research) or a Pass degree (mainly coursework). Within the Government Department students tended to do either the PhD, the Master of Economics or the Master of Arts Degree, although there were rare instances of a Master of Philosophy. By the 1990s greater variety was appearing, with Masters degrees and postgraduate diplomas marking the expansion. In the *Economics Handbook* of 1995, when Stephen Salsbury was still Dean, six coursework Masters degrees were listed, plus a seventh, the Master of Business Administration (MBA), which was taught separately in the Graduate School of Business, still at that time shared with the University of New South Wales. To the traditional MEc was added the MEc (Social Sciences), while the Master of Industrial Relations was an initiative of that department. Government was clearly interested in expanding into this area:

> The Department of Government offers three degrees. The Master of International Studies is for students interested in the national and international politics of the Asia-Pacific region. It is a coursework and thesis degree and usually entails one calendar year on a full-time basis. The Master of Public Policy will be of great interest to those hoping to be employed in

the public sector, while the Master of Public Affairs focuses on the interface between the private and the public sectors. They are both coursework and thesis degrees requiring three semesters on the equivalent of a full-time basis.[5]

It would seem that Government at that time was the most enterprising unit in the Faculty in exploring this new opportunity. However the business departments were starting to gear up, introducing the Master of Commerce in that same year, 1995.

Ten years later, in the Faculty of Economics and Business in 2005, the number and complexity of the postgraduate offerings had increased markedly, with the addition of Masters degrees in Business, Logistics Management, Transport Management, Human Resources Management and Coaching, International Business, and various combined degrees such as International Business and Law. The most strongly marketed postgraduate degrees, in Business and Commerce, offered majors for virtually all disciplines in the Faculty, with the need for many new courses to present to the huge numbers of students enrolling.

The implications for the now renamed "Discipline" of Government in this expansion were that many new units of study designed for these postgraduate courses were needed, but few, if any, extra resources were available. Since staff members were contributing to degrees that attracted full fee-paying students, they expected that extra funding would flow through to pay for the extra teachers needed. However, the great expansion in the early years of the new century was for degrees offered within the School of Business. Proportionately, the School of Economics and Politics was falling behind in attracting the new money, with the result that new teachers went overwhelmingly to the School of Business. Staff in Government and other units of the School of Economics and Political Science were running harder just to stand still. The economic fact that postgraduate students were worth three or four times more than undergraduates was determining decisions about the allocation of teachers. As Rod Tiffen has commented: "Basically we were using the funds from our Masters program to subsidise our undergraduate teaching".[6]

There were also more directly academic consequences. In the highly competitive market for international students the university and Faculty were confronted with a classic commercial dilemma: how high a standard of English should be expected of international students, and how high should standards be set for satisfactory completion of units by students? Admission to the university or Faculty requires a minimum level of English proficiency, generally determined according to a scale developed in a number of international tests. The marketing problem was (and is) that if the bar is raised too high then the potential number of students is lowered — and the aim of the exercise has been to recruit as many students, with their fees, as possible. The Faculty of Economics and Business set the bar at the bare minimum recommended for English proficiency for academic purposes, an IELTS score of 6.5 or the equivalent. Even allowing for a growing level of student cheating in such tests, this was probably adequate for highly technical subjects like Accounting or Econometrics, but was set too low for subjects where English comprehension and expression were more central, such as Business Law or Government. The Teaching and Learning support unit in the Faculty expended a great deal of energy in trying to rescue students who were out of their depth because of problems of English expression, especially in essays and exams, but it still remained true that many students enrolled in postgraduate courses taught by members of the Discipline of Government could barely cope because of language difficulties. Then came the next dilemma: should teachers demand the highest academic standards and fail a significant proportion of students, or should they lower their standards? There is no objective data to indicate what choice has been made, but an honest response from most teachers would suggest that standards expected in postgraduate units of study have not been up to levels traditionally demanded in undergraduate units, especially at an Honours level. Then there is the final dilemma: if such Australian postgraduate degrees involve a measure of dumbing down of standards, then what becomes of the long-term market value of such degrees? There are already indications that, especially in rapidly developing nations of East and Southeast Asia that are the main catchment for the Australian international education market, local universities are providing an excellence in tertiary education that seems to be in question in Australia.

Meanwhile, many units of study have been taught by short-term contract lecturers who have little contact with either students or other Government staff outside the classroom schedule. Some are dedicated and effective teachers, but as a general principle students are better served when taught by teachers whose qualifications are guaranteed by the testing process of tenured staff appointment.

The experience of the department or discipline with postgraduate Masters degrees has been mixed. Although virtually first into the field among the departments in the faculty, its own offerings have not prospered as was hoped. The Master of Public Affairs (MPA) was dropped from the program when it was decided that the small enrolments did not warrant the significant allocation of resources. The Master of Public Policy (MPP) was seriously undercut by the arrival of the Graduate School of Government, as well as strong

---

Hazards of tutorials

One of Hogan's tutorials provided a particularly embarrassing moment for me. It was 1995 and I was waxing lyrical about how John Howard's triumphant return as opposition leader would be short-lived. He was no match for the political brawler/international statesman Paul Keating. As my diatribe veered towards the personal, I earned a few nods, raised eyebrows and the odd chuckle. These responses, however, were at my expense. I had not yet had the opportunity to be introduced to Melanie Howard who was sitting opposite me.

Troy Bramston, 6 February 2014

competition from Macquarie University, and has had difficulty finding staff to teach in its courses. In 2014 the department offers three Masters degrees in international relations; the Master of International Studies (MIntS), the Master of International Relations (MIR), and the Master of International Security Studies (MISS). It is unlikely that a sufficient number of students can be found to continue with all three, so that some rationalisation is likely in the future.

Kolej Antarabangsa

During the 1990s a number of Australian universities moved to establish outposts in Asia, either as overseas affiliated campuses graduating their own students or as twinned units in overseas countries designed to funnel students back to the parent Australian university. The foundation of the Kolej Antarabangsa (International College) in Penang, Malaysia, fitted the second of those models, with the University of Sydney having a dominant role in a consortium

Kolej Antarabangsa, Penang, Malaysia (Photo courtesy of Michael Leigh)

of eight universities (Sydney, Melbourne, ANU, Adelaide, Western Australia, Queensland, Tasmania, Deakin). The initiative also suited the interests of Malaysia and the State of Penang, insofar as it provided relief for ethnic Chinese families who were otherwise constrained by government policies setting a quota for Malaysian universities that favoured ethnic Malay students. An important partner in the enterprise was one of the largest development companies in Malaysia (Sheffield Enterprise Sdb Bhd), which contributed land and the Kolej building as part of a larger housing development on the southern outskirts of the city of George Town on Penang Island. An agreement was signed between the University of Sydney and Sheffield Enterprise at the end of 1991, although only the Faculty of Economics was directly involved in the academic program. Classes began in 1994. English was the language of tuition.

The academic program comprised three levels: the matriculation program was much the largest, offering the Australian-recognised Higher School Certificate (HSC) that facilitated entry to Australian universities, along with concentrated English language courses; a small undergraduate program that aimed to replicate a typical first year undergraduate course of an economics, management or business degree in Australia; and a smaller postgraduate program that offered courses that could be counted towards Masters degrees in a number of Australian universities. In 1995, the second year of operation for the Kolej, 241 students were enrolled in the HSC, 38 in the undergraduate courses, and 21 in the postgraduate program. In later years the undergraduate studies segment doubled its numbers, but its numbers never challenged those in the matriculation program. Students who did well in the HSC could compete for direct entry into Australian universities without having to spend the introductory year in Penang.[7]

The University of Sydney (in effect, the Faculty of Economics) controlled both the admission of students and the appointment of staff. In the undergraduate program Dr Lily Rahim, from Sydney's Department of Economic History (who later transferred to Government), taught both Economic History and Government. In the postgraduate program Dr Felix Patrikeeff (seconded from Government) taught central elements of the Master of International Studies degree (MIntS) that was offered at Sydney. The Academic Director of the Kolej was Professor Michael Leigh, who had been head of the Department of Government during the period of negotiations for the establishment of the Kolej. Probably more students at the Kolej were interested in an eventual business degree rather than a social science education, but the involvement of the Department of Government was more evident than any other part of Sydney's Faculty of Economics.

Students progressing from the Kolej to Australian universities – either directly from the HSC or after the year of undergraduate study in Penang – generally performed well when they studied in Australia. However, the numbers were always quite small, especially when they were spread over all the participating Australian universities. For

Kate Harrison

With a First Class Honours degree (BA, 1977) and a PhD (1986) in Government, Kate Harrison is one of the Department's most distinguished graduates. Her doctoral thesis, on "Television licence renewal inquiries: a study of accountability and participation" reflected a lifetime interest in connections between media and the law. During her postgraduate study she tutored in various courses in the Department. She completed a law degree at UNSW and later gained a Master of Laws at Columbia, and is admitted to practice in NSW and New York. She was a foundation director of the Communications Law Centre at UNSW. She spent a number of years as a senior advisor in the Rudd Government before returning to her leading role in the law firm of Gilbert + Tobin, where she is head of the firm's litigation group and specialises in the area of intellectual property, copyright and trade practices. She is listed in the "Legal 500" guide to the nation's top lawyers.

the University of Sydney it soon became clear that the benefits in numbers of full fee-paying students did not warrant the considerable expense involved in staffing, administration and supervision of the Kolej Antarabangsa. A much greater number of overseas students could be achieved through the less expensive procedure of regular marketing of Australian education opportunities in the countries of Asia, and in the use of education agents in those countries. The initial agreement of cooperation had always been fairly open-ended, and the University of Sydney withdrew from the arrangement early in the new century. In the business of university education it had not been a profit-making exercise.

Hung out to dry in a business school (1999-2008)

When Professor Stephen Salsbury, Dean of Economics for much of the 1980s and 1990s, died in office in the mid-1990s, the Vice-Chancellor, Gavin Brown, took the opportunity to instigate a search for a new Dean who could bring the Faculty into the new corporate environment. For a number of years the Faculty had been vacillating about how to achieve an international standard of excellence in business education, especially in the programs for a Master of Business Administration (MBA). The main question seemed to be whether it was best to cooperate with Sydney's main rival in that area, the University of New South Wales, or to engage in direct competition. Sydney's Graduate School of Business was, for most of the 1990s, a cooperative endeavour with UNSW. The Vice-Chancellor clearly

> **In the business school**
>
> *And all is seared with trade; bleared, smeared with toil;*
> *And wears man's smudge and shares man's smell: the soil*
> *Is bare now, nor can foot feel, being shod.*
>
> Gerard Manley Hopkins, "God's Grandeur"

preferred a model of direct competition, which would involve beefing up the independent resources needed for such business education. In 1999 Professor Peter Wolnizer was appointed Dean, presumably with a mandate to promote the business credentials of the Faculty. Wolnizer was a scholar in accountancy, who had taught in the Faculty's Department of Accounting a few years before.

One of the first tasks of the new Dean was to meet with the members of his Faculty to explain his plans for renewal and to seek some consensus on how they were to be put in place. The main problem – or opportunity? – was that many of the teaching resources available were more concerned with social science rather than business education. Departments like Government, Economic History, Economics, Industrial Relations, along with the special Political Economy group, were likely to resist attempts to narrow the scope of their interests to that of business education. It should not have surprised anyone in the emerging corporate environment that the major item for discussion in the meeting was how the new Faculty was to be re-branded. The result was majority agreement in the meeting on a new name: "Faculty of Economics, Business and Politics". This clearly reflected a compromise between the business focus demanded by the Dean and the interests of some of the largest departments, especially Government, which was still the most productive in terms of research output in the Faculty, as well as being one of the most popular teaching schools. However, the name also reflected a choice between two competing models of business education – a narrow professional skills-based education favoured by many American business schools, and a broader, research and theory oriented style more typical of European universities. For members of the Department of Government the new name put the Faculty along the path of a model made famous by the London School of Economics and Political Science (LSE), which was already one of the top business schools in Europe.

That re-branding was not to be. At the next Faculty meeting the Dean reported back that the Vice-Chancellor had refused to accept the proposed name, imposing the shorter formula: "Faculty of Economics and Business" (E+B). Since the word omitted was "Politics" there was little doubt about the target of official disapproval. Nor was there much doubt that the Vice-Chancellor had not been happy with the proposed title. No doubt pressure had been applied from university and faculty links with the "big end of town" who had little regard for the Government Department that (along with Political Economy) was perceived as espousing leftist, if not Marxist values. However, the responsibility for the rejection of the proposed title for the new Faculty should be given to the Dean himself. As a newly appointed official charged with reforming the Faculty along the lines presumably outlined in pre-appointment interviews, and armed with a firm consensus gained at his first meeting with the Faculty, the new Dean was in a position to demand support from the Vice-Chancellor in his first substantive decision. Not to do so suggests extraordinary timidity, or, more probably, that Peter Wolnizer agreed with the Vice-Chancellor and, by extension, disagreed with the decision of his Faculty meeting.

During the rest of 1999 the Faculty was restructured to meet the plans of the Dean, although some of the readjustments took extra time. From 2000 the Faculty took on its new name, and soon after the various departments were renamed as "Disciplines", to be integrated into one of the two new Schools that became the basic administrative units. The School of Business absorbed the discipline areas of Accounting and Business Law, Finance, Marketing, Transport and Logistics and the old Industrial Relations, now rebranded as Work and Organisational Studies. The School of Economics and Political Science grouped together the discipline areas of Economics, Economic History, Econometrics and Business Statistics, Political Economy and the re-branded Government and International Relations (dropping

> **Andrew West**
>
>
>
> Andrew currently presents the Religion and Ethics Report on ABC Radio National. He graduated with Honours in Government (BA Hons 1992), writing a thesis that applied Robert Michels' "Iron Law of Oligarchy" to community groups and ostensibly non-political organisations. Since then he has been a senior journalist for the *Sydney Morning Herald*, the *Sun-Herald* and *The Australian*, and had his material published in leading American, Asian and Australian journals. He did his Masters degree at Columbia University in New York, and spent a brief period teaching journalism at the University of Canberra before returning to the coalface. The alumni of the University of Sydney recently elected him a Fellow of the Senate, the University's governing body. He remembers his time in the Department of Government: "It truly was my great awakening. My rather modest high school education was suddenly turbo-charged with just a few brilliant first-year lectures by the likes of Ken Turner and Helen Nelson. The later teaching of Michael Hogan, Deb Brennan, Michael Jackson and Lex Watson did more than ready me for a career. They prepared me to be an active citizen. That's so much more important."

any reference to Public Administration, which had been the origins of the old department).

The Dean presented the new organisational structures as enabling an innovative approach to business education, putting the best face on the social science disciplines that were still a large part of the Faculty. In his "Welcome to Students" in the *Faculty Handbook* he asserted:

> As a student you will benefit greatly from our restructuring. Built on the rich diversity of learning offered by the Faculty, our new organisational arrangements give impetus to innovation in teaching and learning through a cross disciplinary approach to curriculum and program design. Our distinctiveness is that we locate the key business disciplines in their economic, political and social contexts.[8]

However, his actions over the next few years, starting with the suppression of the separate Discipline of Economic History in

2003, and continuing in the preferential treatment given to the School of Business, suggests that he was not convinced that such "distinctiveness" was desirable for a business school. Indeed, within a few years even the Vice-Chancellor expressed some disquiet about the dominance of business concerns over those of social sciences.[9] Some of the senior members of the Discipline of Government of the time have suggested that the Dean's commitment to the social science development of the Faculty was genuine enough at the beginning, but had evaporated within about three years. According to Graeme Gill the change of mind was probably associated with the high priority given by the Dean to affiliating his Faculty with various international consortia of business schools. The clear preference was for bodies dominated by American business schools where the stress was on a narrow professional training of accountants and managers with little interest in a social science agenda.[10]

For the life of the new Faculty the Department of Government became the Discipline of Government. This led to some jests about the title of the "head of discipline", or the notice outside the office in the Merewether Building advertised as "Discipline Administration". Jokes aside, the reorganisation meant that what little autonomy remained was even further eroded. Administrative decisions depended upon the head of School. At least for the first couple of years the interests of Government were treated sympathetically since the first holder of that office was its own Graeme Gill. After a three-year term, a search produced a new head of School, Professor Stephen Nicholas, (2003-6) whose expertise was in the field of International Business. In the event Nicholas was no less committed to efficient and just administration of the School than was Gill, but his appointment to a school of social science disciplines sent very clear signals about the priorities of the Dean.

There had been arguments about the suitability of the name "Government and Public Administration" since the beginning of the

> **Mock advertisement for a Chair in Government**
>
> The University of Sydney invites applications from suitably qualified persons. The following attributes are deemed essential:
>
> - *international relations (but must be American trained)*
> - *comparative politics (with a speciality in an area of major world significance which is not, however, the preserve of any existing member of staff)*
> - *public policy and administration (this can be widely interpreted, as this strand is too boring to indulge in internecine warfare)*
> - *political sociology (but not a sociologist per se)*
> - *political theory (preferably arcane)*
>
> *It is automatically assumed that any candidate will be – or will immediately become – an expert in Australian politics. To ensure that the Department gets value for money, the successful candidate will be expected to assume a teaching load at least equal to that of staff who could otherwise have been employed i.e. 3 tutors or 2 lecturers, whichever is greater. ....*
>
> Beyond the Cringe: the retreat from excellence, (occasional newsletter of Department of Government) Vol.2, No.1, Winter 1989.

department in 1947, reviving with some energy and frustration in the 1970s, and renewed within the department when it was reassessing its teaching and research priorities in the 1990s. Not only did the emphasis on public administration, added to government, seem to restrict the definition of politics to a narrow concern over what governments did or did not do, but it left the ever-growing area of international relations seemingly ignored. In an era of university administration when marketing principles were the most urgent consideration, the substitution of "international relations" for "public administration" gave a better idea of what the department (or discipline) actually taught. The loss of a link with its own history, as well as the downgrading of a traditional strength in public policy and administration, meant that some staff members expressed regret over the change of name. Nevertheless, the inclusion of the name "international relations" was overdue. It suited the interests of the

Faculty, where an international dimension to business was central, but it also reflected majority support in the Discipline itself, as indicated clearly by a decision taken by a meeting of the Discipline. The survival of the old name remained only in the title of the chair held by Graeme Gill since 1990 – Government and Public Administration. That lapsed on his retirement at the end of 2014.

It was all very well for the head of School to be sympathetic to the interests of Government, but it soon became very clear that there was competition between the two schools for resources, especially staffing, and that the School of Business had priority. When the two Schools were established in 2000-1 there were five discipline areas in each; by 2006 there were eight in the School of Business, and only four in the School of Economics and Political Science (SEPS). New disciplines had been created in the former for Business and Information Systems and International Business, while Business Law was separated from Accounting. Some of these new units had to be staffed from scratch. Meanwhile the small group of Economic History had been abolished in the other School. The harsh truth was that the Faculty had access to a finite share of university and community resources, and consequently any significant expansion of the business school (which was the point of the whole restructuring) would have to come at the expense of the social science disciplines.

The early years of the new century were a difficult time for Government staff members. There was a high turnover of staff, and replacements for resigning or retiring teachers were either postponed or frozen. There is routinely a lead-time of nearly two years between a resignation and the arrival of the replacement teacher – and that is if a replacement is allowed. In the period when Government was located in the Faculty of Economics and Business (2000 to 2007) well over half the members of staff either retired or resigned – Fred Teiwes, Patricia Springborg, Martin Painter, Deb Brennan, John Hobson, M Ramesh, Randall Stewart, Peter Dauvergne, Michael Di

Francesco, Joanne Kelly, Jason Sharman, Devon Hagerty and Darryl Jarvis, while Louise Chappell departed the following year. Some were long-time stalwarts of the department; others were scarcely in place before they moved on. Many were people whose individual loss was to diminish the department significantly, while the departure of so many near the one time had a major impact on the strength of teaching and research. There was also a cut-back on appointing full-time contract lecturers. By 2008 there had been 10 tenured replacements, but since most were early career scholars it was not surprising that research output had declined. Staff-student ratios oscillated wildly from a healthy figure of about 20 (2001 and 2005) to a worrying level of about 30 (2002, 2003).[11] Meanwhile, the extra duties of teaching postgraduate coursework increased the workload for all.

As part of the restructuring of the Faculty, it was made explicit to the Discipline of Government that a greater effort was expected to make undergraduate and postgraduate courses attractive to students of business. This involved a reorientation of teaching – indeed, a radical reassessment of the priorities of the Discipline. In an endeavour to come to terms with the need for such a review a number of live-in "retreats" were organised – at Wollongong, in the Blue Mountains, and another extended set of sessions in the nearby Darlington Centre. Discussions were vigorous, with much disagreement. This was not surprising since in some ways a review of teaching priorities had been postponed since the 1970s, and no one was happy to be forced into such an exercise. The result of the process was the decision of the Discipline that it was best placed in Economics rather than in a Faculty such as Arts, and that it would cooperate with the demands of the Dean to teach courses appropriate for a business school.

This ongoing review of research priorities had narrowed the scope to a list of four: democracy and democratisation; public policy; international risk and security; and globalisation and governance.

Since teaching and research are closely related in any healthy university discipline, some regret was expressed by staff members at the downgrading of areas such as Australian politics, media studies, area studies, or political sociology which had been strengths of the department in earlier years, but there was no doubt that some rationalisation had been needed for many years, and there were always bound to be winners and losers.

The review also confirmed the decision of the discipline to make a commitment to the faculty and to its aim of business education. A few years later Deb Brennan, as Chair of Discipline, expressed the frustration of Government people that this had not been recognised (and rewarded). Writing to the head of school, Professor Nicholas, to express her dismay about the growing rumours in 2004 that Government was to be moved out of the faculty and located into Arts, she argued:

> In the last few years the Government Discipline has been exceptionally proactive in aligning our teaching and research efforts more closely with the Faculty's mission. While we are a diverse group, the intellectual focus and research interests of staff are firmly cemented within the Faculty. We have, for example:
>
> - introduced new units of study such as 'International Business and Politics', 'Business, Government and Society', 'Government/Business Relations' and 'Government and Business Ethics';
> - embraced the opportunity to embed a new unit in the Bachelor of Commerce in 2006;
> - initiated majors such as 'Business and Society' and 'Governance' within the Master of Business;
> - been key players in School/Faculty ventures such as the Bachelor of International Studies and the major in public policy.

> My colleagues have been dumbfounded by the suggestion that we might be moved to a new location.[12]

As well they might be dumbfounded. At the end of the letter Brennan made explicit her belief about "the strong possibility of staff departures in search of more stable academic environments". That very quickly came to pass, including the departure of Brennan herself.

The question of the appropriate faculty location for Government had a long history. Some of the most obvious academic synergies were with departments such as History or Philosophy that were central to the Arts Faculty, while there was a troubled relationship with Arts about the availability of Government as a central major sequence for Arts students as long as it remained in Economics. Within the Economics Faculty there was never a strong relationship between Government and Economics staff – a matter of some expressed regret for Dick Spann – although there were close links with Industrial Relations, especially in the production of the journal *Labour History*. However it was not any logic of academic groupings that determined the continued resolution of department staff members to stay in Economics whenever the question arose over the years. It was perceived self interest. The Faculty of Economics was better funded than Arts, and was generally managed more efficiently. Moreover, there were many years in the later part of the 20th century when funding cuts were much in evidence in the Arts Faculty, which had been consistently overspending its income. Moreover, in Economics there was an established policy of giving salary loadings for staff who could demonstrate large disparities with salaries that could be expected in the private sector. It did not matter that few Government teachers could satisfy those conditions; there was the hope that such generosity would spread across the Faculty. By the beginning of the 21st century the matter was being complicated by a growing awareness in the university, especially after the foundation of the Department of

> **Rebekah Grindlay**
>
> Currently a senior Australian diplomat, Rebekah graduated with First Class Honours in Government in 2001, with a thesis on conflict in Indonesia, before gaining a Masters in Public Policy at Princeton University's Woodrow Wilson School.  She has worked for the United Nations in Cambodia and Vienna and served in diplomatic assignments in New York, the Solomon Islands, Iraq and Pakistan, where she was Deputy High Commissioner from 2008-2011. She was recently Energy and National Security Fellow at the US Congress in Washington, and then Director of Australia's United Nations Security Council Taskforce. She has worked or travelled in over a hundred countries, and her curiosity about the world began early. While she was at Sydney University she travelled to Africa over the Easter break to climb Mt Kilimanjaro on her 21st birthday, and Professor Michael Jackson suggested she read Hemingway's *The Snows of Kilimanjaro* along the way. She subsequently discovered it was a subtle hint that she should stop writing dreadful waffly sentences, and instead emulate Hemingway's precision of thought and language. It was a lesson that has served her well.

Sociology within Arts, that the teaching of social science should be rationalised and given a higher profile.

A major reason for disquiet among Government staff in the years of the Faculty of Economics and Business was a growing fragmentation of the teaching of politics within the university. In a discipline as varied as political science there were always likely to be significant overlaps with other departments who wanted to teach aspects of their own concerns that had a strong political orientation. One could not seriously expect, for example, a History Department not to teach about war or international security, or a Philosophy Department not to teach political theory. Some replication was to be expected and was not an issue. For example, Government was initially not concerned over the activities of the small Centre for Peace and Conflict Studies in the Arts Faculty, one of whose founders had been Government's Peter King, but this accord came under pressure in 2005 when CPACS was allowed (or encouraged) by the Faculty of

Arts to offer undergraduate programs.[13] Similarly, the US Studies Centre, much of whose concern is with American politics, was not seen as a problem, and members of its staff have become associates of the Department of Government. In the early years of the new century, however, two new bodies were established in the University of Sydney that had politics as central concerns.

The first academic unit to threaten the interests of Government was the Graduate School of Government (GSG), a member of the wider Australian and New Zealand School of Government (ANZSOG), which was established at the University of Sydney in 2003. It was threatening enough that the very name "Government" was likely to cause confusion, but the added irony was that the GSG aimed to concentrate on public administration and Australian politics just when those matters were being downgraded in the title of the Discipline and in its teaching priorities. One of the few major initiatives in this area, the Master of Public Policy degree offered by the department would be directly threatened. The GSG also moved into an area vacated by the antecedents of the Government Department about 60 years earlier – practical courses in public administration and policy aimed at NSW public servants. The GSG also achieved something similar to what Professor Bland had managed even earlier – a commitment from the NSW Government to guarantee 50 public servants to enrol in the programs. After a meeting of Government staff at the end of 2005 Graeme Gill wrote to the Dean, Peter Wolnizer:

> First, we do not understand how the scoping of the future of the Graduate School of Government (GSG) can be done independently of Government and International Relations. The two are intellectually and practically intertwined.[14]

The letter went on to complain of the flawed consultation process with Government on the issue and the "reliance on external advice only from non-academics". It asked whether the conduct of the issue represented a "changed management process" in the Faculty and threatened that "if that were the case we would expect to bring the NTEU into the negotiation process". That final threat suggested that the issue of the GSG was only one sign of an imminent complete collapse of confidence by Government with the Faculty of Economics and Business. The complaints of Government were ignored, so that the GSG was set up within the Faculty independent of the Discipline of Government. In its early years a number of its courses were possible only by using teachers from the Discipline; in fact, one of them transferred directly from the Discipline to the GSG.

The second controversy concerned an initiative funded by the enthusiasm of a former University of Sydney graduate and noted philanthropist, Sir Michael Hintze, for an elite academic unit to concentrate on matters of international security. The result was the establishment of the Centre for International Security Studies (CISS). When it was first announced in 2005 the proposal was that it would be located in Arts. There it would replicate some of the concerns of the already established but tiny Centre for Peace and Conflict Studies (CPACS). This was at a time when the Discipline of Government was already redefining its mission to give a higher emphasis to international relations and international risk. More importantly it seemed to give weight to a suspicion that the Faculty of Arts was moving to host its own school of international politics in competition with the Faculty of Economics and Business.

If Arts was to mount its own program of political science, then the issue seemed to threaten the very existence of Government. A protest from Graeme Gill to the Dean of Arts over the perceived threat of a de facto school of politics in Arts received little sympathy from Professor Stephen Garton, the Dean of Arts at the time:

> And to be frank there is plenty of disquiet in certain sections of the Faculty about units run by Government which would

> seem to overlap significantly with offerings in Arts — so this is an issue that definitely cuts both ways.
>
> The claim that there was a systematic campaign to poach Government territory (of course we could have some very interesting debates about which disciplines own what territory and the answers to my mind might not be all that clear cut), and squeeze Government out of our curriculum don't seem to me to be sustainable in the light of later items in the Faculty agenda.[15]

Moreover, Garton made it clear that his preference was for Government to be located in Arts, which did nothing to ease a growing sense of paranoia in Government. In the event, the CISS was eventually established in 2006 within the Faculty of Economics and Business. However, it was completely separate from the Discipline, and in direct competition with it for postgraduate students in international and security studies. Moreover, it was located within the School of Business — alongside the new Discipline of International Business — not in the School of Economics and Political Science. The Dean of Economics and Business was no more sympathetic to complaints from Government than had been the Dean of Arts.

The Vice-Chancellor was little help. Replying to a complaint about the Chair in International Security, Gavin Brown basically admitted he was powerless.

> I am sure that you and your colleagues are aware that I face problems of Solomonic dimensions in balancing inter-disciplinary collaboration with respect for core disciplines especially when more than one Faculty claims them as fundamental to their mission.[16]

If the new corporate model of university management was designed to make the organisation more efficient, then this was an admission of failure by the CEO. Or perhaps — rather more in line with a corporate mentality – he was just clouding the issue until the decision was irrevocable.

Close to the heart of the problem for the Discipline of Government in the Faculty was the dominant belief in the business sections that business was concerned with the private sector, while Government's main concern was with the public sector. (What such people thought of the current fashion in State and Commonwealth governments for public private partnerships [PPPs] is not known.) This assumption became a part of the general discussion when the GSG was located in the Business School of the Faculty and slotted into a culture simply assuming that only accountants knew how to teach management. As Graeme Gill suggested, this was open to challenge:

> Second, I think that you do need to be wary of the argument that public sector and private sector management are essentially the same, and that what the GSG students need is much more accounting. This is not the view that I have heard from the GSG itself, its advisory board, or from within the state public service.[17]

This was not an argument likely to be received well by the Dean, the main participants in the Business School, nor by their supporters in the "big end of town" who were mentioned often in the correspondence.

Throughout 2005 rumours continued that Government would be relocated in the Arts Faculty. The context was the university's decision to begin a wide ranging inquiry into the teaching of social sciences which clearly involved other Faculties than Arts and Economics: Medicine, Social Work, Education and even Science, with disciplines like psychology and human geography, were frequently mentioned. However, the inquiry was initially conducted at management levels of the university – discussion between Deans and Deputy Vice-Chancellors was the main forum. Rumours became open after a

Professor Graeme Gill (Photo courtesy of GG)

university conference at Bowral that featured the matter of social science reorganisation. Dean Peter Wolnizer apologised to the Head of Discipline, Deb Brennan, that the location of Government had been discussed without any consultation with its personnel. He forwarded to her his aide-memoire sent to the Vice-Chancellor confirming that the GSG would be located in the Business School of the Faculty of Economics and Business. The second point was more confronting for Government:

> 2. In accordance with the University's change-management processes and policies, a sincere and collegial dialogue would

> be held with the Discipline about the merits of moving the Discipline, in whole or part, to the Faculty of Arts. If the Discipline were to be moved, it should be designated 'political science' and located, prospectively, within a new school of Social Sciences in Arts.[18]

To members of the Discipline of Government this indicated that the deal was already done, and that any "sincere and collegial dialogue" would only be to get Government to accept it. The threat contained in the words "in whole or in part" was particularly pointed; as the Dean of Arts subsequently confirmed, this involved a suggestion in the draft change management plan that some members of Government would be transferred to the GSG.[19] A meeting of Graeme Gill with the Vice-Chancellor, in the presence of the Deans of Arts and Economics and the relevant Deputy Vice-Chancellor, June Sinclair, resulted in the V-C indicating that the decision was not irreversible (to the dismay of his Deputy).

In hindsight it is clear that any discussions or arguments in 2005 were largely irrelevant. Decisions had already been made at the level of the Vice-Chancellor's closest advisors on these matters that the Faculty would become a dedicated school of business along the narrow lines of most American business schools, and that Government's future was in the Faculty of Arts, in a grouping of social science disciplines, whether its members wanted it or not. The only matters to be settled were the terms under which such a transfer would take place.

Late in 2006 the university presented a draft of its "Social Sciences Review", that demanded responses both from the Faculty of Arts and the Faculty of Economics and Business. The Deans of both Faculties were in agreement with its main points, which included the transfer of Government to the Faculty of Arts. Only details of the recommendations of the Review were likely to be modified. The head of Government wrote a strong response, arguing that it should remain with the business oriented disciplines. In December 2006, after a Strategic Retreat of the Faculty Executive Committee (FEC) in October, the FEC rejected the arguments in the submission from Government, although it left some room for further negotiation. The FEC determined that the two controversial politics units, the Graduate School of Government and the Centre for International Security Studies, "both intersect with business, government and public policy, and fit strategically within the Faculty in terms of research and (potential) program and unit-of study offerings". It expressed a desire to keep the discipline of Economics united with its cognate disciplines within the Faculty. On the other hand, the attitude to Government (GIR) was dismissive:

> GIR as it is currently constituted could contribute to and greatly enrich the Faculty, while still retaining its disciplinary focus. However, it is felt that GIR has consistently failed to demonstrate a strategic fit with the Faculty, particularly as the latter moves towards an internationally-competitive business/management school model. The Dean stressed that it is up to the discipline to present a convincing argument as to how they will help meet the University's expectations of the Faculty as a business school (for example, how they will contribute to the major programs and initiatives of the Faculty). FEC believed their submission to the Social Science Review did not make this case.
>
> The area of political science, in particular, could be of great value to a business/management school. It was asked whether the Faculty could formally separate the political science from the humanities/social science areas, with the former remaining in the Faculty and the latter moving to Arts. But it was questioned whether this would be worth the effort it may require, as GIR has declared itself as strongly united. Alternatively, this separation may be 'naturally' achieved

through a process of self-selection by discipline members once they are faced with the choice of going or staying.

Subsequent to the FEC meeting of 6th December, the Dean and Marcus O'Connor met with Leanne Piggott, Graeme Gill, Rod Tiffen and Michael Jackson from GIR. The group's response to the Social Science Review report was discussed in terms of its failure to mention business/management education and to demonstrate strategic good fit with the Faculty into the future.

The Dean requested that the group prepare a subsequent submission making a stronger case for their remaining in the Faculty. This second submission was discussed by FEC on 12th December. FEC expressed concern that, while the second submission adds to the first and raises a number of very relevant points, it still does not make a strong case for the strategic fit of GIR in a business/management school. Nor does it provide any concrete strategies for change at the discipline level.[20]

That seemed to be that. Despite the genuine attempts of Government to accommodate its teaching and research to the concerns of a business school, as outlined by Deb Brennan in the quotation above, those were deemed to be not sufficient. The business school wanted the international politics and the explicitly public policy people, but not any of the others. Australian politics, political theory, media studies, feminist or youth studies, and anything else was seen as not relevant to the concerns of business. What kind of business world were they envisaging, one could ask?

In one way – which did not alter the likely result of negotiations – Government had made the situation worse for itself at that period. The head of Discipline was a senior lecturer, Leanne Piggott. This had come about because all the professors and associate professors had declined to accept the position – most with reasons such as already having served their terms, or wanting to do some research, or being already in demanding administrative roles – but it was a pity that not one of them was willing. A group of senior lecturers had tried to force the issue by themselves refusing to accept the role. In the event Leanne was persuaded to accept the appointment but, through no fault of her own, no one so junior and so inexperienced was likely to be influential at such a difficult time.

When the university announced the results of its definitive Social Sciences Review in 2007 most members of the Discipline of Government accepted the result with a sense of inevitability. There was still some anxiety about the possibility of Government losing some resources by moving to a poorer and indebted faculty (fears which so far have not eventuated). Some concessions had been achieved. The whole group would be moved into a social science unit in the Faculty of Arts, meaning that the obvious desire of some leaders in the Faculty of Economics and Business to split the group had been denied. Another small victory was that the suggestion of changing the name of the department to "political science" did not eventuate; there would still be a Department of Government.

There had been no surprise at the eventual decision for Government and Political Economy to move. Both the two controversial politics units, the Centre for International Security Studies and the Graduate School of Government, were to be moved with Government to Arts, although their future relationship with Government remained to be determined.

What was a surprise was the later inclusion of the main Discipline of Economics in the shuffle – moving into the grouping of social science disciplines in Arts, but separating from its close relationship with disciplines such as economic statistics and finance which remained in the business school. That happened in 2012. What had been the old Faculty of Economics since the 1920s no longer had room for Economics! This simply accentuated the perception among many Government staff members that the losses from the Faculty of Economics and Business (soon to be rebranded as the School of Business) were gains for the Faculty of Arts and Social Sciences.

---

1 Bruce Williams, *Liberal Education and Useful Knowledge: A brief history of the University of Sydney 1850-2000*, Sydney, Chancellor's Committee, University of Sydney, 2002, p. 59.

2 Bruce Williams, ibid.

3 Interview with Graeme Gill, 23 April 2014, in Department of Government Oral History Project.

4 Dr Michael Crozier, Honours Benchmarking Report. Department of Government and International Relations, Faculty of Economics and Business, The University of Sydney, December 2003.

5 *Faculty of Economics Handbook, 1995*, p. 39.

6 Interview with Rod Tiffen, 29 April 2014, in Department of Government Oral History Project.

7 "Report on Developments. Kolej Antarabangsa (International College), Penang, 1994-1996", by Michael Leigh, in Hogan Papers, Leigh File.

8 *Faculty of Economics and Business Undergraduate Handbook, 2000*, p. iv.

9 Graeme Gill to Peter Wolnizer "Meeting with VC", 23 June 2005, in Hogan Papers, Gill File.

10 Interviews with Graeme Gill, 23 April 2014 and Rod Tiffen, 29 April 2014, in Department of Government Oral History Project.

11 See Table 4.2 in chapter 4.

12 Deborah Brennan to Stephen Nicholas, 23 September 2004, circulated to members of the Discipline's Board, 21 June 2005. Copy in Hogan Papers, Gill File.

13 Graeme Gill to Chair of the Academic Board, 6 October 2005, in Hogan Papers, Gill File.

14 Graeme Gill to Peter Wolnizer, 24 November 2005, in Hogan Papers, Gill File.

15 Stephen Garton to Graeme Gill, 19 October 2005, in Hogan Papers, Gill File.

16 Gavin Brown to Graeme Gill, 12 December 2005, in Hogan Papers, Gill File.

17 Graeme Gill to Peter Wolnizer, 23 June 2005, in Hogan Papers, Gill File.

18 Aide memoire of Peter Wolnizer to Gavin Brown, in Peter Wolnizer to Deborah Brennan, 21 June 2005, in Hogan Papers, Gill File.

19 Stephen Garton to Deborah Brennan, 20 June 2005, in Hogan Papers, Gill File.

20 Faculty of Economics and Business, "Summary of Key Discussion Points: Faculty Executive Committee Meetings 6th and 12th December 2006", Minutes of the Faculty of Economics And Business, 2006.

8

Into the Faculty of Arts and Social Sciences

Although the basic decisions about the placement of the Department of Government had been made progressively during 2005 and 2006, much negotiation and fine tuning would take place before they could be implemented. A meeting of the Executive Committee of the Faculty of Economics and Business reported in July 2007:

> Social Sciences Review
>
> The Dean advised that the Provost has approved the separation of the disciplines of Government and International Relations, and Political Economy from the Faculty of Economics and Business and their transfer to the Faculty of Arts with effect on 1 January 2008. Although the logistics of the transfer have not yet been finalised, both Mr Nigel Smith and Ms Prue Castleden are assisting in the process. The name of the School (possibly the School of Political and Social Enquiry) has not yet been confirmed, and accommodation for staff is still being sought. Any requests from staff who do not wish to move to Arts must be considered and agreed by both Deans.
>
> He reported that teaching of core mandatory units in Faculty programs is to stay with Economics and Business and noted that although current doctoral students supervised by Government and International Relations and Political

Economy will be considered Arts students from 2008, they will continue to reside within this Faculty. Negotiations about the financial arrangements between the Faculties are yet to be finalised, however he hopes that the changes do not place students at a disadvantage.[1]

As mentioned, there were still some details to be ironed out. The name of the Arts Faculty was to be changed to "Faculty of Arts and Social Sciences", while there was still some discussion before the name of the new School would be settled. Very soon it changed from a school of "enquiry" to one of "sciences" to match with the title of the Faculty. Thus the tentative title became "School of Political and Social Sciences", but it was quickly realised that the acronym for such a body would become SPSS, which guaranteed confusion with the name of a popular statistical software package that was in general use in some departments. The eventual branding, adopted without substantial disagreement, was "School of Social and Political Sciences" (SSPS).

Mark Scott

After dropping out of a law degree Scott spent some years teaching, then moved into the political orbit of the Greiner NSW Government, as an advisor to Education Ministers Virginia Chadwick and Terry Metherell. At the same time he took the opportunity to return to study, graduating with an MA in Government (1992). His thesis topic assessed the coverage of education reform under the Greiner Government by the *Sydney Morning Herald*, a topic he knew well from personal involvement. He went on to do further study of public administration at Harvard before returning to join the *Sydney Morning Herald*, where he soon became news editor and a member of the executive committee of Fairfax. He gained a reputation as a tough negotiator in industrial relations with journalists. In 2006 he was appointed Managing Director of the ABC as one of the late decisions of the Howard Coalition Government. He was confirmed for a second term in 2010, this time under a Labor Government. His time at the ABC has been marked by rapid technological change of digital and online media, which has required constant organisational reform, and by threats to levels of government funding.

One of the first signs of welcome for the department in the Faculty of Arts and Social Sciences was the unloosening of the freeze on replacing some of the jobs that had been stripped in the final years of the Faculty of Economics and Business. There was the promise that future jobs would be made available equitably in the new School according to traditional measures such as staff-student ratios and the need to fill significant gaps in the teaching program. Moreover, general university guidelines for staffing were amended at this time to give greater weight to research record in staffing decisions, which certainly benefitted the department. The size of the department more than doubled over the first five years in the new Faculty. The improvement can be seen in Figure 4.2, where new arrivals boosted the staff-student ratio from a worrying 31.1 in 2010 to a more comfortable 18.4 within four years. Part of this improvement (from 2013) was the addition of the CISS staff to the department, explained below. Nevertheless, there are still concerns in this area; even with a larger staff, important areas like public policy and Australian politics are underrepresented, while there is still a noticeable gender imbalance.

The leadership of the new SSPS was an important consideration. The job was advertised internationally and attracted a strong field. Meanwhile, Associate Professor Tim Fitzpatrick was seconded from his base in the departments of Italian and Performance Studies to become acting head. He had no institutional prejudices and so was in an ideal position to adjudicate any potential departmental rivalries between big disciplines such as Government and Sociology as they settled into a new management structure. The choice for a permanent head fell on Professor Simon Tormey, a political theorist who had a strong record of research and administration at the University of Nottingham, who took up his appointment in 2009. Although appointing a political scientist carried the risk of awakening rivalries with other social sciences such as anthropology and sociology, his status as coming from outside the university, and his skilful administrative style, have largely averted such risks. He has continued his publication record; the recent revised edition of his 2004 book, *Anti-Capitalism: a Beginner's Guide*, addresses the crises and developments in worldwide capitalism in the late 20th and early 21st Centuries.

The new School brought together at the beginning of 2008 departments such as Anthropology, Sociology and Social Policy, along with Government and International Relations (GIR) which once again became a department, and Political Economy, which was now formally a department for the first time. Also in the School was the Centre for Peace and Conflict Studies (CPACS), the Centre for International Security Studies (CISS), and the Graduate School of Government (GSG). Some of the concerns for Government about a fragmentation of the teaching of politics still remained, but further structural changes were being considered.

When the CISS had been established following a generous donation to the university from Michael Hinze in 2006, it was envisaged that a review of its operations should take place after five years. This review was put in place by the Faculty of Arts and Social Sciences in 2011, with professors Glenda Sluga, Stephen Castles, Graeme Gill and Malcolm Cook asked to report. There were special concerns about the pattern of funding, the strength of research and the teaching program. The review committee had no doubts about the worth of the Centre or the value of its research, but did have some questions about problems of both overlap and isolation. The committee "agreed that in this transitional phase the Centre is relatively disconnected from the intellectual life of the Faculty and its School". It recommended some improved form of integration:

> In line with the University's strategic policy on the Social Sciences, we recommend that the Faculty and SSPS with CISS look at developing structures and processes to improve the integration and coordination of CISS administration,

teaching and research activities in the School, and, more specifically, in relationship with GIR.[2]

What form such relationship between the Centre and the department should take was left for the Faculty and University to decide. The decision, made in 2012, was that the Centre would maintain its identity and name, but would be integrated into the Department of Government for coordination of teaching, research and funding. That came into full effect in 2013. This was a disappointment for most staff in the Centre, whose submissions to the committee had supported its continued independence, but it was welcomed in the Department of Government since it brought in a strong addition not just to numbers of staff but to the strength of teaching and research in international relations. Not surprisingly, some disagreements and stresses still need to be addressed in the day-to-day working out of the relationship.

The Graduate School of Government and the Centre for Peace and Conflict Studies did maintain their independence, but they were now placed in the same School of Social and Political Sciences, where the expectation of greater cooperation between all units was part of its reason for being. The surprise reorganisation, also in 2012, was the transfer of the Department of Economics from the School of Business to the Faculty of Arts and Social Sciences, that had not been part of the strategic plan of the old Faculty of Economics and Business when it was recommending which units should go and which should stay. Certainly there were problems of transferring just the Political Economy group to Arts and Social Sciences; would it become the de facto preferred strand of economics units within Arts, for example? How comprehensive would a School of Social and Political Sciences be without the inclusion of the Economics Department, many of whose teachers and researchers regarded themselves as social scientists rather than purveyors of business courses? There still remain problems about the teaching of economics in the university – still managed by separate bodies in two Faculties – which is the subject of a university review at the time of writing. For example, while Economics and Political Economy moved into Arts and Social Sciences, the discipline of Econometrics or Economic Statistics, now rebranded as "Business Analytics", remains in the Business School, along with Finance which has traditionally in most universities been regarded as a prime concern of Economics. Even within the one faculty the Department of Political Economy is located in the School of Social and Political Sciences, not in the School of Economics.

In the major project of the teaching of social sciences in the university, the SSPS is still very much in an early stage. The old BEc (Soc Sc) degree, which dates from the 1980s, has provided a matrix for a general social science degree in the new School, but, just as the earlier degree was seen by its authors as merely a stage in a transition towards something more comprehensive, so the newer one leaves plenty of room for amplification and improvement. It is a journey worth travelling. Similarly, the new School aims at bringing about greater cooperation between cognate social science disciplines and their teachers and researchers. That, also, is in a very early stage

Michael Knight

The highlight of Michael Knight's political career (NSW MP for Campbelltown, 1981-2001) was his role in making the Sydney Olympic Games such a successful event. He was Minister for the Olympics (along with other portfolios) from 1995 till 2001, as well as chair of the Sydney Organising Committee for the Olympic Games (SOCOG). Earlier he had graduated BA, with first Class Honours in Government (1979). At the time he was employed by Campbelltown Council, which gave him the material for a fascinating thesis topic: "A participant observer study of a local council". In 2007 he was appointed chair of the Sydney Olympic Park Authority, which maintains a link with his former achievements.

of development, but can only be seen as a worthwhile continuing endeavour.

When the first students enrolled in Government in 1948, after its establishment as a separate department, all were progressing towards a Bachelor of Economics. By 1950 the first few students studying for a BA started attending lectures. By 1962, when a full sequence of Government was available for Arts students from first year, Government also started becoming an occasional choice for students in other Faculties such as Science, Music, even Medicine, but these were never more than a tiny proportion of the enrolment. Then combined degrees were introduced, which made Government available for example, for students in Arts/Law and Economics/Law. The next major degree featuring Government was the Bachelor of Economics (Social Sciences) introduced in the 1980s. When the department moved to the Faculty of Arts and Social Sciences (FASS) the subject was available for a number of degrees in the new School of Business, but there has been very little interest since such a choice excludes another possible business oriented course. Overwhelmingly, now, Government is studied by students in the FASS. However, besides the simple BA, which still has strong support, there is the BA (Advanced)(Honours), BA (Asian Studies), BA (Languages), BA (Media and Communications), and the Bachelor of International and Global Studies (BIGS), while the old BEc (Soc Sc) has given way for a new Bachelor of Political, Economic and Social Sciences (BPESS). With the new School of Economics located in the FASS, the BEc is now part of the Faculty. The future is likely to see this list expanded. In many of these degrees some study of Government is highly recommended. There has been an associated multiplication of combined and double degrees.

---

1 Faculty of Economics and Business, Minutes of meeting of Faculty Executive Committee, 12 July 2007.
2 University of Sydney, "Review of Centre of International Security Studies 2011", p. 16.

9

In Australian political science

Political science has had its own institutional identity in the University of Sydney since the appointment in 1917 of two teachers as lecturers in Public Administration in the Faculty of Economics. There is little doubt that this was the beginning of the first school of politics in any Australian university. There are many other questions about the place of the Department of Government in a wider Australian context that spring to mind: How does it rank among all the schools of politics in the country? Does it have a recognisable character compared with others? What has it contributed to the discipline of political science in Australia? Has it achieved or wasted its potential? This chapter is an attempt to place the department into its Australian context and suggest answers to some of those questions.

A defining character?

Some political science schools in Australian universities have a reputation of striving for leadership in some particular aspect of the discipline. So, for example, the department in the University of Melbourne was for many years associated with a strong interest in the relationship between politics and psychology, while other universities have chosen to locate political science in a school of Australian society or perhaps to concentrate on international relations. To have a reputation for leadership in some aspect becomes a benefit when there are questions about the location of a "centre of excellence", and such a reputation becomes a pointer for postgraduate students when choosing their institution.

For at least half the lifetime of the department (and even before it was an established department) the Sydney school was recognised as the leader in the field of public policy and administration. Under Professors Bland, Partridge and Spann the name expressed the reality – first "Public Administration", then "Government and Public Administration". This does not mean that other fundamental strands of modern political science – political theory, institutional and regional politics, international relations, political sociology, etc. – were not offered, but the department was renowned for its expertise in public policy and administration. Dick Spann was the acknowledged leader within the department until his retirement in 1981, but his work was supported by people of the calibre of John Power, Ross Curnow, Tom Kewley, Joan Rydon, Trevor Matthews, Martin Painter, Helen Nelson, Peter Nelson and a number of others who had an interest in a particular policy area, even if public policy was not their first concern,

Don Harwin

Harwin joined the Liberal Party while at Sydney University, where he graduated BEc Hons (1985) with a thesis on the conservative "Call to Australia" movement founded by Rev Fred Nile. After graduation he worked for a number of Liberal State MPs and Ministers, gaining considerable expertise in electoral matters. He became President of Young Liberals (1988-90), and served on the State Executive of the party, providing strategic  advice on elections and redistributions. He was elected to the Legislative Council in 1999, becoming Opposition Whip in that chamber in 2003. He was a member of the Premier's committee to advise on publications for the "Sesquicentenary of Responsible Government in NSW, 1856-2006". After the election of the O'Farrell Coalition Government he became President of the Legislative Council in 2011, a position he still holds.

such as Henry Mayer and Rod Tiffen. Even after Spann's retirement the focus was retained with the recruitment of Christopher Hood as professor, and the appointments of Deb Brennan, Martin Laffin, Louise Chappell and Barbara Page, while into the present century they were followed by Allan McConnell, Paul Fawcett, Lyn Carson, John Mikler, Peter Chen, David Schlosberg and Anna Boucher, along with others having an interest in particular policy areas.

Despite a well entrenched and recognised excellence in this area, a deliberate decision was taken in 2000 as part of the rebranding of the Faculty of Economics and Business discussed in the previous chapter, to downgrade the relative significance of public policy and administration when the department was re-branded as a "Discipline", and its name changed to "Government and International Relations". It would be hard to make a case in the present century that the restored and renamed department is still a national leader in public policy as it was for so long. A recent preliminary Australian survey of academic disciplines – the ERA ranking of 2010 – rated "Policy and Administration" (Code1605) at the University of Sydney at level 2, which is below the international standard (although few Australian universities ranked higher).[1] Moreover, that is probably a little harsh, as the policy areas favoured by current staff members – the environment, immigration, and relations between government and business – merge seamlessly into international relations where a much higher ranking would be appropriate. Nevertheless, in the first years of the new century the department lost public policy specialists such as Martin Painter, Deb Brennan and Louise Chappell, who all primarily sought professional advancement, but no doubt they also could read the signals pointing to a reduced status for public policy studies in the newly renamed Faculty of Economics and Business.

The change of name to include "International Relations" clearly reflects a redirection of the department's public image and also of its recruitment policies. In an earlier chapter it was noted that

Troy Bramston

Troy earned his BEc Hons in 1998, writing a thesis on "Australian political leadership: the Keating years". Leadership has remained an interest for him, resulting in books on the Whitlam, Hawke and Wran governments, as well as a collection of "great Labor speeches that shaped history". He has worked as an advisor to Labor in opposition and in government, including a time as principal speechwriter for Kevin Rudd. He is now a notable  journalist, writing a regular column for the *The Australian* and contributing to *Sky News*. He remembers his time as a student in the Department: "The many academics who taught me in the years 1994 to 1998 did much to spark not only my interest and expand my knowledge but also taught me to think critically and analytically while maintaining one of the most important qualities in any writer or researcher: curiosity. I have very fond memories of lectures and tutorials with Martin Painter, Barbara Page, Lex Watson, Ernie Chaples and many others. Michael Jackson provided an unparalleled insight into Machiavelli's *The Prince* and memorably had us act out the infamous writer's play, *La Mandragola*. Rod Tiffen on the media and its interaction with politics was unparalleled. Randal Stewart was an encouraging honours thesis supervisor. Michael Hogan's knowledge of education policy and religion, and his lectures on Australian politics were always informative."

international relations was slow to develop as a strong strand in the department in the 1950s and 1960s, although it gathered strength in later decades. There is no question that there is a very strong demand from students for courses in international relations, especially boosted by the increased proportion of overseas students at the University of Sydney and the success of postgraduate degrees such as the Master of International Studies. The recent incorporation of the Centre for International Security Studies into the department has given a substantial boost to personnel and to the prospects for good graduate students, and there is no doubt that Sydney now has one of the strongest schools of international relations in Australia. Despite this assertion of excellence it is hard to claim international relations as a pointer to a defining character that might distinguish Sydney from other schools of political science in Australia, since virtually every other school regards it as a priority market that must be serviced.

There has always been a strong attention to comparative politics in the department – even in the years of Professor Bland, and it was given a central place in the curriculum under Dick Spann in the 1950s and 1960s – with courses in second year devoted to British, American and European variations on the liberal democratic model. This emphasis was reinforced with the reform of the curriculum in the 1970s, when there was a blossoming of courses in, for want of a better name, area studies. Southeast Asia featured strongly, especially Vietnam, Burma and Indonesia. Units on China and the Soviet Union were usually popular, as were those on Japan, Western Europe, the Middle East and the United States. Australian politics also has a place in that list. However, there has always been a reluctance of staff in the reformed curriculum to face directly the teaching of comparative politics rather than area studies. (One exception was a Government I semester unit offered by Graeme Gill comparing Australian and Soviet politics, but that course was not repeated.) The reason for a wariness about comparative politics is probably that the level of theory in the worldwide discipline of political science about comparative politics has always been disappointing. In the 1970s the dominant theoretical framework was still the American tradition of systems analysis and functionalism, leaning heavily on Parsonian theory. Textbooks such as Almond and Verba's comparison of five democratic regimes in *The Civic Culture* were occasionally set for students, but effectively for the sake of rejecting such a theoretical framework as of any worth for the areas being studied.[2] Consequently most of these courses have concentrated directly on wider democratic theory, highlighting economic development and underdevelopment, or authoritarian politics and military involvement. Most of the areas studied also have their own body of theory, as the literature on, for example, China or Russia, presents a variety of interpretations of the political history and culture of each state. So it can be said that area studies, rather than comparative politics, have been a feature of the Department of Government in a way that distinguishes it especially from smaller schools of politics that usually need to be less expansive in such courses. However, since the refocusing of teaching priorities within the department in the 1990s and the early years of the new century, area studies have lost their special place in the curriculum. Interestingly, many of the current applications from students wishing to enroll in a doctorate in the department (largely international students) nominate topics that assume a continued expertise in area studies.

General political theory and philosophy have always had a place in the curriculum, and the department has recruited a notable list of top-flight political theorists over the years – Percy Partridge, Henry Mayer, Carole Pateman, Patricia Springborg, Michael Jackson and, in recent years, John Keane and Alex Lefebvre, while theory is only one of the strengths for Pippa Norris. The current Dean of the Faculty of Arts and Social Sciences, Duncan Ivison, and the head of the School of Social and Political Sciences, Simon Tormey, are both renowned political theorists who are associated with the department. The department now co-hosts Pippa Norris' vast "Electoral Integrity Project", which is already producing an impressive amount of research and publication. Yet political theory has a low profile in the teaching program; courses have rarely been very popular except for a devoted clientele of students, and most students gaining a pass degree with a major in Government are able to avoid the courses completely – and do so.

It may seem surprising to suggest that Australian politics may be one of the key distinguishing strengths of the Department of Government in comparison with other politics schools in Australia. In the 1950s and 1960s that claim could be made based on the work especially of Henry Mayer in publishing the ground-breaking volumes of *Australian Politics: a Reader*, where many chapters were contributed by members of the department. However, in more recent times regular books on Federal elections have issued from other universities, and have featured only occasional contributions from this department. Similarly, a glance through articles on Australian politics in the two main local journals, the *Australian Journal of Political Science* and the *Australian Journal of Politics and History*, does not suggest that members of the Department of Government are taking a leading role. The main public intellectuals given a voice in the media on Australian politics are not from Sydney (as they were when Mayer was in his prime). Nevertheless, those measures would give a misleading impression of the reality. The strength of the department has not been primarily in national politics but in State and local politics. In 1954 Henry Mayer and Joan Rydon put together what can claim to be "Australia's first elections study" with a study of *The Gwydir By-election 1953: a study in political conflict*. This was followed in 1962 by Rydon and Spann's political chronicle of New South Wales politics, and later by the 30 or more volumes resulting from the committee for the "Sesquicentenary of Responsible Government in New South Wales 1856-2006", and the four volumes of NSW electoral studies from 1843 to 1999 in *The People's Choice*. No other State has a body of literature on its politics even remotely to compare with New South Wales.[3] Overwhelmingly, the contributions have come from the Department of Government and its graduates. (A member of the Sesquicentenary Committee commented correctly that virtually all members of the committee were former colleagues or students of Ken Turner.) At the local level there has been a continuing interest dating from Mayer & Rydon's study of the Gwydir by-election, to Connell and Gould's 1967 study of right wing politics in the Warringah electorate, to John Power's concentration in the 1965 State election in Manly, to Chaples and Nelson's 1985 compilation of local electoral case studies, to Michael Hogan's 2004 history of the Labor Party in the Sydney suburb of Glebe.[4] Some indication of the strength of this aspect can be seen in the recent welcome promotion of Rodney Smith to a Chair with the title of Professor of Australian Politics; belatedly Government joins Sydney's History Department which has a Chair of Australian History (from 1988), and English which has its Chair of Australian Literature (from 1968).[5]

Despite the prominence at various times in its history of studies in public policy and administration, international relations or Australian politics, it is probably fair to say that the Department of Government has not aimed for excellence in any one area at the expense of others. It has not tried to define itself by narrowing the scope of political science. Instead, it has endeavoured to cover the field, as was made possible by the relatively large size of the teaching faculty since the 1960s. It probably reflects the general state of the discipline in Australia in that it has always been an eclectic school of politics, refusing to mirror an American model reliant on statistical analysis, and willing to accommodate a wide range of theoretical and ideological approaches. Recruitment of staff has seen the appointment of new members trained primarily as historians, sociologists, anthropologists

---

Antony Green

With Sydney degrees in Science (1981), majoring in Mathematics and Computer Science and also in Economics (1989), with Honours in Government, Antony had the perfect background to become Australia's foremost psephologist, or election analyst. His Honours thesis, unsurprisingly, was a study of "The Senate and the Australian Voter". Within a few years of his graduation he was employed by the ABC, commentating on the NSW election of 1991. His own computer program has become the database upon which ABC TV commentary and graphics has been based since that time, although Antony's amazing memory for names and facts would enable him to comment very well without it. He is the author of numerous monographs and book chapters on electoral matters, and his journalist skills are sought by various newspapers and journals when an election is in the offing. He was an honorary recipient of the Doctor of Letters from the University of Sydney in November 2014.

or philosophers, as well as statistically literate political scientists. If one approach is characteristic of the department it is probably a preference for an historical perspective on political issues. That has come about partly because of the large proportion of area study specialists over the years for whom history cannot be ignored, and from the era (before the 1980s) when Australian history seemed to be regarded by the History Department in the University of Sydney as barely worth studying. The eclectic nature of the department can be regarded as a strength or, especially for advocates of a narrower scientific definition of political science, a weakness.

Ranking the Department of Government

In the current era of the corporate university attempts to give a ranking to the achievements of universities, faculties, departments and even individual staff have come to occupy a central place in the administration of higher education. On the resulting scores depend funding, the shape of future restructuring, and even the academic tenure of individual teachers. The academic marketplace needs to know which product is best, or which at least provides value for money. The usual criteria in the academic world make comparisons of: research productivity – measured by grants awarded or by actual publications, citation indexes, and peer reputation; teaching standards; supporting infrastructure; international affiliations; and a host of other measurable factors such as numbers of undergraduate and postgraduate students, or effective placement of postgraduates. It is easy to be scornful of the reliance on numbers to reveal quality, but a desire to know which academic institution is better than another has a tradition going back into the dawn of history. The modern world is merely committed to a set of measures that promise to advance beyond the traditional assumption that "everyone knows that Oxford/Paris/Bologna/Edinburgh/Salamanca/ is best, while red-brick or colonial colleges are for people who can't afford that standard". The motto of the University of Sydney – "*Sidere mens eadem mutato*" – is testimony to the strength of that mentality in the mid-19th century; "we are Oxbridge in the southern hemisphere"! It is wise to be suspicious of how adequate some of the numbers are to do the job, but the task itself demands a response.

So, how does the Department of Government at the University of Sydney compare with other schools of politics within Australia and in the world? Within the University of Sydney the department has always had the reputation among students as providing some of the best teachers and among staff as having a remarkably fertile record of published research. While it was located in the Faculty of Economics, and then of Economics and Business, the numbers of published articles, chapters and books were almost always well above any other section of the Faculty. However, that reputation, although it has helped attract students and aid recruitment of good staff members, means little for a wider comparison.

Since the 1970s the Sydney department has always been among the larger schools of politics in the country. After the spectacular rise in student numbers the full-time academic staff settled down to average about 25 during the 1970s, which usually included about five tutors or lecturers on short-term contracts. By 1995 there were 27 on the establishment staff, plus three Associate Lecturers. In 2005, by then suffering the freezing (or deliberate stripping) of positions in the Faculty of Economics and Business, the numbers of establishment staff had declined to 19 (although there had been no reduction in student numbers). After transferring to the Faculty of Arts and Social Sciences, and incorporating the Centre for International Security Studies, the staffing position improved markedly, so that by 2013 the staff list contained 40 positions, including half a dozen who were generally unavailable for undergraduate teaching duties because of commitments to administration or research. Size is an important consideration in any comparison across Australia; it is difficult to make fair comparisons between large and small institutions.

The QS World University Ranking, an international index that incorporates information about most of the criteria mentioned above (international reputation, employer reputation, citation index for staff, publications), has published data for four years (2011-14). The latest version ranked "Politics and International Studies" at Sydney as 24th of 200 universities surveyed – a high ranking exceeded in Australia only by the Australian National University (seventh).[6] Moreover, Sydney's ranking has been improving each year. The index has been criticised for methodological reasons, notably by the Australian Group of Eight Universities, which analysed a number of international university rankings and noted that "all the indexes are deficient methodologically" and that universities should not place too great a reliance on any of them.[7] Nevertheless, there does tend to be considerable agreement among all indexes about the place of Australian universities in the world higher education market – and this is one of the few that provides comparative data on individual disciplines.

One of the principal guides to excellence is the research output of staff members. One measure used by universities – following government guidelines – ranks the amount of money that comes to each unit through grants awarded either from government sponsored bodies like the Australian Research Council (ARC) or from industry or other sources. In any one year it is possible to make a rough comparison by examining the list of grantees and noting their university and departmental affiliation. In 1989, for example, the *APSA Newsletter* recorded that almost half of the ARC grants in Australian political science for that year came from Sydney researchers, with major grants for Gill, Teiwes and Painter.[8] However, a fair comparison would need to be over a period of four or five consecutive years, and even then there are so many distinct categories of grants, and so many projects where grants are shared in ways that are not immediately obvious, that the task of comparison would need the help of a substantial ARC grant, and would still be tentative. What can be asserted is that the record of members of the Department of Government has been outstanding. At the beginning of 2014, 13 members of the department held current ARC grants. Pippa Norris holds an Australian Laureate Fellowship that gives employment to a number of researchers attached to the department. To that list should be added another for an Emeritus Professor, Fred Teiwes. Some of these, notably Graeme Gill and Fred Teiwes, have held multiple ARC grants over the years. Many others held grants in earlier years but not currently. And it should be pointed out that looking only at ARC grants overlooks many other people who have been successful in winning awards and grants from international and national specialist research organisations, such as the NSW Sesquicentenary fund, and from different levels of the University of Sydney.

A more direct – and arguably better – measure of research is to examine actual published research in the form of articles, books, book chapters, conference papers and publications in other reputable media. There are also problems of comparison here. Academic journals can be ranked so that in each academic discipline there are top journals and also-rans. How does one achieve a fair quantification of the worth of an article in the top journal and another in a lesser ranked publication? In recent years the Australian government has sponsored a project to assess "Excellence in Research for Australia" (ERA), designed by the two main funding agencies, the ARC and NHMRC. A trial survey of the ERA was conducted in 2009, and more comprehensive (but still not complete) surveys in 2010 and 2012. Publications for each university are assessed using the Field of Research (FoR) clusters of coded discipline areas. Thus for example, an academic writing an article on environmental initiatives of the United Nations might report the work under relevant codes for political science (Code 1606), and policy studies (Code 1605), and environmental management (Code 0502), or any of another half dozen possible codes. The 2012 ERA

Report has offered a comparison of each Australian university for most of these codes. Institutions are ranked on a five-point scale so that a score of three signifies that the institution has reached a standard equivalent to an international average of quality, while scores below three are less, and those above three are better or much better than the international standard. The report on political science (Code 1606) indicates that the University of Sydney has achieved a ranking of five on that scale. Only three other Australian universities – the Australian National University, University of Queensland and Griffith University – have achieved the same grade. It needs to be stated that this is not directly a ranking of departments but rather of discipline areas. Publications coded as political science may issue from any number of units in the university. At the University of Sydney, for example, it is highly likely that some publications from the Graduate School of Government and the US Studies Centre, and perhaps the Department of Political Economy, would be reported with the same code. Nevertheless, according to Professor Graeme Gill, who prepared the local report for the ERA, more than 80% of the material came from the Department of Government.[9] One would like to follow such a ranking over a period of years to have greater confidence in the results (the University's ERA score for political science in the 2010 survey was four, for example, along with Griffith, Melbourne and Queensland, where only the ANU was awarded five). It is safe to say that, according to such published rankings, the Department of Government is at present one of the best publishing schools of political science in the country. As it always has been.

Another set of indicators which are difficult to quantify point to the reputation of the department in the world of political science in Australia and worldwide. Reputation affects the kind of people who seek to gain appointment to the department or who enrol for postgraduate study. In both these areas the reputation of Government has held up strongly from the beginning to the present day. Any advertisement for an academic position attracts a field of top class applicants, so that to be appointed to the staff already carries the connotation of excellence. Similarly, for reputational reasons any department pays close attention to the number and quality of its prospective research students. The Sydney department attracts many more applicants for doctoral study than it can possibly accept, while the level of candidates accepted and guided through to completion is extremely high.

Contribution to the discipline

One of the shortcomings of the kind of measures mentioned above is that they all tend to be snapshots for a short period of time. The ERA, for example, involves listing publications over the previous six-year span. Yet the worth of an institution like the Department of Government, which in one form or another is now nearly a century

Rodney Cavalier

Already an activist on the left of the Labor Party, Cavalier graduated with an Honours Arts degree (BA, 1977) in Government, writing his thesis on: "An analysis of the Australian Labor Party, NSW Branch, 1971-75". After a term on Hunters Hill Council, he won the marginal seat of Fuller in the "Wranslide" of 1978, holding the redistributed seat of Gladesville in 1981 and 1984. He served briefly as Minister for Energy and Minister for  Finance in early 1984, but his major contribution was as Minister for Education from 1984 to 1988. He saw himself as a reforming Minister, intent on combatting the policy stranglehold exercised by the militant Teachers' Federation. Not surprisingly it was a period of policy confrontation, with Cavalier emerging with a technical knockout over the Federation. After losing his seat in 1988 he became a journalist, writer of Labor history and a harsh internal critic of developments in the modern Labor Party, as evidenced in his influential book, *Power Crisis: the Self Destruction of a State Labor Party* (CUP, 2010). He was the chair of the Committee for the Sesquicentenary of Responsible Government in NSW, set up by Premier Bob Carr. He is a notable cricket "tragic", and for 13 years he was a high profile Chairman of the Sydney Cricket Ground Trust.

Terry Metherell

Metherell was a doctoral graduate of the History Department at the University of Sydney, where his thesis examined the conscription issue in Australia during the Great War (PhD, Arts, 1972). He came to the Department of Government as a full time tutor from 1973 to 1975, where his Afghan jacket and general demeanor proclaimed him a radical leftist, crossing swords with Henry Mayer on the issue of democratization in the Department. It came as a surprise to his former colleagues, therefore, when he won the solid Liberal seat of Davidson in 1981, holding it till his resignation in 1992. He became a controversial Minister for Education and Youth Affairs in the Greiner Government (1988-90), intent on dismantling many of the reforms introduced by his predecessor, Labor's Rodney Cavalier. He, like Cavalier, crossed swords with the Teachers' Federation, to such an extent that placards appeared on Sydney highways: "Come back Rodney, all is forgiven". His resignation from Parliament in 1992, after being offered a public service job by the Premier, was the occasion for the downfall of Greiner who was found by ICAC (a finding later overturned) to have acted corruptly in making such an offer in order to get Metherell to resign.

old, needs to be put into a much longer historical context. In a sense all the earlier chapters of this book have this task in mind, although there has been no attempt to make constant comparisons with other schools of politics. Yet there does exist one measure of excellence that can be traced over those years – its academic staff.

Any large university department, in any discipline, will tend to have the occasional passenger among its members. That is true of the Department of Government, if the opinions of other staff members are sought. Yet there have been very few over the years, and it is very difficult to find any who have not contributed significantly. There have been occasional members who have not been up to expectation in research and publication, but virtually all have been excellent teachers and contributors in other ways. There have also been occasional members who have been regarded by their colleagues as not pulling their weight in teaching responsibilities, but the names that come to mind over the years have all been highly productive in research. What is genuinely remarkable is that most of the best researchers, with outstanding publication records, have also been dedicated and popular teachers. Some of the professors have led the way in this regard – Francis Bland, Henry Mayer, Dick Spann, Graeme Gill and Michael Jackson, to name the outstanding ones. Their influence has been contagious among their colleagues.

In Appendix A is a list of full-time academic staff from the establishment of the department in 1947, with a few part-time members for the earlier period. There are 101 names, and readers are invited to peruse the list and make their own judgements about the standard of recruitment adopted over time. One piece of information that emerges from the list is the remarkably high number of teachers in the department who have been promoted or progressed to chairs, either in the University of Sydney, at other Australian universities, or to overseas institutions. The names marked with an asterisk number 40, which is well more than a third of the total. That does not include others, such as Dick Spann, who were appointed as professors to the department from outside and stayed in Sydney. Nor does that figure include an extra 14 names of non-tenured staff, graduates or research staff of the department who have later been promoted to chairs, bringing the total so far to 54. Within Australia, staff members and graduates of the Department of Government have been appointed to chairs in most of the Group of Eight universities (ANU, Melbourne, Queensland, Adelaide, Western Australia, UNSW and Sydney) and to a host of other institutions. There has been no attempt to provide a comparison with other Australian schools of politics, but it would be very surprising if any other school came even close to such a record.

In the early years that saw the establishment of political science as a strong discipline across most Australian universities the role of the department, especially of Henry Mayer and Dick Spann, in setting up the Australian Political Science Association (APSA), and creating the journal which later became the *Australian Journal of Political Science (AJPS)* has already been discussed in an earlier chapter. That coordinating role has continued, with the department providing various presidents of APSA, hosting conferences, and providing editorial committee members for many national and international journals. The Australian study of political science was put on its feet largely by the example, the organisational drive and the diffusion of personnel coming from Sydney in the 1950s, 1960s and 1970s.

Looking at the comparative index data, along with an historical perspective, at least two confident assertions can be made. First, the Department of Government is one of the strongest schools of politics in Australia, one of only a few that can compete on even terms for prestige with the Australian National University, given all the advantages which that institution has had since its creation as a research centre in any comparison (although some of that advantage has recently been reduced).

Perhaps more important: over a period of nearly a century, but especially in the last 70 years, the Department of Government at the University of Sydney has been the cradle of political science in Australia.

---

1 http://www.arc.gov.au/era/outcomes_2010/Institution/SYD, accessed 11 September 2013.
2 Gabriel Almond & Sidney Verba, *The Civic Culture: Political Attitudes and Democracy in Five Nations*, Princeton, Princeton University Press, 1963.
3 Henry Mayer & Joan Rydon, *The Gwydir by-election: a study in political conflict, 1953*, Canberra, ANU Press, 1954; Joan Rydon & RN Spann, *New South Wales Politics, 1901-1910*, Melbourne, Cheshire, 1962. Michael Hogan & David Clune (eds.), *The People's Choice: Electoral Politics in 20th Century New South Wales*, Sydney, Parliament of NSW and University of Sydney, (3 vols.), 2001; Michael Hogan, Lesley Muir & Hilary Golder (eds.), *The People's Choice: Electoral Politics in Colonial New South Wales*, Sydney, Federation Press, 2007. Quotation by Murray Goot in the "Henry Mayer" entry in Brian Gallagher & Winsome Roberts (eds.), *Oxford Companion to Australian Politics*, Oxford, OUP, 2007, p. 334.

4 RW Connell & Florence Gould, *Politics of the Extreme right: Warringah 1966*, Melbourne, Cheshire, 1967. John Power, *Politics in a suburban community: the NSW election in Manly, 1965*, Sydney, SUP, 1968. Ernie Chaples & Helen Nelson (eds.), *Case Studies in New South Wales Electoral Politics*, Sydney Department of Government, University of Sydney, 1985. Michael Hogan, *Local Labor: A History of the Labor Party in Glebe 1891-2003*, Sydney, Federation Press, 2004.

5 In 2014, 18 professors were listed by the Department of Government as members, emeriti, associates or affiliates.

6 http://www.topuniversities.com/university-rankings/university-subject-rankings/2014/politics#sorting=rank+region=+country=+faculty=+stars=false+search=. Accessed 16 September 2014.

7 Go8 Backgrounder, *World University Rankings: ambiguous signals*, October 2012. http://www.go8.edu.au/__documents/go8-policy-analysis/2012/go8backgrounder30_rankings.pdf. Accessed 13 September 2013.

8 *Beyond the Cringe*, (Occasional Newsletter of the Department of Government), Winter 1989, p. 8.

9 Interview with Graeme Gill, 23 January 2014, in Department of Government Oral History Project.

10

Challenges and opportunities

The task of an historical narrative is to open up the past – among other reasons so that its consequences in the present may be suggested. Historians are not expected to be prophets nor even to hazard guesses about the future. Nevertheless, by observing the evolution of an institution over time it is possible to see some of the developments of the present that will demand future change and accommodation. What direction those changes might take is a matter only of speculation. There are at least two contemporary phenomena that will inevitably force the department to adapt or decline – the technological pressures of the digital revolution, and the political and economic trend towards further corporatisation of Australian universities.

The competitive university

As discussed in Chapter 7, since the late 1980s a fundamental change has been introduced into the funding and management of Australian universities. The Commonwealth Government (of whatever political colour) has been withdrawing more and more from being the guarantor of adequate funding, leaving universities to make their own arrangements in an increasingly competitive environment. The most obvious changes so far have been as a result of the decision to allow them to charge overseas students full fees for degree programs. The Commonwealth Budget for 2014-15 threatened to extend that licence to Australian students and to lift all restrictions on the level of fees that can be charged, so that elite universities such as Sydney will be looking at very considerable increases in all student fees. No matter what is the political fate of that controversial Budget, some such development is virtually inevitable in the near future. The University of Sydney will become, even more than at present, an elite institution. Despite assurances by the Vice-Chancellor that the ability to pay high fees will not determine who gains entry, it seems certain that the overwhelming catchment for future students will be found among the well-to-do, with a limited scholarship opportunity for gifted students without that background. One can speculate about the social impact of such developments, but who knows what impact they will have on the student base of the Department of Government?

The constant ranking of universities and disciplines in what is now an international higher education market indicates pressure on every level of a university to make the – sometimes tough – decisions to adapt, so as to be more competitive and to attract students and resources that might otherwise be directed to other Australian and overseas universities. At the departmental level it is impossible to say what decisions and choices will be made, but some guesses can be made about their likely nature. For example, to cement its position as one of the best schools of politics in Australia, in the terms discussed in Chapter 9, questions will almost certainly be asked about continuing to attempt to be an eclectic school that covers the field of the study of politics without having a core of internationally ranked excellence in one or two areas. Will a future department see its future as building further on its current strength in international relations? Will that mean that recruitment of staff will focus on teachers and researchers in that area, with other strands such as Australian politics or public policy left to wilt?

Emily Scanlon

Emily Scanlon graduated with an MEc (Soc. Sc.) in 2002, writing a thesis on a "Machiavellian analysis" of civil and military relations in the 21st Century. She later earned an MA in International Law (USYD) and a MA in Journalism (UTS). During her undergraduate degree she was awarded the Mayer Prize for Best Student in Political Theory and studied International Mediation and Conflict Resolution at both Rotterdam and The Hague. She has worked as a journalist in the ABC (2004-7) and a media liaison officer with the Department of Foreign Affairs and Trade (2006-9) before making a career change to become a registered psychologist. In this capacity she has become a valued member of the External Advisory Committee of the Department of Government.

Another choice that will be presented lies in the relative importance between undergraduate and postgraduate teaching. The past 30 years has seen some adjustment already, with relatively greater attention to coursework Masters degrees than in previous years and a strengthened doctoral program. Will the Department of Government aim to build its reputation on its postgraduate school – possibly at the expense of an established excellence in undergraduate teaching? There are suggestions, discussed below in the section on the ongoing electronic revolution, that online teaching will become more easily adaptable for undergraduate courses than for research degrees. There will certainly be temptations to release more permanent staff for postgraduate teaching and research if undergraduate courses can be staffed by part-timers who can correspond online with undergraduate students in courses merely designed by senior and permanent staff.

Two changes that have already been signalled in the University of Sydney have a yet uncertain future. One – that is driven by the importance of staff research profiles in determining both current funding for departments and their international ranking – is the fashion of appointing "star" professors, who do little or no teaching, but are expected to boost the departmental profile with further publication and successful grant applications. This is a pattern that has a long history in elite American universities, but which seems to be experiencing some resistance in Australian departments. Departments are likely to prefer short-term appointments of junior research-only staff to tenured appointments of senior "stars" whose best work may be behind them. The most important factor is likely to be economic. Graeme Gill has pointed out that: "I think the Faculty has a real problem in terms of those who are producing money and those who aren't, and there are a lot of research-only positions in departments that can't sustain them."[1]

The other is a recent suggestion of the Vice-Chancellor that more scope be given for the appointment of teaching-only staff. That is part of the history of the Department of Government, when the rank of Senior Tutor or Principal Tutor was a tenured position until the 1970s. Henry Mayer, Ken Turner and Lex Watson began their careers in that way, while numerous tutors and contract lecturers in the 1970s and 1980s served with distinction as full time teachers without tenure. The contemporary environment, however, where research profile is so highly esteemed, means that such non-research appointments will come only at the expense of proven researchers, and is likely to be resisted. But who knows what will be the future relative demands of economic contribution from accomplished researchers as against the need for dedicated undergraduate teachers?

The continuing electronic revolution

A significant 1986 entry in the occasional Departmental newsletter, *Beyond the Cringe,* heralded a fundamental change in the way both staff and students went about their tasks. Lynne Thomson, a treasured research assistant attached to the department, gave a report on the introduction of computers in the department in a column entitled "Technobabble":

> This was the year we became computerised. New arrivals included 3 IBM clones and a big fat IBM PC-AT with 30mb of memory. These acquisitions have enabled more staff to become adept at word processing, given us powerful in-house statistical analysis capability, and opened up the world of data bases and graphics for the Department. A modem was also added, putting the Department on-line to the University Computing Centre. ...
>
> Next year, hopefully, will see the addition of another IBM PC-AT (or at least a hard disc for one of the clones) and some super software (dBase III+ for one). So now we are off and running.[2]

To think that staff members in the Department of Government lusted after "a big fat IBM PC-AT" with a clunky screen that took two people to lift onto a desk and a whole 30mb of memory! These words are being typed on a machine with a cardboard-thin screen and 8 gigabytes of memory – in the order of 270 times more powerful. A reader of these lines in the third or fourth decade of the current century will smile at the pathetic memory and speed of both machines. Thompson's column had the postscript (necessary for most of the academic staff at that time): "Translations of this article are available from the author". In fact the department was rather slow off the mark. The Economics Faculty office had been using a dedicated word processor and a dot-matrix printer for a few years before that, and some staff had been using a separate keyboard, with a one-line read-out, and with work saved to a tiny matchbox-sized cassette, that could transfer the file to the Faculty word processor for editing and printing. In some scientific Faculties mainframe computers had been essential tools from the 1960s. By the 1970s the University Computing Centre had mainframes and workstations available for academic use – which was exploited by at least one Government course taught by Ernie Chaples.

Thomas Moore

With a brilliant undergraduate career at Sydney (BA Hons 1, 1999, University Medal, Professor Joan Rydon Scholarship), Moore completed his doctorate at the University of Edinburgh. His interests are in political theory and international relations. He is currently a Principal Lecturer in the Department of Politics and International Relations at the University of Westminster, where, according to his own account, his research "explores the geopolitical and ethical dimensions of contemporary just war theory". He remembers learning about power in Michael Jackson's class: "We had a fantastic workshop on Machiavelli which involved us reading Mandragola (the Mandrake Root), and this has always stuck with me as one of the most enjoyable experiences at the University of Sydney. We laughed, but we also learned about looking beyond the formal dimension of politics to see how politics manifests itself within popular discourses".

The general introduction of personal computers in the 1980s was to revolutionise academic life, as it did most other aspects of society. The first obvious impact in the Government Department was on non-academic staff, rather than academics. The first PCs went to the professorial and general office secretaries, who found that it transformed the work of typing that had dominated such jobs for many years. No more painting white-out over typing errors, and no more complete retyping of second and third drafts of academics' articles and books. No more having to decipher Henry Mayer's or Peter King's illegible handwriting. However, as soon as academics themselves began to have access to the machines an unanticipated change took place in the relationship between academic and non-academic staff. Academics were expected to do their own typing and to learn keyboard skills – and then do their own photocopying. Non-academic staff, at the same time, were relieved of those major and time-consuming responsibilities. Within a very short time they were expected to become managers and administrators (as professorial secretaries already were), with the result that extra qualifications were demanded beyond the customary business school training in typing and shorthand. The University offered courses for non-academic staff to update their skills to understand electronic spreadsheets, databases and other programs.

At the University of Sydney, as in most other similar institutions, this development occurred at the same time as the university was moving towards a more corporate structure modelled on commercial management. New recruits to university non-academic staff would tend to be graduates and given management tasks at a Faculty level. In the Faculty of Economics, for example, the change in the numbers and role of general staff between the 1980s and the end of the century was remarkable. In 1980 the Faculty Office on the northern wing of Level 2 of the Merewether Building was the size of three standard academic rooms. By 2000 that space had been incorporated into a new extension to the building that housed a dozen Faculty officers while others were scattered through the two buildings of the Faculty. Meanwhile, in the Department of Government by 2000, one person attended the department office for enquiries, a graduate assistant was shared between Government and Political Economy, while professorial secretaries, general typists and general research assistants had disappeared.

The early years of the revolution moved fairly slowly, as more teachers gained the use of their own PCs and printers and started to learn new-fangled software as well as keyboard skills. The corridors of the Government Department hosted frequent informal discussions about the relative merits of different word processing programs; *Microsoft Word* was just coming in, while programs like *Multimate* or *Wordperfect* had their champions until *Microsoft Office* swept all before it. One has to wonder how many academic hours, days and weeks have been spent learning new software, updating to newer versions (while swearing at the way learned routines have been consigned to unknown corners of the program), and waiting for help from overworked support staff when either the hardware or the software wouldn't respond. This has become a major part of academic life, especially with the addition of local university programs to check salary payments, get information for tax returns, apply for grants and do a hundred other administrative tasks. Of course, there have been compensations of time and convenience as more and more information has become available without travel, while frustrations about finding a desired journal missing from the library shelves have largely disappeared.

In the 1980s there was still a popular feeling that computer technology was not going to change anything substantial in research and teaching. One discussion in the department about what computers could contribute to the study of history concluded that the answer was: not much. Then came the internet. Some scientific departments at the University of Sydney had been using a similar network that connected them to other universities across the world since the late 1960s, but the modern internet did not arrive until the protocols were made commercially available at the beginning of the 1980s and eventually resulted in the familiar World Wide Web in 1989. Staff in the Department of Government were using email facilities by the beginning of the 1990s, and soon learned of the new world of rapid information transfer, chat groups, blogs and the whole array made possible by the commercialised WWW. It was to completely transform the way both teaching and research would be conducted.

Probably the most telling symbolic demonstration of the impact of information technology on both teaching and research has been the gradual transformation of Fisher Library from a vast deposit of books to an electronic hub for access by staff and students to resources that previously had only been available after spending considerable sums of money on travel and postage. The academic time that was seemingly wasted on learning the technology is returned generously by almost instantaneous access at the terminal to international journals and databases, as well as contact with colleagues on the other side of the world. It comes as a shock for old-timers to wander through Fisher and ask where are the books. There are, of course, still books in the library, but most space is given over to desks and computers where scholars can reach out to the world (or ignore it and have a good gossip!).

Researchers spend their working time at their computers. There is very little difference whether the computer is at the office or at home, so most teaching staff prefer to work from home, where they are not disturbed by students and colleagues. In the new century the corridors of the Department of Government are usually almost empty and there are very few open doors. At the beginning of each semester, or at times for handing back essays, students still crowd around the doors of the department office or the course supervisor, but normally teachers are present only when they are to take a class or for the few hours of scheduled office consultation with students. It is pointless for a student to wander along the corridors hoping to drop in on their teacher, as was the custom in a former age.

Teachers still give lectures and take tutorials, but a great deal of communication with students is via email and dedicated teaching programs like *Blackboard* and its variants. Since students have access to the same instant flow of information on every subject under the sun, part of a teacher's task is to convince students that *Wikipedia* and *Google* are not automatically authoritative sources. Moreover, unlike in pre-IT days when mediocre students were faced with a problem of finding some worthwhile readings for a particular essay topic, now the problem is that there are too many, and it is difficult to teach discrimination between academically relevant sources and popularised rubbish. Then there is the problem of plagiarism, which has always existed in universities, but has now become endemic, especially since high schools teach students how easy it is to get information online so that many students are completely bemused by the very concept

Annie Corlett

Annie earned a Bachelor of Economics in 1980 from the University of Sydney, majoring in Government. She was an Executive Director of two publicly listed mining companies. Annie was elected a member of the University of Sydney Alumni Council in 2009. She is currently President of the Alumni Council and Chair of the Regulatory Taskforce, as well as a member of the External Advisory Committee for the Department of Government. Annie has had a long time involvement and active engagement in the not for profit sector. Currently, she is a National Board Member of Lifeline Australia. Her involvement with Lifeline began in 2007 as an accredited Lifeline Telephone Crisis Supporter. She has also been a Lifeline Facilitator and Supervisor on Call. She supports the Homicide Victims Support Group (NSW) as a Volunteer Court Supporter/Counsellor and volunteers on the Support Line for this group. Annie is a mother of four university graduates.

of plagiarism. Teachers also have access to programs that can identify plagiarised work, but the problem is more notional than bureaucratic, as the very concept of plagiarism has become foreign to many students for whom the internet is where they live. Cut-and-paste is how they write.

In lectures most students have a laptop or pad in front of them, which can be a wonderful resource if the teacher wants to switch between internet sites or give references to sites from which students can download interesting information. However, perhaps the student is writing an essay for another subject, sending emails to friends, or playing games? There is strong pressure from students for teachers to make available taped copies of lectures or at least the electronic slides from the *Powerpoint* presentation. One has to ask, what is the point of face-to-face lecturing if most information is transferred electronically? Part of the response is to insist that lectures should not be about imparting information but about asking important questions. There have always been arguments questioning the educational worth of lectures to large groups of students, but there is now an awareness that the IT revolution is eventually likely to kill off the mass lecture. The question becomes, when is "eventually"? And should the process be resisted?

One would be very rash to assume that the IT revolution in university teaching has run its course. How will courses be taught in 20 or 50 years' time? The answer to that question is as impossible to give now as it would have been if asked in 1980 – the technology and its social implications have been changing at breakneck speed and in unanticipated directions. However, there is one hint of a possible direction of change: the increasing ease and convenience of online courses. The Department of Government has had online units, notably designed for Sydney students studying international relations on exchange at overseas institutions, but this is only a tiny fraction of the department's teaching offerings. A recent communiqué from the Faculty of Arts and Social Sciences on *elearning* initiatives called for expressions of interest from Faculty members in the development of fully online units of study. The Faculty is cautious about where this might lead, but is providing funding nonetheless, as is entirely justified:

> Although the in-class and on-campus experience will remain the primary mode of teaching in our Faculty, it is important that we explore opportunities for providing students with access to high quality online learning opportunities that include a selection of fully online units of study where appropriate.[3]

Given the lifestyle of most contemporary students, who seem more at home with electronic media than with paper, and given the more expensive nature of traditional face-to-face teaching, a good guess would be that the future of tertiary teaching, especially for undergraduate students, is online. It will be interesting to see how the Department of Government responds to the challenge.

The same message from the faculty on *elearning* offered funding for innovative ideas on "blended learning":

> ... to support staff in developing high quality, sustainable blended learning initiatives that will have a demonstrable, positive impact on the quality of our teaching (including 'flipped classrooms', enriched unit of study websites, online assessment initiatives etc).

An earlier generation of teachers and students will have to guess at the meaning of terms like "blended learning" and "flipped classrooms", but they are part of the language of modern tertiary education. In general, however, the University of Sydney has not made any significant commitment to online courses, unlike a number of its competitors (ANU, Macquarie, Monash, Curtin, Griffith, RMIT, UWA, USA, Swinburne, UNE) who have embraced the technology as a means of extending the possibilities of a much older tradition of distance education. In some sense and to some degree, almost certainly the future of tertiary education is online.

For many years scientific and would-be scientific disciplines have sought to simplify (and cheapen) assessment by the use of multiple-choice questionnaires in exams and other tests. These have never been popular in the Department of Government. However, the digital revolution is reaching further and further into assessment. For example, for the three major tests of English proficiency used by most Australian universities for international students, there is a clear trend towards automatic (that is, computer-rated) testing: the British-based *IELTS* test is still completely graded by humans; the American-based *TOEFL* test is partly automatic; while the newcomer to the field, the Pearson *PTE Academic* test is completely automatic, with humans used only for back-up.[4] Meanwhile, some American universities are already using software that grades student essays by scanning for desirable and undesirable characteristics.[5] Automatic testing cannot easily be dismissed as less reliable or accurate than grading by human markers, especially when human markers are largely left to their own devices and prejudices, although there are serious doubts about how effective such assessment can be for the student's learning. There are choices here that will face the Department of Government in the not-too-distant future.

Perhaps more of a challenge to traditional university study is the phenomenon known as MOOCs (Massive Open Online Courses). These courses are free, unconstrained by national borders, and demand no gatekeeper level of high school grades. Moreover, many of them offer certificates or degrees on completion. A 2014 article in the *Guardian* noted the serious problems of low MOOC completion rates, not to mention the problem of how prospective employers are likely to regard the accreditation level compared with a degree from a recognised conventional university.6 That is the situation today. A good guess would be that within a relatively short period of time online courses will take up a much greater proportion of university teaching than they do at present. The challenge for universities, as for a future Department of Government, will be either to compete with other online offerings or to demonstrate to prospective students (not just assert) that face-to-face learning is greatly preferable. However, rather than being an alternative to face-to-face teaching, it is clear that MOOC courses are already acting as back-up resources for existing traditionally-taught degree structures. At the internationally ranked Warwick Business School (WBS) of the University of Warwick, MOOC courses are being used to give high school students and undergraduates a taste of what is involved in their graduate MBA programs. As the Dean of the WBS points out: "If Warwick is not giving potential students a 'try before you buy' offering while our competitors are, then it is likely we will lose out to US rivals in the long run."7 The discussion here is about the value of such online courses as a marketing tool for schools that are in an international competition for the best students. That is precisely the situation faced by the Department of Government.

No institutional structure in modern life is guaranteed permanency. This is even more the case in a corporate environment where restructuring and rebranding are major instruments of management. Will there be a Department of Government in 20 or 50 years' time? Who knows? However, it is likely that some bodies within the University of Sydney will continue the tasks of undergraduate and postgraduate teaching, and advanced research into political and social questions. The teaching of social sciences in the University, the role of the School of Social and Political Sciences, and the future directions to be taken by the Department of Government are all part of a task that is still very much in progress. That is as it should be. And, at least for the Department of Government, it is a much more optimistic journey than seemed likely in the early years of the new century.

---

1 Interview with Graeme Gill, 23 April 2014, in Department of Government Oral History Project.
2 LT [Lynne Thomson], "Technobabble", *Beyond the Cringe*, Vol. 1, November 1986, p. 1.
3 Faculty of Arts and Social Sciences, University of Sydney, "New funding schemes for elearning initiatives", 29 January 2014.
4 An official explanation by Pearson of their use of automatic scoring can be found at: http://pearsonpte.com/SiteCollectionDocuments/AutomatedScoringUS.pdf; while the TOEFL overview of their scoring system is at: http://www.ets.org/toefl/english_programs/scores/; both accessed on 19 May 2014.
5 John Markoff, "Essay-Grading Software Offers Professors a Break" *New York Times*, digital edition, 5 April 2014: http://www.nytimes.com/2013/04/05/science/new-test-for-computers-grading-essays-at-college-level.html?pagewanted=all&_r=1&, accessed on 19 May 2014. A version of the same article can be found in the print version of the *New York Times*, 5 April 2013, p. A1.
6 Louise Tickle, "Are MOOCs the best chance we have to satisfy a global thirst for education?", *Guardian*, 20 January 2014, http://www.theguardian.com/education/2014/jan/20/moocs-global-thirst-education, accessed 21 January 2014.
7 Stephen Hoare, "How MOOCs are changing education", *CORE, Journal of the Warwick Business School* (WBS), Edition 2, 2014, p. 49.

Appendix

Staff List (1917-2014)

Those marked with an asterisk (*) were later promoted or appointed as professors in this or other universities. People who arrived in the Department already as Professors, such as Dick Spann, are not marked with an asterisk.

Tenured staff

Dennis Altman (*La Trobe), Des Ball (*ANU), Betsi Beem, Coral Bell (*Sussex), Ian Bell, Francis A Bland (*Sydney), Anna Boucher, Deborah Brennan (*UNSW), Ian Campbell, Lyn Carson (*UWS), Ernie Chaples, Louise Chappell (*UNSW), Minglu Chen, Peter Chen, Bob (Raewyn) Connell (*Macquarie, California, Sydney), Ross Curnow, Alastair Davidson (*Monash), Peter Dauvergne (*UBC), James Der Derian, Michael Di Francesco, Charlotte Epstein, Paul Fawcett, Anika Gauja, Graeme Gill (*Sydney), Ben Goldsmith, David Goodman, Ryan Griffiths, Ian Grosart, Devin Hagerty (*Marylands), Justin Hastings, John Hobson (*Sheffield), Michael Hogan, Christopher Hood (*LSE, Oxford), Bob Howard, Terry Irving, Darryl Jarvis (*Hong Kong), Yuan Jindong, Brian Jinks, Adam Kamradt-Scott, Michael Jackson (*Sydney), John Keane, Joanne Kelly, Tom Kewley, Peter King (*PNG), Martin Laffin (*Singapore), Alexandre Lefebvre, Michael Leigh (*Malaysia, Melbourne), Peter Loveday, Doug McCallum (*UNSW), Megan McKenzie, Robert Macneil, Allan McConnell (*Sydney), Diarmuid Maguire, Trevor Matthews, Ross Martin (*ANU), Henry Mayer (*Sydney), Gil Merom, John Mikler, Ivan Molloy, Rex Mortimer (*PNG), Helen Nelson, Peter Nelson, Pippa Norris, Barbara Page, Martin Painter (*Hong Kong), Susan Park, Percy Partridge (*Sydney, ANU), Carole Pateman (*California), Sarah Phillips, Leanne Piggott, Gian Poggi (*Virginia, Florence, Trent), John Power (*Melbourne), Jia Qingguo, Lily Rahim,

M Ramesh (*Singapore), John Ravenhill (*ANU), James Reilly, Jim Richardson (*ANU), Andrew Rosser, David Schlosberg, Roger Scott (*UQ), Jason Sharman (*Griffith), David Smith, Frank Smith, Rodney Smith (*Sydney), Dick Spann, Patricia Springborg (*Sydney), Randall Stewart, Bob Taylor (*London), Fred Teiwes (*Sydney), Rodney Tiffen (*Sydney), Simon Tormey, Ken Turner, Ariadne Vromen, Lex Watson, Percy Watts, Linda Weiss (*Sydney), Peter Westerway, Colin Wight, Thomas Wilkins, Neville Wills.

Non-tenured staff

The list above, with a few exceptions, is of tenured and full time teaching staff. It omits people appointed full time under various titles such as tutor, teaching fellow, assistant lecturer, associate lecturer and contract lecturer. Many of the people listed below were stalwarts of the Department's teaching program for a number of years, and include some of its best teachers. The teaching program could not have been managed without them. Most of them went on to important positions in academia, business, law, politics, and the public service. Nor does this list include the hundreds of people who have served as part-time and casual teachers over the years. This list does not include a significant number of tenured members of the Department staff who started as tutors or casuals and later gained tenure (Anika Gauja, Michael Hogan, Peter King, Doug McCallum, Henry Mayer, Rod Smith, Ken Turner, Lex Watson, Peter Westerway.

Rebecca Albury, George Angelides, Ruth Atkins, John Brookfield, AW Coady, Peter Curson, Peter D'Ews Thomson, Frank Frost, Fran Gale, Florence Gould, Caroline Graham, Christopher Green, Jeff Groom, Fran Hausfeld, Lisa Hill (*Adelaide), Ann Hooper, Michael Howard, Jennifer Hutchinson, Kanishka Jayasuriya, Christine Jennett, Craig Johnston, Peter Lemon, Barbara Levy, Gillian McDonald, Roger Markwick, Angus McIntyre, Fiodor Mediansky, Terry Metherell, Ben Moffitt, JT Monaghan, Janice Nicholson, Warren Osmond,

Francesca Panzironi, Ralph Pettman (*Wellington, Melbourne), Marilyn Pietsch, Roderic Pitty, Juliet Richter, Paul Rutherford, Shelley Savage, Bernadette Schedvin, A Sealy, Peter Searle, Tony Smith, Roger Spegele, Kerry Stubbs, Elaine Thompson, Judith Walker, Virginia Watson, David Wells, Jennifer Westacott, Sue Wills.

Students and other staff who have become Professors
Bernard Carey (BA Hons, 1975, PhD, 1987 – Macquarie, UWS); Alex Coram (PhD, 1986 – UWA); Kath Gelber (PhD, 2000 – UQ), Murray Goot (BA Hons, 1968; Research Fellow – Macquarie); Andrew Jakubowicz (BA Hons, 1970 – UTS); Ken Knight (BEc Hons, 1952 – UQ); Martin Krygier (BA Hons, 1970 – UNSW); Robert Parker (BEc Hons, 1937 – ANU); Tim Rowse (BA Hons, 1974 – ANU, UWS); Joan Rydon (R/A – Latrobe); Peter Spearritt (BA Hons, 1973 – UQ); Ted Wolfers (BA Hons, 1965 – Wollongong).

Note: Since I have not had access to University of Sydney employment records, and since the Department of Government has been remiss in retaining its own records, there are likely to be errors or omissions in these lists. Please let the Department know if you recognize any.

Bibliography

Books

Almond, Gabriel & Verba, Sidney, *The Civic Culture: Political Attitudes and Democracy in Five Nations*, Princeton, Princeton University Press, 1963.

Altman, Dennis, *Homosexual: oppression and liberation*, New York, Outerbridge & Dienstfrey, 1971. Published by Angus & Robinson in 1972, and by Penguin Australia in 1973.

Butler, Gavan, Jones, Evan & Stilwell, Frank, *Political Economy Now! The struggle for alternative economics at the University of Sydney*, Sydney, Darlington Press, 2009.

Chaples, Ernie & Nelson, Helen (eds.), *Case Studies in New South Wales Electoral Politics*, Sydney Department of Government, University of Sydney, 1985.

Coleman, Peter, *Memoirs of a Slow Learner: An intimate and personal memoir*, Sydney, Angus & Robertson, 1994.

Connell, RW, *The child's construction of politics*, Melbourne, MUP, 1971.

Connell, RW and Irving, TH, *Class Structure in Australian history: documents, narrative and argument*, Melbourne, Longman Cheshire, 1980.

Connell, RW & Gould, Florence, *Politics of the Extreme right: Warringah 1966*, Melbourne, Cheshire, 1967.

Corpolplan, Corporate Political Planning, a unit in the Department of Government University of Sydney, *Political Scenario for Qantas Airways Limited*, 3 vols. for private distribution, Sydney, 1973.

Foster, Leonie, *High Hopes: the Men and Motives of the Australian Round Table*, Melbourne, MUP, 1986.

Gallagher, Brian & Roberts, Winsome (eds.), *Oxford Companion to Australian Politics*, Oxford, OUP, 2007.

Greer, Germaine, *The Female Eunuch*, London, McKibbon & Kee, 1970.

Groenewegen, Peter, *Educating for Business, Public Service and the Social*

Sciences: A History of the Faculty of Economics at the University of Sydney 1920-1999, Sydney, SUP, 2009.

Hogan, Michael, *Local Labor: A History of the Labor Party in Glebe 1891-2003*, Sydney, Federation Press, 2004.

Hogan, Michael & Clune, David (eds.), *The People's Choice: Electoral Politics in 20th Century New South Wales*, Sydney, Parliament of NSW and University of Sydney, 2001, 3 vols.

Hogan, Michael, Muir, Lesley, & Golder, Hilary (eds.), *The People's Choice: Electoral Politics in Colonial New South Wales*, Sydney, Federation Press, 2007.

Hogan, Michael & Dempsey, Kathy (eds.), *Equity and Citizenship under Keating*, Sydney, PARC, University of Sydney, 1995.

Ker Conway, Jill, *The Road From Coorain*, New York, Alfred A Knopf & Random House, 1989.

Kewley, TH, *Social Security in Australia*, Sydney, SUP, 1965.

Kewley, TH, *Social Security in Australia from 1900 to 1972*, Sydney, SUP, 1973.

Kuhn, Thomas, *The Structure of Scientific Revolutions*, London, University of Chicago Press, 1962.

Mackinolty, John and Judy (eds.), *A Century Down Town: Sydney University Law School's First Hundred Years*, Sydney, Sydney University Law School, 1991.

Mayer, Henry (ed.), *Australian Politics: a reader*, Melbourne, Cheshire, 1st & 2nd editions, 1966, 1969.

Mayer, Henry & Nelson, Helen (eds.), *Australian Politics: a third reader*, Melbourne, Cheshire, 1973 (4th ed., 1976, 5th ed., 1980).

Mayer, Henry & Rydon, Joan, *The Gwydir by-election: a study in political conflict, 1953*, Canberra, ANU Press, 1954.

Mill, John Stuart, *Considerations on Representative Government*, London, Parker, 1861.

Pateman, Carole, *Participation and Democratic Theory*, Cambridge, CUP, 1970.

Pateman, Carole, *The Disorder of Women: Democracy, Feminism and Political Theory*, Cambridge, Polity Press, 1989.

Power, John, *Politics in a suburban community: the NSW election in Manly, 1965*, Sydney, SUP, 1968.

Rhodes, RAW (ed.), *The Australian Study of Politics*, Melbourne, Palgrave Macmillan, 2009.

Roberts, Stephen, *The House That Hitler Built*, London, Methuen, 1937.

Rydon, Joan & Spann, RN, *New South Wales Politics, 1901-1910*, Melbourne, Cheshire, 1962.

Smith, Rodney, *Politics in Australia*, Sydney, Allen & Unwin, 2nd and 3rd editions, 1993, 1997.

Smith, Rodney & Watson, Lex (eds), *Politics in Australia*, Sydney, Allen & Unwin, 1989.

Smith, Rodney, Vromen, Ariadne & Cook, Ian (eds.), *Contemporary Politics in in Australia: theories, practice and issues*, Melbourne, CUP, 2012.

Summers, Anne, *Damned Whores and God's Police: the colonization of women in Australia*, Ringwood Vic., Penguin, 1975.

Summers, Anne and Bettison, Margaret, *Her Story: Australian Women in Print 1788-1975*, Sydney, Hale & Iremonger, 1980.

Vromen, Ariadne & Gelber, Katharine, (eds.), *Powerscape: contemporary Australian political practice, Sydney*, Allen & Unwin, 2005.

van Holsteyn, Joop, Mon, Reineke, Smit, Ineke, Tromp, Henk, & Wolters, Gezinus (eds.), *Perspectives on the Past: 50 years of FSW*, Leiden, Faculty of Social and Behavioural Sciences, University of Leiden, 2013.

Weber, Max, *Wirtschaft und Gesellschaft*, published in English as *Economy and Society: an outline of interpretive sociology*, New York, Bedminster, 1968.

Williams, Bruce, *Liberal Education and Useful Knowledge: a brief history of the University of Sydney 1850-2000*, Sydney, Chancellor's Committee, University of Sydney, 2002.

Wills, Sue, "The politics of sexual liberation", unpublished PhD thesis, University of Sydney, 1981.

Wills, Sue, "The Philosophy Strike: the view from the Department of Government", *Australian Feminist Studies*, vol. 13

Wills, Sue, Cox, Eva & Antolovich, Gaby, *Attitudes to Sexuality*, Sydney, Canberra, AGPS, 1977.

Articles and Unpublished Theses

Anon. "Joint Staff-Student Action", *Honi Soit*, 23 June 1965.

Allen, Pam, "A Preliminary Sketch of the Role of Women in the NSW Branch of the ALP", Government Final Honours thesis, 1974.

Bennett, Garry, "Toilet Lid Closes", *Honi Soit*, 19 October 1976, p.26.

Bongiorno, Frank, "British to their boot heels too: Britishness and Australian radicalism", Trevor Reese Memorial Lecture 2006, London, Menzies Centre for Australian Studies, King's College London, 2006.

Cooper, RG, "The Women's Suffrage Movement in New South Wales", MA, University of Sydney, 1970.

Curnow, Ross, "Intellectual Stance: RN Spann", *Australian Journal of Public Administration*, Vol.39, (3-4), September 1980.

French, Robert, Obituary: "Lex Watson, leading gay activist and trailblazer", *Sydney Morning Herald*, 28 May 2014.

Hoare, Stephen, "How MOOCs are changing education", *CORE, Journal of the Warwick Business School* (WBS), Edition 2, 2014, p.49.

Hollingsworth, D, "Sydney Women's Liberation and the Problem of Revolutionary Praxis", Government Final Honours thesis, University of Sydney, 1971.

Krygier, Martin, "Obituary. RN Spann 1916-1981", *Quadrant*, September 1981.

John Markoff, "Essay-Grading Software Offers Professors a Break" *New York Times*, digital edition, 5 April 2014: http://www.nytimes.com/2013/04/05/science/new-test-for-computers-grading-essays-at-college-level.html?pagewanted=all&_r=1&, accessed on 19 May

2014. A version of the same article can be found in the print version of the *New York Times*, 5 April 2013, p.A1.

Parker, RS, "Departments and God Professors: some suggestions", *Vestes*, March 1965, vol.8 (1).

Parker, RS, "F.A. Bland's contribution to public administration in Australia", *Public Administration (AJPA)*, September 1948.

Parker, RS, "Understanding Public Administration: a Comment", *Australian Journal of Public Administration*, Vol. XI, No.3, September 1981.

Scott, Roger, "Political Science and Public Administration: The Saga of a Difficult Relationship", *Australian Journal of Public Administration*. Vol. 62, No 2, 2003.

Spann, RN, "Political Science in Australia", *Australian Journal of Politics and History*, Vol 1 No 1. 1955.

Spann, RN, "Political Studies: A Conference Report", *AJPH*, Vol 4 No 1, 1958.

Spann, RN, "Understanding Public Administration: Reflections on an Academic Obituary – 'Alas, Poor Yorick' ", *Australian Journal of Public Administration*, Vol. XI, No.3, September 1981.

Tickle, Louise, "Are MOOCs the best chance we have to satisfy a global thirst for education?", *Guardian*, 20 January 2014, http://www.theguardian.com/education/2014/jan/20/moocs-global-thirst-education, accessed 21 January 2014.

Thompson, Elaine, "Henry Mayer as a Teacher", *Politics*, 20 (2), November 1985.

Wills, Sue, "The politics of sexual liberation", unpublished PhD thesis, University of Sydney, 1981.

Archival and Manuscript Material

Archives of the University of Sydney: Spann Papers; Department of Government folders; some employment records; Minutes of the

Senate, Professorial Board, Academic Board; University Calendars; photo resources.

Beyond the Cringe, an occasional newsletter prepared by the RAs in the Department of Government. Vol.1, November 1986; Vol.2, No.1, Winter 1989; Vol.3 No.1, September 1990. (To be deposited in the University Archives)

A file of ephemera collected during the 1970s political upheavals, especially of the strike over the dispute in the Philosophy Department and issues of democratisation in the Department of Government. Probably collected originally by Frank Frost, then to Lex Watson, Graeme Gill and Michael Hogan. It will be deposited in the University Archives.

Gill Papers. A file of correspondence about challenges faced by the Discipline of Government and International Relations during the period of the Faculty of Economics and Business, kept by Graeme Gill. It will be deposited in the University Archives.

Department of Government Oral History Project. Recorded and transcribed interviews with Ross Curnow, Graeme Gill, Bob Howard, Terry Irving, Sue Irving, Judith Keene, Peter King, Michael Leigh, Fred Teiwes, Rod Tiffen, and Ken Turner. In the University Archives.

Timeline of Department of Government

1915　First mention of lectures in "Government", in a WEA course on Municipal Government, taught by George Beeby (former NSW Labor Minister and future Chief Justice). The WEA had an arrangement with the University of Sydney, where the University provided some lecturers as part of its extension teaching.

1916　FA Bland, PR Watts and CM Collins lecturing in "Public Administration" for WEA extension courses in Sydney and the Illawarra. Bland claimed that he took over from Beeby.

1917　Appointment of Bland and Watts as half-time Lecturers in Public Administration in the Department of Economics, University of Sydney. Bland also appointed to help manage extension courses in the University's Department of Tutorials.

1929　Decision made to establish Diploma in Public Administration especially designed for NSW public servants. Taught for the first time in 1930.

1935　Chair of Public Administration established from a special NSW Government grant.
Francis Armand Bland appointed Professor of Public Administration without advertisement.
Department of Public Administration established within Faculty of Economics.

1943-5　Diploma in Public Administration curtailed then abolished.

1947　Establishment of Department of Government & Public Administration.

Advertising of Chair of Government & Public Administration.
Chair offered to Percy Partridge.

1948 At mid-year Bland retires and Partridge arrives.
First courses in "Government" for Economics Faculty students. Not taught in first year, but, in a four-year BEc, taught in years 2, 3 and 4.

1950 Qualified approval of Government for Arts students.
Not available for first year students. A three-year sequence with the first year specified as a prerequisite of History or Philosophy, followed by two years of Government.
Arrival of Henry Mayer as Teaching Fellow.

1951 Partridge resigns to go to ANU.
Location of Department in the Mills Building, with overflow of junior staff occupying the "Lecturers' Hut".

1954 Arrival of Dick Spann in December.

1957 Beginning of three-year Bachelor of Economics degree.
Government I available as a first year course for Economics students under the New By-laws, but not for Arts students or Economics students under Old By-laws.

1962 Government available for first year students in Economics and Arts.
Start of rapid expansion in numbers of students studying Government.

1966 Beginning of the arrival of the "baby boom" children.
Rapid expansion in students and staff numbers.

1969-76 Years of student and staff activism on issues such as Vietnam, conscription, women's liberation, gay liberation,

apartheid, and attempts to impose student co-management of the Department. Splits in Departments of Economics and Philosophy.
Arrival of a cohort of American lecturers.

1974-80 Revision of the curriculum to provide a wide choice of semester-length courses in Government II/III, and then in Government I. (The University still maintained a three-Term arrangement until general semesterisation was introduced in 1990).

1986 The first personal computers are made available to staff in the Department of Government.

1990 Appointment of Professor Don McNicol as Vice-Chancellor signals the transformation of the University into a corporatised body adopting the principles of private enterprise and line management rather than collegial decision making.

1999 Arrival of Peter Wolnizer as Dean of Economics with a brief to achieve a world-class business school.

2000 Re-branding of Faculty of Economics to Faculty of Economics and Business.
Name change to: Department of Government and <u>International Relations (GIR).</u> Graeme Gill, Head of School of Economics and Political Science (2000-3)

2001 Name change to: <u>Discipline</u> of Government and International Relations.

2003 Discipline of Economic History disbanded.
Graduate School of Government starts, partly in competition with GIR.
Stephen Nicholas Head of School, 2003-6.

2005	Announcement of the new Centre for International Security Studies (CISS), initially intended for the Arts Faculty but then located in the Faculty of Economics and Business, and completely separate from the Department of Government and International Relations.
2008	Department of Government and International Relations relocated into the Faculty of Arts and Social Sciences, in the School of Social and Political Sciences.
2012	University decision to provide partial integration of the CISS into the Department of Government and International Relations, while maintaining its own identity. This took effect in 2013.

Index of Names

Aitkin, Don 62
Albanese, Anthony 116
Albury, Rebecca 257
Aldrich, Robert 131
Altman, Dennis 62, 91, 109-10, 130-1, 134, 137-9, 150, 166, 177, 256
Anderson, John 5, 36, 62
Angelides, George 257
Armstrong, David 134
Ascot, Phillip 137
Association for Cultural Freedom 56, 63
Atkins, Ruth 25, 44, 46, 51, 65, 257
Atkinson, Meredith 3, 9
Australian Political Science Association (APSA) 26, 62, 234, 239-40

Ball, Desmond 256
Ball, McMahon 27-8
Barlow, Kate Colour insert
Barraclough Sir Henry 24
Bavin, Thomas 14
Bell, Coral 256
Bell, Ian 256
Beeby, George 7-8
Beem, Betsi 256
Benjafield, David 65
Bettison, Margaret 122, 150, 261
Black, Hermann 14
Bland Francis A 5-20, 22-30, 32, 34, 36-8, 40, 43-4, 46, 48, 67, 71, 159-60, 207, 225, 228, 239
Borrie, WD 36
Boughton, Bob 137
Boucher, Anna 226, 256
Bramsted, Ernest 65
Brennan, Deborah 202, 204-5, 211, 214, 216, 226, 256
Brett, Judith 3, 15, 28-9
Brick, Jean 124
Brookfield, John 257
Brown, Gavin 196, 209, 216
Burgmann, Meredith 112
Browne, WF 38
Buckley, Ken 129, 131
Burnheim, John 133
Butlin, Sidney 14, 18, 67

Calwell, Arthur 83
Campbell, Ian 256
Campbell, Keith 132
Carey, Bernard 137, 258
Carboch, Dagmar 68
Carson, Lyn 226, 256
Castles, Stephen 220
Chaples, Ernie 79, 91-2, 141, 151, 171-2, 230, 241, 256, 259
Chappell, Louise 203, 226, 256
Chipp, Don 129
Chen, Minglu 256
Chen, Peter 226, 256

CISS (Centre for International Security Studies) 208-9, 213, 215, 219-20, 227, 233
Coady, AW 25, 46, 257
Cole, Ed 91, 170
Coleman, Peter 37, 53, 58, 80, 257
Collins, Jock 116
Connell, Bob (Raewin) 91, 144-5, 149, 152, 170, 230, 241, 256, 259
Conway, Jill Ker 62-3, 80, 260
Cook, Ian 76, 81, 261
Cook, Malcolm 220
Corbett, Pitt 5
Cordeus, Klaus 137
Corkery, Laurence 39
CPACS (Centre for Peace and Conflict Studies) 206, 220-1
Crisp, LF 76, 87
Crosland, Tony 64
Crozier, Michael 188, 216
Curnow, G Ross 18, 29-30, 54, 62, 80, 91, 103, 108, 137, 151, 165, 170, 177, 225, 256, 262, 264
Currey, Charles H 5, 14, 24
Curson, Peter 257
Curthoys, Jean 132-4

Daniel, Marcia 50, 64
D'Arcy, John S 10
Dauvergne, Peter 202, 256
Davidson, Alastair 98, 256
Davis, Ian 137
Davis, Rufus 15
Dawkins, John 179

Deeble, John 68
Delarue, Barbara 50
Der Derian, James 256
D'Ews Thompson, Peter 257
Di Francesco, Michael 202, 256
Duncan, WGK 6, 24

Epstein, Charlotte 256
Evatt, HG 83

Fawcett, Paul 226, 256
Feith, Herb 62
Fell, Liz 124
Fisher, Joyce 51
Fitzgerald, Arthur 39
Fitzpatrick, Timothy 219
Freedman, Lyn Colour insert
Freire, Paulo 115
Fogarty, Cliff 137
Frost, Frank 257, 264

Gale, Fran 257
Garton, Stephen 208-9, 216
Gauja, Anika 256-7
Gelber, Katherine 76, 80, 258, 261
Gill, Graeme 118, 150, 185, 200, 202, 207-8, 210-2, 214, 216, 220, 228, 234-6, 239, 241, 245, 255-6, 264
Goldsmith, Ben 256
Goodman, David 256
Goot, Murray 76, 80, 240, 258
Gorton, John 83, 102, 129
Gould, Florence 230, 241, 257, 259

GSG (Graduate School of Government) 207-8, 210-2, 220
Graham, Caroline 124, 257
Green, Christopher 257
Greenwood, Gordon 34
Greer, Germaine 121, 124, 130, 150, 259
Griffiths, Ryan 256
Groenewegen, Peter 1, 14, 28-30, 33, 52-3, 66, 80
Groom, Jeff 257
Grosart, Ian 91, 256

Hagerty, Devon 203, 256
Harman, Grant 36, 52
Harris, Shirley 50
Harrison, Wilfred 54
Hastings, Justin 256
Hausfeld, Fran 150, 257
Heinius, Daniel 1
Higgins, EM 66
Hill, David 115
Hill, Lisa 257
Hinze, Michael 220
Hobson, John 202, 256
Holmes, Jean 62
Hogan, Michael 29, 53, 81, 108, 118-9, 137, 150-2, 177, 216, 230, 240-1, 256-7, 260, 264
Hogan, Warren 114-5
Hood, Christopher 94, 98, 176-7, 226, 256
Hooper, Ann 257
Howard, Michael 257

Hughes, Colin 15
Hughes, Thomas 128-9
Hurley, Brian 39
Hurley, Michael 137, 151
Hutchinson, Jennifer 257

IPA (Institute of Public Affairs) 17
Irvine, Robert F 7, 9, 43
Irving, Terry 79, 81, 91, 100, 109-10, 133-5, 139, 144-6, 149-52, 177-8, 256, 259, 264
Ivison, Duncan 229

Jacka, Liz 132-4
Jackson, Michael 6, 29, 91, 101, 118, 214, 229, 256
Jaensch, Dean 62
Jarvis, Darryl 203, 256
Jayasuriya, Kanishka 257
Jennet, Christine 257
Jindong, Yuan 256
Jinks, Brian 256
Johnson, Betty 126, 147
Johnston, Craig 130-1, 137, 257

Kamradt-Scott, Adam 256
Keane, John 229, 256
Keene, Judith 124, 264
Kelly, Joanne 203, 256
Kewley, Tom 6, 13-14, 18-19, 23, 25, 27, 37, 39-40, 42, 44, 46, 48, 50-1, 53-4, 58, 63, 67, 71, 73, 90, 225, 256, 260
King, Peter 91, 108, 112, 133-4, 137,

139, 151, 247, 256-7, 262, 264
Kolej Antarabangsa 193-6
Krygier, Martin 56-7, 80, 137, 258
Kuhn, Rick 116
Kuhn, Thomas 115, 149

Laffin, Martin 226, 256
Lang, John T 14, 18
Leahy, Gillian 130
Lefebvre, Alexandre 229, 256
Leigh, Michael 67, 80, 91, 98, 101, 150, 152, 173, 178, 195, 216, 256, 264
Lemon, Peter 257
Levy, Barbara 124, 257
Lipsius, Justus 1
Loveday, Peter 67, 73, 90, 256

MacCallum, Duncan 6
MacCallum, Sir Mungo 14
McCallum, Doug 65-7, 90-1, 256-7
McCallum, JA 26
McConnell, Allan 226, 256
McConaghy, Professor 131
McDonald, Gillian 257
Mackinolty, Chips 137, 139, 151
McIntyre, Angus 257
McKenzie, Megan 256
McKnight, David 137
Macneil, Robert 256
McNicol, Don 181
Maguire, Diarmuid 256
Markwick, Roger 257

Matthews, Trevor 90, 100, 150, 225, 256
Mayer, Henry 34, 40, 44, 50-1, 57, 59, 61, 63-4, 66-7, 70, 72-3, 76-7, 79-80, 83, 85, 87, 90-2, 95-9, 107, 110, 121-4, 129, 131-2, 135-8, 140, 145-6, 149, 151, 153, 155, 165-6, 168, 170, 178, 184, 226, 229-30, 239-40, 245, 247
Martin, Ross 90, 256
Mediansky, Fiodor 257
Merom, Gil 256
Metherell, Terry 137, 257
Mikler, John 226, 256
Mills, RC 14, 17, 51-2
Moffitt, Ben 257
Molloy, Ivan 256
Monaghan, JT 25, 46, 257
Moran, James 39
Mortimer, Rex 91, 94, 100, 110, 118, 135, 137, 144, 256
Myers, Beatrice 66

Nelson, Helen 76, 80, 101, 118, 225, 241, 256, 259-60
Nelson, Peter 91, 225, 256
NSW Constitutional League 17-18
Nicholas, HG 54
Nicholas, Stephen 200, 204, 216
Nicholson, Janice 257
Norris, Pippa 229, 235, 256

O'Neil, Bill 133
Osmond, Warren 124, 257

Page, Barbara 226, 256
Painter, Martin 118, 202, 225-6, 234, 256
Panzironi, Francesca 258
PARC (Public Affairs Research Centre) 77-9, 81, 172
Park, Susan 256
Parker, Robert S 14, 16, 29-30, 34, 65, 143-5, 151
Partridge, Percy 5, 21, 23-4, 26-8, 34-53, 59, 67, 110
Pateman, Carole 123, 127-8, 137, 150-1, 229, 256, 260-1
Patrikeeff, Felix 195
Peterson, Kathi 116
Pettman, Ralph 258
Phillips, Sarah 256
Piddington, Mark 135
Pietsch, Marilyn 258
Piggott, Leanne 214, 256
Pitty, Roderic 258
Poggi, Gianfranco 97, 256
Poll, Christabel 129
Pollard, Mary 50, 147, 183
Portus, GV 9, 14-15
Power, John 67, 90, 110, 165, 225, 230, 241, 256

Qingguo, Jia 256

Rahim, Lily 195, 256
Ramesh, M 101, 202, 257
Ravenhill, John 93, 257
Rawson, Don 59, 61, 80, 87

Reilly, James 257
Ricardo, David 115
Richardson, Jim 91, 113, 118-9, 257
Richter, Juliet 110, 137, 150, 258
Roberts, Paul 116
Roberts, Stephen 4, 29, 261
Rosser, Andrew 257
Rutherford, Paul 258
Rydon, Joan 51, 62, 66, 225, 230, 240, 258, 260-1

Salsbury, Stephen 119, 189, 196
Savage, Shelley 258
Schedvin, Bernadette 258
Schlosberg, David 226, 257
Scott, Roger 23, 30, 90-1, 257, 263
Scott, Sue 126, 147
Scotton, Dick 68
Sealy, A 258
Searle, Peter 258
Sharman, Jason 203, 257
Simkin, Colin 114-5
Simpson-Lee, Geelum 115
Sinclair, June 212
Sluga, Glenda 220
Smith, Adam 115
Smith, David 257
Smith, Francis 257
Smith, Rodney 76, 80-1, 230, 257
Smith, Tony 258
Spann, Richard N 12, 16, 27, 239-40, 256-7, 261-3
Spegele, Roger 258

Spigelman, James 111-2
Springborg, Patricia 202, 229, 257
Stevens, Bertram 14
Stewart, Randall 202, 257
Stilwell, Frank 116, 119, 149, 259
Stone, Julius 6
Stout, Alan 5-6, 18, 21, 29
Stubbs, Kerry 258
Summers, Anne 62, 121-4, 133, 150-1, 261
Sydney Studies in Politics Series 77
Symons, Dorothy 129

Taylor, Robert 91, 257
Teiwes, Frederick 91, 150, 202, 234-5, 257, 264
Thompson, Elaine 62-3, 80, 246, 258, 263
Thomson, Lynne 245, 255
Tiffen, Rodney 101, 168, 177, 191, 214, 216, 226, 257, 264
Tormey, Simon 219, 229, 257
Turner, Kenneth I 46, 51, 53, 62, 68, 73, 84-6, 88, 90, 92, 96, 99-100, 106, 114, 118, 133-4, 146, 152-3, 155, 157, 177, 184, 230, 245, 257, 264

Vromen, Ariadne 76, 80-1, 257, 261

Walker, Judith 258

Wallas, Graham 8
Walter, Jackie 50, 126
Ward, John M 116, 181
Ware, John 129
Waters, Bill 110, 115
Watson, Lex 76, 80, 110, 129-31, 150, 157, 184, 245, 257, 261-2, 264
Watson, Virginia 258
Watts, Percy R 7, 8, 10, 13, 17-21, 27-8, 30, 67, 257
Weiss, Linda 257
Weller, Patrick 17, 26-8, 30
Wells, David 151, 258
Wertheim, Peter 137
Westacott, Jennifer 258
Westerway, Peter 46, 66-7, 73, 85, 90-1, 155, 257
Wheare, KC 32, 54, 67
Wheelwright, Ted 116
Whitlam, EG 68, 83, 148, 179
Wight, Colin 257
Wilkins, Thomas 257
Williams, Bruce 52, 115, 181, 216
Wills, Neville R 23, 25, 42-4, 50, 53, 54, 67, 110
Wills, Sue 108, 123-4, 130-1, 150, 258
Wolnizer, Peter 197-8, 207, 211, 216
Wotherspoon, Garry 131
Wright, John 39

www.ingramcontent.com/pod-product-compliance
Lightning Source LLC
Chambersburg PA
CBHW070019010526
44117CB00011B/1637